The Guys in the Gang

—————— and other stories ——————

JAMES T. JOYCE
AND
JAMES T. JOYCE

iUniverse, Inc.
Bloomington

The Guys in the Gang
(And Other Stories)

iUniverse books may be ordered through booksellers or by contacting:

iUniverse
1663 Liberty Drive
Bloomington, IN 47403
www.iuniverse.com
1-800-Authors (1-800-288-4677)

Because of the dynamic nature of the Internet, any Web addresses or links contained in
this book may have changed since publication and may no longer be valid. The views
expressed in this work are solely those of the author and do not necessarily reflect the
views of the publisher, and the publisher hereby disclaims any responsibility for them.

Any people depicted in stock imagery provided by Thinkstock are models,
and such images are being used for illustrative purposes only.

Certain stock imagery © Thinkstock.

ISBN: 978-1-4697-7768-9 (sc)
ISBN: 978-1-4697-7769-6 (hc)
ISBN: 978-1-4697-7770-2 (e)

Library of Congress Control Number: 2012903386

Printed in the United States of America

iUniverse rev. date: 2/28/2012

Contents

Preface

I've been thinking about writing this book for thirty years, ever since reading a *Chicago Tribune* column by Bob Greene. Bob suggested we should all write something about ourselves for our posterity. I paraphrase: Wouldn't you cherish something your great-grandparents wrote about their lives and times, even if it was as simple as what they saw out their window when they woke up?

I have finally taken pen in hand and, as is my bent, gone over the top by writing a book instead of merely relating the view out my bedroom window, which, today, is trees. There have been many others: A brick wall, the river, a city street, Army barracks, a jungle, rice paddies, a trailer park, a swimming pool, Black Angus, a ski slope, the Rockies, Route 53, the Smokies and the Gulf of Mexico to name some. This is not normal.

My life started out normal enough. I grew up in a nice blue-collar neighborhood in Chicago and spent four years attending college in Cleveland. Then normal ended. The Army took me to Virginia, Alabama, Georgia, South Vietnam and back to Alabama. Business found me back in Georgia, then Florida, Colorado, Illinois, North Carolina and back to Florida. If you connected those dots it would be a peculiar circle.

All that moving around is symptomatic and so, too, is the disparity of my occupations: cab driver, pilot, land salesman, condo salesman, concrete salesman, newspaper columnist, author, psychoanalyst, construction supply salesman, chemical grout salesman and owner of assorted enterprises. I've had a diverse life (some would say bizarre). This book will lay out much of it, but not all – there are parts that are none of your business.

So dear offspring and offspring's offspring, you are about to learn a lot about your ancestors and, perhaps in the process, a little about yourself. If we were not in your past, you would not have been born. When you finish this book, you may find that a scary thought.

A theme running through *The Guys in the Gang* is my preoccupation with religion. Starting as a little kid, and up to today, it has been a source of wonderment and befuddlement.

Helping me with these stories is James T. Joyce. You did not misread. His name and mine are the same - James Thomas Joyce. Only our Confirmation names are different: his Patrick and mine Peter. We have been friends since childhood. We are not related. In the book he is called "Carpenter Joyce." I'll explain later.

Jim is well known in Chicago where much of this book takes place. Unlike me, he has been stable and today he's the retired Commissioner of the Chicago Fire Department. Walking through the Loop with him takes time. Everybody knows him, or thinks they do, and they want to chat. Jim is approachable. A good guy. He's also a good writer. I had an editor read the manuscript and she said, "Bringing in the other James Joyce was brilliant! He has the eye of a writer," she gushed, "so perceptive!"

I thank Jim for his contributions. One day I hope he takes the lead and writes a more extensive book about himself. He has a keen sense of humor both on the page and in person and he has the stories. Boy, does he have the stories.

Jim and I have always been of a mind but once we agreed to disagree. Thirty-seven years ago he and Janet came to visit us in Durango, Colorado. I had just begun the process of becoming a psychoanalyst and was enthusiastically explaining the brilliant theories of Sigmund Freud - the unconscious, the repetition compulsion, the Oedipal conflict and so on. I was really getting into it when Jim held up his hand. "Stop right there," he said, "I don't believe in any of that mind shit." I completely understood and stopped right there. (However, from time to time I point out some of his neuroses, which doesn't faze him.)

But this book has nothing to do with the psyche. I already wrote one of those, *Use Eagles if Necessary.* This book is simply stories from our lives and we hope you enjoy them. The stories are true to the best of our recollections. When you see an asterisk* following a name, that's a made-up name. We don't want anyone embarrassed.

Brief bios: Jim (Carpenter) has been married for forty-six years to Janet. Four children: Jennifer, Jim, Jarrett and Joe.

I've been married twice. Eight years to Mary. Two children: Jim,

Jr. and Walter. Thirty-four years to Barbara. Two children: Alex and Zack.

READERS PLEASE NOTE: This book contains offensive figures of speech and bad words. It also frequently paints us James T. Joyces as bad examples. So we ask our offspring not to read it until they've reached the *real* age of reason, about forty-five.

ALSO: Carpenter Joyce's contributions are noted at the beginning of his chapters. The rest were written by me, Ada Joyce.

And speaking of cherish? Our friendship of fifty-seven years and counting...

DEDICATIONS

I dedicate these snippets of my story to the unique Sabina neighborhood and the strong friendships forged there. These early years of my life's journey shaped not only my adolescence, but still impact me even today as a husband, father and grandfather. My connection to "The Guys in the Gang" has lasted for almost sixty years and I continue to be grateful for it.

–Jim "Carpenter" Joyce

To my parents, Peter and Mildred, my siblings, Bob and Mary, the Catholic Church and Sigmund Freud.

And to my grandchildren: Anna Katherine Joyce, Claudia Prevost Joyce, James Walter Joyce and other offspring to come. May you live in peace, hurt no one ... and have fun.

–Jim "Ada" Joyce

SECTION I
Raised Catholic

CHAPTER 1
Saint Sabina

I was eight years old when Monsignor William Gorey died. Moments after he exhaled his last breath a priest at his bedside gave the signal to ring the bells. I was asleep at home, two blocks from the rectory.

"Jimmy," my mom whispered, "Wake up and listen to the bells. Monsignor Gorey is on his way to heaven."

I sat up and saw the old, white haired man, in his long black cassock, slowly ascending – gong by solemn gong – into the sky. "Say a prayer for him, Jimmy."

St. Sabina had thousands of parishioners back then. In their bungalows and apartments, on the streets and in the taverns, they all listened to the bells. Heads were bowed, prayers were uttered, and glasses were raised to the soul of Monsignor Gorey. He'd been their pastor and they'd respected him as a man of God. Unlike some men of God at that time, Monsignor Gorey was a nice man. He would be missed.

Our St. Sabina (suh-Bye-nah) Church complex was (and still is) bordered by 78th Street on the north, 78th Place on the south, Throop Street on the west and Racine Avenue on the east. In this half square city block is the church; its size and grandeur would qualify it as a cathedral in most places. Here also is the grammar school, a convent for nuns, a rectory for priests and a gymnasium. The rectory is on two levels. Under one wing was a garage for the monsignor's car, a big, black Chrysler. Few parishioners owned cars in those days and none of the mere priests. Monsignors were like royalty, they thought they deserved big cars and no one thought otherwise.

St. Sabina was one of the largest parishes in the Chicago. Its neighbor to the east, St. Leo, was even bigger. It also had a monsignor as its pastor, one Patrick J. Molloy, who was not always a nice man. In fact he could be somewhat of a prick, but I'm getting ahead of myself and, in fairness, Molloy had a problem Gorey never thought of.

St. Sabina in the 1940s and 50s had three classes for each of the eight grades with over forty children per class. Only two of our teachers were laypersons, Mrs. Madigan and Mrs. Johnson. All the rest were Dominican nuns, twenty-two of them. There was also a full-time music teacher nun and another nun or two who performed domestic chores in the convent including washing, ironing and starching the elaborate habits that every sister wore.

The relatively few women who enter Catholic religious orders today keep their own names: Sister Sonya, Sister Karen, Sister Lynda and so on, but for centuries when nuns completed their final vows they took the names of holy people, usually saints, from the past. For instance, at Sabina we had Sisters Brendan, Brenda, Pius, Dominic, Imelda, Sarah and so on. The principal was a stern-faced nun, a humorless disciplinarian who had taken the name of a holy angel. I never saw the connection.

The massive, gray stone church was on two levels called "the upstairs church" and the "downstairs church." There were ten masses on Sundays, five on each level and all but the very early ones were packed. Half-dozen or so priests lived in the rectory with the pastor. They said the masses, baptized us, confirmed us, married us and buried us. Besides daily masses there were Novenas, Stations of the Cross, public recitations of the rosary and other services I can't recall.

You should have seen the upstairs church on Saturdays when we all lined up for Confession. There were four built-in confessionals and, prior to Christmas and Easter when even more sinners showed up, two temporary ones in the sanctuary were added. We told the priests our sins and he then, as God's emissary, forgave us after issuing a penance. This could be as light as "Three Hail Marys" or as daunting as fifteen decades of the rosary. The penance depended on the severity of our sins and the severity of the priests. We jockeyed for position to get in line where the lenient priests were hearing. You could tell by how fast the lines were moving.

Protestants accuse Catholics of cheating life with the concept of Confession. "They can do whatever they want then tell a priest and they're forgiven," they say. Not true. You not only have to confess your sins, but then agree to "never do them again." Without that promise a Confession is invalid. There's the rub.

Sins are the bedrock religions are built on but religions don't always agree on sin. For instance, the Mormons of old and some Muslims today think having multiple wives is just fine. The Pope and Billy Graham beg to differ. Following is an abbreviated list of some Catholic mortal sins, the kind that could send you straight to hell but can be wiped off your soul by Confession.

- Taking any role whatsoever in abortion.
- Practicing artificial birth control including condoms, IUD's, pills, tubal ligations, vasectomies and onanism (both kinds)
- Missing Mass on Sundays or Holy Days of Obligation
- Entertaining sexual thoughts about someone other than your spouse.
- Petting anyone other than your spouse.
- Fornication
- Pre-meditated murder.
- Calumny
- Stealing more than $100 (adjusted for inflation).

Note: Eating meat on Fridays used to be a mortal sin but Vatican II changed that. Now it's only Fridays in Lent plus Ash Wednesday that are meatless. Don't forget.

Our first Confessions were at age seven, the so-called "age of reason," and were held the day before our First Holy Communion. We were fully prepped by the nuns. Each Confession began with: "Bless me Father for I have sinned. It has been (say how long) since my last Confession." Then our sins were enunciated in hushed tones so the people outside the confessional couldn't hear us. When we were done we said, "That's all I can remember, Father."

The priest then dispensed advice, if he was so inclined, and then gave us our penance. "Now make a good Act of Contrition," he'd say.

"Oh my God I am heartily sorry for having offended thee and I detest all of my sins, not because of your just punishments but because they offend you, my God, who are all good and deserving of all my love. I firmly resolve with the help of thy grace to confess my sins, do penance and amend my life, Amen."

"Your sins are forgiven," the priest would say. "Go in peace and sin no more." And that was it.

You came out of there feeling like a million bucks.

Once a year traveling priests, who were particularly gifted public speakers, visited St. Sabina to conduct a two-week long "mission." The first week was for men and boys and the second for women and girls. Every night those missionary priests filled the church. We parishioners of St. Sabina were immersed in our Catholic faith.

In the mid-twentieth century the neighborhoods of the south side of Chicago were known by their parishes; to some extent it is true to this day. When asked where they lived, Southsiders didn't give street addresses; they just said they lived in Sabina, Leo, Ethelreda, Christ the King, etc. Everyone knew where the parishes were.

Parishes had individual characteristics, which were also telling: St. Sabina was on the upper end of blue collar. Visitation was a notch or two down. If you said you lived in Christ the King or St. Barnabas you probably had money. If you lived in St. Gabriel's, you probably worked for the city and were beholden to the mayor.

We Catholics of that era followed the rules under pain of sin. When entering the church we dipped the middle finger of our right hand into a holy water font, then made the sign of the cross: wet finger to our forehead, chest, left shoulder, right shoulder. We did it again as we left the church. When going past a Catholic church – be it on foot, in a car, on a bicycle or a bus we also made the sign of the cross. (Hat-wearing men could get by with a tip of hat.) Whenever we heard Jesus' name we reverently bowed our heads.

Inside a church males had to remove their hats. Women, conversely, had to cover their heads with hats, scarves or "chapel veils," lace pieces found in every Catholic woman's purse. They looked like doilies. Some younger women fudged this rule by using bobby pins to attach hankies to their hair. This practice was frowned upon, but tolerated, by the nuns and priests.

The nuns' headdresses, called wimples, completely covered not only their hair but also their ears and necks. Once, in the fourth grade, I saw, to my horror, an errant tuft of a nun's hair sticking out from her wimple onto her cheek. I liked this nun (she was young, beautiful and nice) and thought I should tell her before others saw it, but I was too awed and just stared at the brown tuft. To a nine-year-old it was a fascinating, frightening and erotic sight. I can clearly picture it today.

The nuns were preoccupied with the salvation of our souls and encouraged us children to wear scapulars. These were cloth necklaces which carried "plenary indulgences," which meant if we died while wearing a scapular we would bypass Purgatory and go straight to heaven (assuming we had no current mortal sins on our souls).

Another way to get a plenary indulgence was to say the words, "My Lord and my God" at the moment of consecration of the bread and wine at mass. But this had to be done twenty days in a row. Plenary indulgences are not transferable, and nobody needs more than one, so I took the easier route to instant heaven, wearing the scapular. I wore one throughout my childhood, my tour of duty in Vietnam, and for a few years thereafter.

"Ejaculations" were a big part of our lives. The nuns encouraged us to make many of them throughout the day. Ejaculations are mini-prayers, not orgasms. I still say them in times of crisis: "Dear God, please let my child get well soon; Dear Lord, please help me make this sale because my company needs the business; Sweet Jesus, please don't let Bush get re-elected." Sometimes they work and sometimes they don't.

We were taught that the devil, like God, is omnipresent. Fortunately we were all issued guardian angels to help keep the devil at bay. Early on I learned life was not fair. Some kids had better guardian angels than others.

Genuflect in the aisle before entering your pew. Say grace before all meals; don't eat meat on Friday; pray on your knees before going to bed. No food or water after midnight in order to receive Holy Communion the next day. Mortal sins not confessed to a priest were tickets to hell. Venial sins not confessed piled up time in Purgatory. (Purgatory was like hell but eventually you'd get out.) Praying for dead people, who you assumed were in Purgatory, could lighten their sentences. Nothing you could do to help those in hell. Unbaptized babies who died and would therefore be unable to sin their way to hell, or good their way to heaven, went to Limbo. Limbo was described as heaven without the "Beatific

Vision," another way of describing God. So they'd be pretty happy but not perfectly happy. Not a bad deal.

To assure a safe journey recite this prayer nine times: "Glory be to the Father, the Son, and the Holy Ghost as it was in the beginning, is now and ever shall be, world without end, amen." This is known as saying "The Nine Glory Be's." I still say them for my loved ones and myself when we travel. This prayer never fails.

With so much praying and religious practicing going on at St. Sabina you would think we were kind, loving, and tolerant people. Forget it. If someone was not Irish and Catholic, they were suspect. We had names for them: Dagos, Polacks, Slopes, Spics, Gricks, Nips, Frogs, Hebes, Krauts, Cans, Honkies, Lugans, Wooden Shoes, Chinks, Bohunks and so on. They would have to prove themselves on an individual basis before we accepted them. And who did we think we were? The center of the universe.

But we reserved most of our prejudice for Blacks and Protestants. First I'll tell you about the Protestants, who we really didn't like. We'll cover the Blacks later.

Just to set foot inside a Protestant church required a special dispensation from a priest. Even weddings and funerals of relatives required this dispensation and if it was not obtained you committed a sin. Anything smacking of Protestant was to be avoided. At 81st and Racine, in the middle of the parish, a YMCA was built. Although the YMCA was not a religion, we were told that because the "C" in YMCA stood for "Christian," a religious association was implied. We Catholics could have nothing to do with the place. Although Catholics are, of course, Christians, we were Catholics first. To simply call oneself a Christian implied grave theological error. Frankly, in St. Sabina, Christian was a bad word.

This rule was unfortunate for us kids because the YMCA had an outdoor basketball court available at any time. Our Catholic basketball courts were inside the gymnasium and were frequently unavailable. At a Sunday mass one of our parish priests devoted his entire sermon to the evils of playing basketball at the new "Y." He stated, in no uncertain terms, that to do so was committing a sin.

No youngster dared question his pronouncement, because priests spoke for God, but I do remember thinking – at the age of twelve and for the first time ever – that I disagreed with a priest's pronouncement. It was the first personal chink I experienced in my Catholic indoctrination and as I listened to Father Kelly* rant and rave about basketball and the "Y," I decided he was nuts. But I didn't tell a soul.

I was an altar boy and served hundreds of masses, but I only remember one. Fortunately it was a daily mass with few people in attendance. Immediately I noticed the priest wasn't right. He was staggering and had to put his hands on the altar to steady himself. Then he fell down. I helped him up and leaned him against the altar. Then I ran to the rectory as fast as I could with my surplus flying and my knees bumping against the cumbersome cassock. The rectory was connected to the church by a hallway. I saw a priest and told him there was something wrong with Father McGuire*. "I think he's sick," I said. The priest hustled with me to the sacristy and escorted McGuire, who was drunk, off the altar. The mass was ended, go in peace. (I only remember that one mass out of hundreds I served? Shame on my human mind and me.)

The depth of anti-Protestantism that was grilled into us was far reaching. After I graduated from college I had six months of nothing to do while waiting for my date to enter the Army. So I took a job driving a taxicab simply to kill time during the day and to earn a little spending money. I was living at home and didn't need much.

The first day on the job one of my fares was a Catholic priest. When we arrived at his destination I refused to take his money. He was delighted. A few days later I picked up a couple of nuns and did the same thing. They, too, were most pleased and called me, "A nice Catholic boy." A week or so later a Protestant minister, with his wife and two kids, got into my cab. They were going to O'Hare, a long and expensive ride from the south side of the city.

All the way to the airport I silently debated if I should treat him as equal clergy. It was a moral dilemma. On the one hand I wanted to be fair to all the clergy I carried. On the other hand I knew St. Sabina Catholic dogma would consider a free cab ride to a Protestant minister as aiding and abetting the enemy.

When they were departing the cab the minister asked what he owed me and I heard the words in my mind, "Father Kelly was nuts." I told the minister the ride was on me. He was overwhelmed and said, "God bless you." And I said, "God bless you, too, Reverend." All the way back to the south side I wondered how much Purgatory time I'd just racked up. Father Kelly made *me* nuts.

In retrospect I've found it interesting that Jews were spared the venom we directed toward Protestants. We were taught in church and school "the Jews killed Christ." This should have made them Enemy Number One, but it didn't.

Perhaps it's because when the Jews killed Christ, He was one of their own. His Church and new religion were formed after He died. The Protestants, on the other hand, abandoned the Catholic Church after 15 centuries and formed their own, competing, religions. When Luther, Calvin, Knox, Henry XIII and the rest told Rome to buzz off, the Catholics who remained loyal took this rejection personally. Let the hatred begin. In our case, at St. Sabina, four hundred years after the Reformation, we remained pissed at the Protestants.

In our family the normal animosity of Catholics toward Protestants was a sticky, inconvenient issue. My mom's father, Edward Wurtz, was a baptized, albeit non-practicing, Lutheran. So were his siblings and their offspring, many of whom did practice their faith. Many were farmers and were the most decent of people. We spent lots of time with them at family gatherings when I was growing up. But Mom and my Granny, Edward's wife, wanted him to convert to Catholicism. I won't say they hounded him but they certainly made their wishes known up to, and on, his deathbed. Yet even though he was not a Catholic they both loved him (worshipped him really) for his goodness. A paradox I grew up with.

Nuns and priests of St. Sabina began defining us from the first grade onward. They expanded and strengthened our superegos, thwarted our burgeoning ids and made us terrified of our latent libidos. Their goal, it seems to me now, was to pass along their own fears and guilts, thereby making us like little saints. Then we, too, would become priests and nuns. They constantly encouraged us to "pray for a vocation." I remember in high school praying that I would *not* get a vocation and admitting that, even today, is a tad guilt producing. How could I not have wanted to be a priest, the highest calling of all?

Being taught by the nuns at St. Sabina was not a pleasant experience for me. Some were patient and kind, but the ones who mostly stick in my mind were mean spirited and emotionally unstable. They were screamers, meting out physical punishment as though that was a normal thing to do and, in those days, it was. We got our faces slapped, our cheeks pinched, our butts whacked, our knuckles rapped, our hair pulled and our shoulder-bones skewered by bony nun fingers. Not all the time, of course. A kid could go years at St. Sabina without experiencing corporal punishment; many went the whole eight years, but the threat was always there.

But I'm speaking as a male student. My sister, Mary, claims she loved St. Sabina Grammar School and has nothing but pleasant memories of the nuns. So maybe they only had it in for us boys. Whatever the truth was, it no longer matters. That species of nun is now extinct. I was a happy boy when I graduated and was no longer under their control.

CHAPTER 2
Leo High School

Because there was no Catholic girls' high school within walking distance of St. Sabina Parish, the girls in our class chose from four or five schools on the Southside. City buses went to Mercy, Aquinas, Longwood, (Academy of our Lady), Loretto and others.

We boys were fortunate that Leo High School was an easy walk from St. Sabina, less than a mile east on 79th Street to Sangamon. Most of us chose to go there. Please note: Although Leo High School was located in St. Leo parish they were not affiliated. The parish was named after St. Leo the Great; the school after Pope Leo the XIII. Now you know.

Our teachers at Leo were members of a religious order founded in Ireland called The Christian Brothers of Ireland. The word Ireland in the name apparently took the heresy out of the word Christian because everybody in Ireland was Catholic. In their Roman collars and black cassocks they looked like priests, but they were not ordained so could not say mass or administer the sacraments. Technically they were closer to nuns than priests. Both took vows of chastity and obedience and lived communally.

Whereas I remember too many nuns as mean spirited, I remember too many brothers as sadistic. One of them, a roly-poly little man who taught geometry, punished misbehaving students by making them stand in front of him, with their arms down their sides like soldiers at attention. He would reach way back with his short yet muscular arms and with as much force as he could muster he'd clap his hands together with the student's face in between. This was extremely painful and almost impossible not to instinctively defend against, but to do so brought more slaps.

Once he did this to Bill Nelligan, a tall, muscular athlete and who played on the football and basketball teams. When he stood on his tippy toes to reach Bill's face, he misjudged the distance and clapped his fat, puffy hands against Bill's ears. The pain was excruciating and brought involuntary tears to Bill's eyes. But Bill did not break down. On the contrary he gave the brother a look of disdain I will never forget and, apparently, neither did the brother. That was the only time he ever hit Bill Nelligan. Had he tried it again I believe Nelligan would have killed him.

Another sadistic faculty member at Leo High School, Brother Hennessey, taught algebra. His form of punishment was to have us stand at the front of the room and remove any contents from our back pockets. We then had to bend over as he proceeded to strike us on the butt with a drumstick. This may not sound cruel or painful but, trust me; it was the equivalent of being whipped. The blinding pain went from your butt to your toes to the top of your head. "It's all in the wrist, boys!" he'd gleefully announce as the punished student was reduced to tears.

The brother who taught us world history liked to walk up behind us as he wandered the classroom lecturing. He would suddenly stick his fingers deeply in front of our collarbones and squeeze them against his thumb. In moments we were kneeling on the floor in agony. This sadist was a tall, skinny man whose prides were that he was left-handed and smoked cigarettes, "Just like the Pope," he'd brag, "I, too, am a great man."

Brother Sloan, our religion teacher, did not have any favorite ways to punish or torture. If you pissed him off he'd simply flail away at you slapping, punching and kicking. But these attacks were not premeditated which, although frequent, made them seem less cruel. Because of his short temper Sloan was the most famous disciplinarian at Leo High School and he was nuts. "You'll never get away with anything in this classroom, boys. I can hear grass growing," he'd say, and then add, "Keep your arms folded and your eyes on me. If you don't, heads will be rolling down the aisles." We didn't doubt it.

Brother Sloan's erratic behavior was a tip-off to his mental condition. From time to time he'd tell us to close our eyes and put our heads on our desks. Then he'd pretend to be a jockey at an Irish steeplechase using a broomstick as a horse. He'd race around our desks yelling at the horse to slow down. He called the horse "Big Fella." You want to take it from here, Dr Freud?

Brother Comack, a young, tall, well-built guy was usually quite affable. But one time he got pissed off at the entire class and uncharacteristically screamed at us for our lackadaisical attitudes toward his subject, physics. He ended his tantrum by saying, "If you don't shape up I'll make Sloan look like Mickey Mouse!" He then turned around and punched the blackboard, cracking it down the middle. We shaped up.

Brother Kiely was a nice old man who taught mechanical drawing. He was not looking for students to punish, on the contrary, he just wanted peace but if overly provoked he, too, could be aggressive. Kiely caught me and the kid who sat next to me eating our lunches at our desks instead of mechanically drawing. This was about the fourth time he'd caught us doing this and he finally saw red. He grabbed the three-edged ruler off my desk and broke it over my head. At that moment the bell rang and the other kid ran out the door. Fortunately for him Brother Kiely was senile and the next day forgot about it. My head hurt all day.

Brothers who were normal and not inclined to beat us up had the option of punishing us by making us stay after school. This was called "jug." For any infraction we could be handed a "jug slip" which forced us to report to the "jug room" after regular school was out. Brothers took turns being the "jug master."

When we reported for jug we were given one of two choices: Bend over and get whacked five times with a wooden paddle or sit at a desk and copy words from the dictionary for an hour. The only kids who chose the paddle were those who had to work after school. The rest of us mindlessly copied from the dictionary, lying to our mothers about why we were late coming home from school. Once I chose the paddle, a horrible mistake. It hurt almost as much as the drumstick.

When springtime came around there was another option offered to us jug inmates. We could join the Cross Country Team. Cross Country was made into an organized sport for those kids who had lousy eye to hand coordination and couldn't compete in real sports. To get on the team all you had to do was run. It was the most boring of sports and recruiting team members was difficult. So this incentive was offered:

Every day we ran cross-country they'd take away three days of jug. Carpenter Jimmy Joyce and I knew a good deal when we heard one and we signed up. The first day of practice the weather was bad so the team had to run inside the school. We ran to the end of a hallway, then up three flights of stairs, then down another hallway and then down three flights. We had to do this over and over and it soon became torturous. Jimmy and I found a storage closet, slipped into it, and hid.

We stayed in it until time was almost up. As we heard the team huffing and puffing past us we opened the door and joined them, huffing and puffing to the finish line pretending to be exhausted, like the dummies not as clever as us. But our plan was flawed. "Hey, you two Joyces!" yelled the coach, "How come you're not sweating? Let's see you do twenty more minutes by yourselves." It was tough to beat the system at Leo High School.

What you did not want to happen to you at Leo High School was to get sent to the principal's office. Brother Regan was short in height but massive through the body with huge shoulders. He had the whitest hair and the reddest face I'd ever seen. With all due respect, he looked like an Irish ape. Once I witnessed a student being led to his office by a teacher. The door to the office was open, but Regan wasn't in it. As the student got to the door Regan came up behind him and punched him squarely in the back. The kid flew through the door and landed on the floor. Regan followed him in slamming the door. I heard yelling and screaming as I hustled off to my next class. Leo High School could be a violent place.

But there were some nice brothers. Coogan, Finnerty, McCormick and J.C. Collins come to mind. They were gentlemen whose only agenda was to teach and I remember them with fondness.

Some of the brothers were pleasantly out of their minds. Brother O'Dwyer, the librarian, used to recite a long poem that he had composed about smoking cigarettes. It ended with, "So, boys, light up a Lucky, if you're lucky enough to light up!" Then he'd tell us to go out into the alley to do just that. "I'm busy boys. You're botherin' me," was his favorite expression.

Many of the brothers smoked and many of the older ones also dipped snuff, a drizzle of brown goo seeping out of the sides of their mouths to eventually drip onto their cassocks. When a smoking, snuff-using brother stood next to your desk the smell of his cassock made you breathe through your mouth.

My brother, Bob, preceded me at Sabina and Leo by eight years and many of the teachers remembered him. I heard often, "Are you really Bob Joyce's brother?" They remembered him as the perfect, straight A student. All I wanted were Cs and to get the hell out of there. (Bob was one of the few males who went through both schools who was not physically punished.)

I did not enjoy my time at Leo any more than my time at Sabina. School is a difficult, frustrating experience for most kids. Adding the elements of psychological abuse, and the knowledge you could be physically punished at any time made it awful. I hated Leo High School and when I graduated I was the happiest of seventeen year olds and vowed I would never set foot in the place again. I haven't.

So my formal Catholic education on Chicago's south side came to an end. The nuns and brothers prepared me well in the basics of the arts and sciences and I had no trouble being accepted into a good college. For that I am grateful. But I learned later in life that millions of other students in the United States were also qualified to enter good colleges without experiencing unnecessary cruelty. For that I'm resentful.

(I am happy to report that the Irish Christian Brothers are also essentially extinct.)

CHAPTER 3
Mom and Dad

M y religious education was not limited to schools. At home we lived Catholicism. Our house was a mini-church with religious pictures on the walls, statues on the counters and holy water fonts at the entrance to the bedrooms. Few parents took their religion more seriously than mine.

My mom, Mildred Christiana (Wurtz) Joyce, was from Wilmington, Illinois, a small farming community about half way between Joliet and Kankakee on Alt. Rt. 66. She never spent a minute in a Catholic school yet she became, in the minds of many in our St. Sabina parish, "Mrs. Catholic Church."

Dad, a Chicago native, was working at the paper mill in Wilmington. He and mom met at church. One morning after mass Dad asked her if she'd "like to go out for a soda or something." She did and that was that.

Mom and Dad lived in his parents' building, a two flat, on Peoria Street in St. Leo parish until they bought their own house on Ada Street in St. Sabina. Mom then kicked into gear. Over the next twenty years she became the president of: St. Sabina Mother's Club (twice); Leo High School Mother's Club (twice); The Altar and Rosary Society at Sabina (numerous); The South Side Catholic Women's Club (with 200,000 members); and the Chicago Archdiocesan Council of Catholic Women (with a million members).

One of my proudest moments as a kid was seeing Mom seated on the dais at the Chicago Amphitheater for the annual meeting of the National Convention of Catholic Women. On her right, sat His Emminence Samuel Cardinal Stritch, the Archbishop of Chicago. On her left, was Richard J. Daley, the mayor. Mom gave the opening speech to the many thousands of women in attendance. They were from all over the country. I was thrilled and remembered thinking: How could the lady who fixed my breakfast this morning, in her bathrobe, now be sitting with the cardinal and the mayor? I wanted to yell out, "That's my mom!"

Naturally nobody said it but I know I cramped Mom's style when I was born. She and Dad were thirty-nine, my brother, Bob, was 8 and my sister, Mary, was 7. They were in school leaving Mom free to do her most favorite thing in the world, attend daily mass and receive Holy Communion. Then she'd do her errands on 79th Street going from store to store. This could take hours because Mom knew everybody and loved to chat. Then I came along.

I have few memories of my first three years of life so I don't know when mom started taking me to daily mass, but I know she did because she told me so. She said neighbors used to talk about "Mrs. Joyce dragging Little Jimmy to church."

The only memory Little Jimmy has of this is a hazy one. I was down below the pew straddling the kneeler, my head in my hands, bored out of my little mind and thinking Mom had finally found the mass that would never end.

When I was 5, I clearly remember walking to mass one morning with Mom when she slipped on a patch of ice and went down, hard, her arm hitting a concrete stoop. When she got up, she said, "Jimmy, I may have broken it." I was freaked that my mom was hurt but I do recall (shame on me) having the thought: I hope we can skip mass and go to the doctor. Fat chance. We continued to mass, *then* went to the doctor. He put her arm in a cast.

To say Mom crammed religion down my throat is not an exaggeration but I wasn't the only one. Before my friends and I were old enough to drive, sometimes Mom would take us to our family farm for a day. On the two-hour trip Mom always insisted we say the rosary, aloud, taking turns leading the prayers.

One of the decades of the rosary is called "The Agony in the Garden." Billy Callaghan told me years later that he and my friends referred to those trips as "The Agony in the Car." Billy also said that when he became a policeman, he began running five miles a day to stay in shape. To break the monotony he recited the rosary, "always thinking of your mom."

(Fifty years later Billy got cancer. He suffered for months in a hospital. On his tray, always at an angle where he could see it, was a picture. When he went home to die, his wife had a large copy made and placed it on an easel next to Billy's bed. The picture was Jesus on his knees, hands folded in prayer on a rock, face lifted to heaven. "The Agony in the Garden.")

When we started driving and dating a tradition began at Christmas time. After midnight mass we'd take our girlfriends to my house where Mom and Granny would have orange juice, coffee, bacon, sausage, sweet rolls, potatoes, a tower of toast and a mountain of fried eggs. Fried eggs, not scrambled. Mom and Granny did it right.

By the time I was old enough for college, Mom and I became friends and remained so until she died. We were "people" people, so had much in common. She was sincerely interested in all of my friends and what they were doing. When Mom was in her late eighties, she visited us in North Carolina. One afternoon I found her sitting alone on the back deck reading. She had a stack of prayer cards bound with a rubber band. She read them everyday. I hadn't seen much of her in the years hence and had forgotten that ritual. "What are you doing, Mom?"

"Reading my prayers, Dear."

"Mom, you are defined by your religion, aren't you."

"Yes," she said, "And you should be, too."

That Sunday I took Mom to mass at St. Margaret's, a beautiful church in Maggie Valley with spectacular mountain views. It's about ten miles from the house. The kids, my sister Mary, Mom and I got into the car and headed to St. Margaret's. After we'd driven about five miles Mom said, "Jimmy, I don't want to be late. How much farther is it?"

"I don't know, Mom," I said, "I've never been there."

She gasped, the kids and Mary laughed, and then she saw the smile on my face. "Oh you!" she said, but had to laugh. It was fun to tease Mom. She was a good sport.

Unlike me, Mom always sat up front in church. And unlike me she always chatted up the priest after mass. The priest this day at St. Margaret's was old, short, bald, rail thin and effeminate. I'd never seen him before; Mom introduced herself, said she was visiting from Illinois and proudly announced she was eighty-nine years old. The priest took her hand and said, "Yes, dear. It's time we went home." Not the response mom was looking for.

Once I picked Mom up at the farm to take her to our house in Addison, Illinois for Thanksgiving. Both the kids were in car seats and Mom had a walker. We stopped for lunch at McDonalds. Getting back in the car with all the food, drinks, kids, her walker and her was a hassle and I was frazzled. As I was buckling in the squirming kids and worrying about the drinks sliding off the roof of the car, Mom, securely in the front seat said to me, "Jimmy, where should I put this napkin?" I looked at her and said, "Do you really want me to tell you, Mom?" She tittered. (Phew. That smart-alec remark just slipped out.)

Mom lived alone on the family farm in Illinois until into her nineties. Once I had a business trip to Illinois and decided to spend the night with her. I'd picked up steaks in Wilmington and was frying them up, Scotch in one hand, cigarette in the other. Mom and I were having a great time chatting. The subject of religion came up, of course, and she said, "Oh Jimmy, I am so afraid to die." I almost dropped my drink. When I regained my composure I said, "Mom, you've gone to mass almost every day of your life. If *you're* afraid to die, how should *I* feel?" We laughed.

Later that night Mom told me sins she had committed years before. I considered them not worth mentioning, but they were a big deal to her. It was a precious gift from Mrs. Catholic Church to her sometimes-imperfect son.

My dad was an Irish Catholic American, his parents, Peter and Bridgette, came from the area known as "Joyce Country", which straddles Counties Galway and Mayo. Unlike most Irishmen, Dad didn't drink, smoke or swear - the three great vices. He was short of stature, rock solid, quick to laugh and slow to anger. He worked with his hands, prayed on his knees, and feared no one.

Dad was conservative in all things and did not cotton to the grays of life. He knew right from wrong; no wiggle room allowed. His wardrobe told it all. He had three outfits: 1) Dark suit, white shirt and tie. 2) Same suit pants and same white shirt but without the coat and tie. 3) Bib overalls with blue work shirt underneath. Those were the only clothes he ever wore...except for the one time he bought a bathing suit.

Shortly after I was first married we had installed a swimming pool in the backyard of our home in Georgia. We told Dad and Mom about it and when they came to visit, Dad put on the suit to have a swim. It covered his body from his neck to his knees. It had sleeves that went down to his elbows. When we saw it, we couldn't help laughing, and he laughed himself at his old fashioned modesty. Dad liked to laugh at himself, an endearing trait of the Irish. I asked him where on earth he found the suit; no one had seen one like it for fifty years. "Maxwell Street," he said. "They have everything."

Once I asked Dad why he didn't wear shirts that had color. "Too showy," he said. The man could have been a Mennonite.

Peter John Joyce, Jr. was an electrician by trade. He could make, or repair, anything. At his funeral Monsignor McMahon said, "I can see Peter now, walking around heaven with his tool box, asking people if they need anything fixed." Dad was happiest with a tool in his hands: screwdriver, soldering iron, hammer, wrench, wire cutters, shovel and so on. When he and Mom retired to the farm, he insisted that the little guest cottage on the property must have a basement. "Every building should have a basement," he said, as though this was a law.

So he took his pick and shovel, busted a hole in the wood floor, and started to dig throwing the dirt out the window. When the hole was over his head he piled the dirt onto a piece of plywood, filled it up, and then climbed out of the hole. He drug the plywood (there were ropes attached to it) over to the window and shoveled out the dirt. Then back into the hole he'd go.

He was well along on the project when he experienced heaviness in his chest. It was after supper and he thought it was something he ate. He delayed twelve hours before going to the hospital. When a doctor at the emergency room saw him he said, "Get that man on a gurney!" Dad had had a heart attack. A few days later, on Labor Day in 1972, my dad died. He was sixty-eight.

Dad was a self-effacing, un-worldly man. He was friendly to those he met, but he had no personal friends. He didn't want any. His preoccupations were his work, his family and his Catholic faith. His pleasures were simple. For instance, he loved puns. Once he told us he was "taking the month off." We were shocked. Then he went over to the calendar and tore off the month.

When televisions were invented, he thrilled to *Gunsmoke, Lawrence Welk* and *The Saturday Night Fights*, but not during Lent. For forty days and forty nights, the TV in our house was off. He hung a cover over it lest anyone forgot. During those forty days he got up an hour earlier to attend mass and receive communion.

Because Dad worked with his hands they were always dirty. "Good, clean dirt," he'd laugh. (They were as hard as sun dried leather, unless he was feeling your forehead for a fever, then they were lamb's wool.) Whereas the rest of us washed our hands with Ivory soap, Dad used Ajax Cleanser. There was always a canister of it on the bathroom sink. It only partially worked. In his casket his hands, wrapped in a rosary, were still dirty.

Dad had two wakes – the first night in Chicago and the next night in Wilmington, where he is buried. I was outside the funeral home in Wilmington having a smoke with my Uncle Ed. Of seven siblings, Dad was the oldest boy and Ed was the youngest. Ed was a WWII veteran who experienced too many horrors in the South Pacific. When he came home he got a job, with Dad's help, as an electrician. Ed never married and when he wasn't working he hung out in the bars of 79th Street. (My mom said he was a "bar-fly." She was afraid I'd wind up just like him.)

Uncle Ed was beside himself with grief at Dad's sudden death. In Ed's mind, his clean living brother should have lived to a very old age. On the steps of Reeves Funeral Home Uncle Ed told me he would never stop drinking and smoking. "What's the point? Look at Pete." Then he said, with tears in his eyes, "You know what your father's biggest problem was, Jimmy? He thought life was on the square."

Our house on Ada Street was a gathering place for my many friends and Dad liked all but one of them. "Give that guy the gate," he said after meeting him. "He's got shifty eyes," he said, and then added, "Tell me who your friends are, Jim, and I'll tell you who you are." Gulp. Dad especially liked Billy Callaghan calling him "the salt of the earth." Billy became a police commander. His other favorite was the other Jimmy Joyce (Carpenter). "He's going places," Dad said.

When Dad died Jimmy asked if he could have some of Dad's tools as mementos. I said, "Of course, my brother and I wouldn't know what to do with them." So Jim took a few tools, which would have pleased my dad. He also took boxes filled with nails.

Some months later Jim called. "I was swearing at your dad last night."

"Why?"

"I was hanging signs on telephone poles for Jerry." (Joyce who was running for Chicago alderman). "It was ten below zero. When I left the house with the signs, I grabbed a handful of your dad's nails and put them in my coat pocket. I was on the ladder and had the first sign lined up just right. I took a nail from my pocket, but it was bent. I took another and it was bent. I then realized they were all bent! So now I'm on my hands and knees on Western Avenue, in the middle of the night, banging on his nails, trying to straighten them out."

"Jim," I said, "haven't I always told you my dad never threw anything away?"

When I got to college, Dad was somewhat in awe of the friends I'd made, especially Bill Smith, whose dad was the president of Inland Steel and John Breen, whose dad was a prominent Chicago attorney. Both were from wealthy northern suburbs. One time John, who owned a car, came to our house to pick me up for the trip back to John Carroll University. Dad tried to give John money for gas but John refused. "Not necessary, Mr. Joyce."

"Okay then," Dad said, "Much obliged. But when you get to Cleveland make sure Jim buys you a turkey dinner."

Being Irish, a man's man, and a product of the early 1900's Dad never paid attention to his feelings. If things bothered him he'd let them simmer until there was enough fuel to ignite his temper. And what a temper it was – an explosion with harsh words that hurt.

In high school, I was flunking physics at the half way mark. On PTA night, Mom, Dad and I had a meeting with Brother Comack, the one who cracked the blackboard with his fist. He was very nice that night, telling my parents that my grades were improving and he was sure I'd be fine at year's end. I was pleased.

When we got in the car I, like a fool, asked Dad if he would drop me off at the corner so I could hang out with my friends. He said not a word. When we got home Vesuvius blew. Dad began yelling, saying that throughout the meeting I had been scowling at Brother Comack. I would no more scowl at Brother Comack than I would head-butt a bear but that is what dad said and I was not about to argue. Dad never laid a hand on me in anger, but I think he came close that night. (And I think that scared him.) That was the final barrage of anger I received from Dad, and, obviously, I've never forgotten it.

Years after Dad died I told Mom that it seemed to me that he had not been fair in dispensing his anger. She, Bob and Mary were not immune, but I felt like I got it most often. "Do you think that's true, Mom?" I said. "Yes," she said, "you deserved it the most."

You wouldn't know that Dad and I were father and son. Other than our devotion to the White Sox and the Catholic Church we had little in common. I like to be with people. He liked to be with things. I like the arts. He liked the sciences. Dad liked dogs. I don't. (Too needy.) If my toaster breaks I throw it away. His, he would fix. My favorite tool is a pen. His was a welding torch. My idea of a good time is drinking with friends. Dad's was spending time in the basement, alone, re-building a motor. Dad never brought attention to himself. I'm a writer.

Dad didn't tell me "the facts of life." (I'm not sure he knew them.) Anything having to do with sex was bad. Period. I became a psychoanalyst. All we do is talk about sex. I have many prejudices; Dad only had one. He could not stand Germans or those of German descent. "They are arrogant people," he'd say. He called them Prussians.

Dad was obsessed with job security. When he lost his job in the early thirties, he landed another one at the Joslyn Manufacturing Company back in Chicago. He worked diligently and conscientiously for Joslyn Manufacturing for twenty-seven years. The company made streetlights. He was the head of the electrical department with a dozen men who worked under him. He would never have considered a job change. In my case jobs came and jobs went. It seemed to me there was always a more fun way to make a bigger buck, and I would go for it. Dad would call this attitude irresponsible. He'd have a point.

When I was little, I'd sit on Dad's lap as he read me the funny papers. This was our private time together accompanied by hugs, kisses and laughter. But when I became six years old this ended. I had been visiting my grandparents on the farm for a few weeks. When I got home Dad was at the top of the front steps to greet me, as always, with his big smile. I put my arms out to be enfolded into his, but he put my arms down, stood back, and extended his hand. "From now on we shake hands like men," he said. I was stunned. I shook his hand pretending happiness, then went to my bedroom and cried.

Now let's get older and go up to the corner.

SECTION II
The Neighborhood

—————————— ⚮ ——————————

CHAPTER 4
79th Street

There was more to be learned on Chicago's Southside than the reading, writing and religion taught in schools. People of the neighborhood were also our teachers. By observing them we learned how life really is, not how it's supposed to be. The boundaries of St. Sabina parish were also the boundaries of our neighborhood. The church and the school were the neighborhood's head; 79th Street was its spine; its heart was in its kitchens.

79th Street is as straight as a three-edged ruler and runs due west from Rainbow Beach at Lake Michigan until it peters out in a distant suburb some fifteen miles away. In our day as it passed through Sabina, between Carpenter Street and Ashland Avenue, a distance of less than a mile. It bustled with commercial establishments: Three grocery stores (one owned by Jews), one sporting goods store (owned by a Protestant), four drug stores (one owned by another Protestant), three bakeries, an Ace Hardware, two butcher shops (with sawdust all over their floors), two cobblers, three barber shops, four funeral parlors, three florists, two shoe stores, a men's fine clothing store (owned by a Republican), a ladies fine clothing store (Jew), three newspaper stands, a music store, a bowling alley and at least eleven restaurants including a White Castle and a Chinese take-out called Lang Lee's Chop Suey (owned by a Chinaman). There were fifteen Irish taverns.

We also had real estate and insurance offices, a Selective Service office, four gas stations, doctors' and dentists' offices and a haberdashery owned by Freddie Menzer, another Jew. There was a Savings and Loan, a movie theatre, a furniture store, a veterinarian, a Chinese laundry and two dry cleaners. And there was Riley's Trick Shop, where we could buy plastic boogers, fake dog turds, whoopee cushions, hand buzzers, costumes and disappearing ink. Saint Sabina was self-sufficient.

The neighborhood was a colorful place with multiple personalities. Some of the nicknames I recall are: Spooky, Tubby, Wesley Harden, Bub McDoo, Rughead, Pinhead, Red, God, Lightning, Deals, Bells, Smiley, Spoon, Jarbonias T., Farts, Stretch, Stinkey, Chinger, Buzzy, Beansie, The Big Bopper, The Old Dad and the Riordan brothers, in order of birth: Rocky, Stony and Pebbles.

One of the more bizarre personalities was Spike Webb, the strange little man who ran the newspaper stand at 79th Street and Racine, the intersection known as "the corner." The newsstand was at the curb in front of DeLites, a restaurant and our main hang out. Newspapers in those days sold for pennies and when Spike accumulated fifteen cents he would hold the coins between two fingers and raise his arm in triumph. He'd pucker the left side of his mouth and whistle, "Tsweet, tsweet," then scurry across the sidewalk into Chris Quinn's Tavern for a glass a beer, which cost fifteen cents.

In no time he'd be back at his post until he had another fifteen cents and the ritual was repeated. We could not figure out how Spike stayed in business. It seemed like every night he drank up all the money he took in. One time Ronnie Neher asked Spike about this and Spike said, "Tsweet, tsweet."

Spike could talk but his vocabulary was limited. Whenever a customer drove up to his newsstand to buy a paper from the window of his car, Spike would say, "Here comes dat asshole." When the car pulled away Spike always said, "whadda asshole." It was rumored that Spike's newsstand was a front for a book because he discretely stuck tally (betting) sheets inside the folded newspapers when he handed them to his customers, looking both ways as though checking for cops. But you can't run a book if you don't have a brain. Spike was a mystery.

Pizza began its popularity when we were in our early teens and soon a pizza parlor, Fasano's, opened a few doors down from Chris Quinn's. It immediately became a hang out for us kids. A young man named Mike made the pizzas. He'd stand behind the plate glass window that faced 79th and toss the dough way up into the air, then deftly catch it on his fists when it came down. He'd spin it around between his fists for a few seconds then toss it back up. This was repeated over and over until the dough was the proper diameter and thickness. He then flipped it with flair onto a wooden board with a long handle, brushed on the tomato sauce, scattered the other ingredients across the top and shoved it into the oven. It was quite a show.

Although Mike didn't own Fasano's, he was the man in charge. When not making pizzas he took orders and ran the cash register. Mike was a body builder always wearing a T-shirt to show off his rippling muscles. Most of us kids considered him a numbskull but we were a little in awe of him because he was in his twenties. Aside from his pizza tossing talents, and Jack Armstrong physique, he told us stories about things he did on dates with girls. His stories were unbelievable. Once he told us, "girls like to put boys' 'things' in their mouths." What an incredible imagination Mike had and what a bullshitter! We used to laugh about how sick he was.

One night about 10:00 the door of Fasano's opened and a very drunk, very large Irishman staggered in. He gazed around the room, took about four steps, came to an unsteady halt, bent over and threw up. Everyone was stunned, including Mike, but in a few moments he composed himself.

"You drunkin, fuckin' Mick! Get out of here!" He yelled. He put his hand on the counter and vaulted it. He grabbed the Irishman by the back of his sport coat with the intention of whirling him around and pushing him back out the door. But the Irishman was an immovable mass. He didn't budge and he and Mike began to tussle. We were surprised at the deftness of the Irishman, who no longer seemed drunk. In just a few moments Mike slipped in the puke and went down on his back. The Irishman got on top of him and took a bite out of his chest. Blood started spurting and Mike started screaming. The Irishman stood up, squared himself and calmly walked out the door. Mike was taken to the hospital for stitches and a tetanus shot.

The Irish are known for excessive drinking and, for sure, Ireland has produced a million drunks, but problem drinking was not an issue for most of the families of St. Sabina. However, there were many young bucks around, like the biter in Fasano's, who were recently arrived from Ireland and found places to live in the neighborhood's spare bedrooms. They did not always exercise moderation, especially after "The Irish Hour."

On the corner of 79th and Bishop was a larger than normal Irish tavern called Hanley's House of Happiness. It took up two storefronts.

On Sunday nights Hanley's played host to a live radio broadcast called "The Irish Hour," which aired throughout Chicago. The place filled up with men, women and children who gathered to hear the songs, stories and jokes that reminded them of "the auld sod." Many of Hanley's patrons ate their Sunday supper in the tavern, washing it down with mugs of beer.

When the radio show ended, most people went home but the young bucks would adjourn to the bar and begin to drink in earnest. Interspersing their beers with shots of John Powers whiskey, a "boilermaker," it didn't take long for the arguing, shoving and "Fook yoos" to commence. Inevitably a fight broke out. It could be a Kerry man versus a lad from Mayo or perhaps a Dubliner against a young buck from Galway. It didn't matter. Those Irish loved to fight as much as they loved to drink.

Jack and Kathleen Hanley owned the establishment and would not tolerate fistfights in their tavern. The very instant one broke out baseball bat wielding bartenders ousted the combatants with the threat of never letting them come back. The boys (pronounced "byes") would leave Hanley's and go out onto 79th Street and continue to fight.

You'll remember the scene in the movie *The Quiet Man*, when John Wayne was finally goaded into fighting Danaher, his new brother-in-law. The fight was mobile, beginning on a farm and continuing, in intermittent fashion, over hill and dale and ending in a pub. There are no hills and dales on Chicago's Southside but our fighting young Irishmen were also mobile. They'd flail away at each other in front of Hanley's, or any of the other taverns they were ejected from, stop fighting and start walking home. After a hundred yards or so they'd go at each other again. This could go on for blocks.

In my home at 8027 S. Ada Street, two and a half blocks from Hanley's, I would hear them coming on Sunday nights. "You muther foocker!" Whack – Whack. "Fook you, you cook sucker!" Punch – Punch. I'd peek out our front door to see them going by with their up and down Irish gaits. Their fists and faces were bloodied and they'd be pushing, shoving and swearing at each other. They spit teeth and insults as they made their way past the house. Sometimes one would knock the other to the ground, but he didn't take that advantage. He'd keep walking. The Irish didn't fight to maim or embarrass, they fought because it was the thing to do.

It could be ninety-eight degrees in July or twenty below zero in January, but these Irish immigrants wore the same outfit every Sunday night. Heavy boots, rumpled pants, open collared shirts, and tattered, gray-flecked sport coats. A non-descript, shapeless hat topped off their ensemble. The slang name for this breed of Irishman was "Turkey," short for "Turkeybird." This was an insulting label – like "Spic" for a Mexican or "Wop" for an Italian. I don't know where the name Turkey came from but I've always assumed it was because an Irishman talking, especially when drunk, sounds like a turkey gobbling – melodic, even beautiful, and totally indecipherable.

One summer evening, before dark, three or four of us teenagers were walking past Hanley's when the door flew open and a drunken turkeybird was tossed out onto the sidewalk. We stopped to see what he would do.

He lay quiet for a few moments, face down on the concrete, then slowly raised his head. It was bobbing up and down. Then he focused in on something down the street. He managed to get on all fours and began crawling. He didn't notice us as he crawled by. 79th Street has parallel parking and the Irishman crawled about thirty yards until he got to the door of one of the parked cars. He got hold of the door handle on the passenger side and pulled himself to his feet. He then began inching toward the back of the car, steadying himself with his hands on the roof. He made it around the trunk, to the other side of the car, opened the driver's door and got behind the wheel. He fumbled with the keys and then the engine coughed to life.

He did not have enough room to pull away from the curb so he backed up with a lurch, smashing the headlights of the car behind him. We watched in astonishment as he fought the gearshift. Then he paused, nodded to himself, hunched his shoulders and very deliberately pulled away from the curb heading east on 79th, his door still wide open. On-coming cars swerved and honked as he weaved back and forth across the centerline. We watched 'til he was out of sight. It was a miracle no one was killed. We laughed ourselves silly.

A family story, often told, was about the time Mom took my brother Bobby (age 4) to see Santa Claus. At that time my folks still lived in

St. Leo Parish. Santa Claus was at Franks Department Store on 79ᵗʰ St. near Halsted. There was a long line of moms and kids waiting to see him and she and Bobby got in it. Mom didn't know Santa had been drinking until she got to the front of the line and smelled his breath. Too late now. Bobby was already on his lap.

Santa was jolly and having a good time for himself playing the role. He had a rich Irish brogue.

"And what's your name, little fella?" asked the jovial Santa.

"Bobby."

"That's a fine name, Bobby, what do you want Santa to bring you for Christmas?"

"A train."

"And you shall have it, Bobby! Where do you live?"

"On Peoria Street."

"You don't mean it," said Santa. "So do I!"

As part of my training to become a psychoanalyst I attended seminars on drug and alcohol abuse. One time the speaker made this interesting observation. He said the Irish culture did not produce more alcoholics, per capita, than many other nations. He named the Scandinavian Countries, Russia, Poland and Hungary as examples. He said they were actually worse, but he went on to say there was a difference. In those countries getting drunk was a disgrace. In Ireland they found humor in it.

Our main grocery store was Kalk's. The father and son team of Al and Seymour owned it. They were Jews. I remember them as candid, generous and delightfully sarcastic. One afternoon Seymour was eating a pizza at the checkout counter. I'd not seen one before and asked him what it was. He gave me a slice and said, "You won't like it, Jimmy, you're Irish. They don't like anything new."

Another Jew on 79ᵗʰ was Freddie Menzer who owned the haberdashery. He was a soft-spoken, gentle, little old bachelor who gave us kids great bargains on pants, shirts and shoes. When we went into his store, he didn't care if we bought anything or not. He enjoyed our company and liked to tell us stories about when he was a kid in the old country–Russia, I think. His store had no shelves or displays; it was just a bunch of cardboard boxes, literally hundreds of them, stacked to the ceiling. Freddie knew the contents of every one of them.

The other Jews, Mr. & Mrs. Schwartz, had the ladies fine clothing store. Mrs. worked the store and Mr. sat outside on the sidewalk, on a folding chair, eager to engage any passersby in conversation. He was bald; snaggle toothed and had a jolly disposition. I learned on 79th Street that there was nothing wrong with Jews.

That was not the case with Protestants. On our block of Ada Street, between 80th and 81st, lived about one hundred and fifty people and only six of them, three elderly couples, were Protestants. I remember them as being exceptionally crabby people always yelling at us kids for stepping on their grass. "You kids! Stay on the sidewalk! That's what it's for!" they'd shout.

One time I made the mistake of bouncing a rubber ball against the garage door of one of the Protestants. It was a little ball and I'd skip hop it to the door then catch it as it came back. I didn't know the Protestant was in his garage. I never thought about it. But after a few bounces he came running out of the side door and into the alley and yelled at me, "Stop hitting my door with your ball! You're leaving marks on it!" I told him I was sorry and we kids started moving on and then he added, "Why don't you go say your *black* rosary!" It was my first experience with reverse prejudice. Sabina's new pastor, Monsignor John McMahon, had the idea that on Thursday nights the parishioners on each block in the parish should gather together to say the rosary. Host houses were established for this purpose and the practice was soon known as "The Block Rosary."

I was twenty-three years old and in the Army before I became aware that all Protestants were not assholes. My grandfather, and all my other Lutheran relatives excluded, of course.

I can't write about 79th Street without writing about DeLites. It was a restaurant and soda fountain and the neighborhood's main meeting place. It was like hundreds of such establishments scattered across Chicago, owned by Greeks. When you walked in the front door of DeLites, the cash register was on your left followed by a counter with six permanently mounted stools; beyond that were a dozen booths. There were no partitions. Cooking was done on a grill behind the counter. Soda fountain creations were also made there. All very simple, straightforward and in plain view. The food menu was limited; the menu for fountain creations was extensive. The place smelled like ice cream.

Gus and Tula Tsopels, a childless couple in their forties, owned DeLites. When Gus opened the restaurant at 10:00 in the morning he was always in a grouchy mood. He was a Greek, they are all grouchy, and Gus mostly remained that way until about 3:00 in the afternoon. He'd then lighten up a little and by 8:00 at night he was down right pleasant. This mood pattern never changed. He once told us not to speak to him until he'd had at least five cups of coffee and half a pack of cigarettes.

Gus was about 5'9", balding, average weight. He wore a full-length white apron that extended below his knees. He had a perpetual five o'clock shadow like Richard Nixon. Tula was almost as tall as Gus, had a huge bosom and was a little overweight. She always wore a black dress and heels. She had black hair, high cheekbones, a sensuous mouth, and dark eyes. A matronly Sophia Loren. In her youth she must have been stunning. Tula's mood, unlike Gus's, fluctuated throughout the day. Mostly she was all business but was easily distracted by gossip. If Tula was in a bad mood we'd give her a tidbit of neighborhood gossip and she'd perk right up.

One time she and Gus bought new sugar dispensers that were placed on the counter and the tables. They had a hinged metal flap on top. Teenagers can't keep their hands off anything and we would sometimes idly flip the top of the new dispensers. "Tick." This drove Tula crazy. "Whoever's doing that, stop it!" she'd yell across the room. When we became aware of this idiosyncrasy we tried to control ourselves but the things just asked to be flipped.

Spooks Cavanaugh and Tula never got along and he was the main offender. He'd wait until the place was full and then do a "tick, tick, tick." With all the people talking, it was hard for Tula to pinpoint the "ticks" but she soon learned it was always Cavanaugh. She'd walk back to his booth and order him out – barring him for the rest of the day.

My friends and I hung out at DeLites during our teen years. Many guys and girls from the Sabina classes ahead of us and a few from behind us also spent time there. The place symbolized a rite of passage from adolescence to adulthood; from the neighborhood to beyond.

It was at DeLites that I became aware you could make a living without being a policeman, fireman or working in a factory. Jack Moran* was a regular. It seemed like he was there most of the day drinking coffee, smoking cigarettes and pouring over racing forms. Jack was a lawyer, about 40, always dressed to the nines in suit, tie, tie-pin and hat. He had a physical deformity. When he stood he leaned forward at a 45-degree angle like his spine was fused in that position and he couldn't turn his head. He walked side to side like a duck. To look right or left he had to twist his whole body.

Jack was the most pleasant of people, enjoying conversation with all the patrons be they young or older. The only thing that would interrupt a conversation was an ambulance. When one went screaming by DeLites, Jack would bolt from his booth, put on his hat, and hustle as fast as he could (not that fast) to his big white Cadillac and off he'd go. When he returned Gus always asked, "How'd it go, Jack?" Almost always Jack would smile and say, "Got him!" He'd then return to the racing forms.

When I was fifteen and first started going to DeLites, Gus and Tula intimidated me. His gruffness and her haughtiness made me want to be invisible to them. I'd slink in and out and do my best not to "tick" the sugar shakers. When I paid my bill, Gus called me "boy." Although I'd become a regular he never acknowledged that he'd seen me before. When I turned sixteen, I got my drivers license and sometimes drove my dad's car to DeLites parking behind it. One day Gus was taking out the garbage and saw me get out of the car. I said, "Hi, Gus." He ignored me.

I went inside and joined some of the other guys in our gang. When we were about to leave, Gus came to our booth. "Jim," he said (My God, he knows my name!), "I can't get a cab for Tula. Can you take her home? I'll give you money for gas." I couldn't get out of the booth fast enough.

At this time in my young life I was in love with Elizabeth Taylor. I used to fantasize going horseback riding with her and then, later, kissing her, chastely, in the barn. If Gus had said, "Jim, you have two options: a date with Elizabeth Taylor or driving Tula home," I would have chosen the ride with Tula. To me she and Gus were the most important people on 79th Street – making them the most important people in the world. Liz could wait.

Gus and Tula lived in an apartment on Blackstone Street on the east side of Chicago. This was about a twenty-five minute drive from the corner. Tula chatted me up the whole way, prying me for information about other guys in the gang. "Who are they dating? How are they doing in school? Who's trustworthy? Who's a jerk?" I gave her all the information she asked for and embellished it when I could. By the end of our ride she asked if I'd like to work at DeLites washing dishes. I said yes immediately, not even asking what it paid. Acceptance! A Gus and Tula *imprimatur* was placed on me! I was thrilled. I had just become *somebody* on 79th Street.

CHAPTER 5
Jobs and Shopping
Coauthor –Jim Carpenter Joyce

To further enrich your understanding of 79th Street and Leo High School the other James T. Joyce, Jim, now enters the picture.

Jim and I went to part of St. Sabina grammar school together, all of Leo High School and part of college. The teachers at Sabina and Leo differentiated us by the streets we lived on, calling us Joyce Carpenter Street and Joyce Ada Street. I'm Ada. (To our friends in our street corner gang he was Big Jimmy and I was Little Jimmy because he started out taller than me. Eventually I caught up and passed him, and am now at least a half inch taller (and probably even more), but to gang members I'm still Little Jimmy. That's what old friends are for – to keep you from growing.)

Jim Carpenter's Narrative

I enjoyed working as a kid and always had a job. And that's a good thing because it was necessary. All seven of us "siblings" (I recently learned that word's meaning and it's now firmly in my vocabulary) went to Catholic schools. Leo High School at that time cost $150.00 a year. Our dad was a fireman and that kind of paper did not grow on trees. My first real job was at Cornell's meat market on 79th Street between Elizabeth and Throop Streets. I worked after school and on Saturdays. I loved those two old guys, George and Bill, who owned the place. They were probably in their forties.

The shop was small with the standard white porcelain refrigerator display cases, butcher blocks and sawdust on the floor. I wore a white apron and was in charge of mixing the brine in wooden barrels where they corned the beef. I scrubbed the cutting blocks with a wire brush and swept up the bloodied sawdust at the end of the day. My favorite part of the job was on Saturday when I delivered the meat orders all over the neighborhood on a bicycle. They were wrapped in white butcher paper and loaded into the big wire basket on the front. I swear it could hold half a steer, or whole pig. I enjoyed the tips, too. Most people were generous.

What I found most fascinating about George and Bill was their irreverence toward women. It was shocking. I'd never heard that kind of talk. They'd come up with some of the most unbelievable things to say about women's body parts and the various cuts of meats and the myriad combinations of the two. I was blushing most of the time I was on the clock at Cornells. "Oh, hi, Mrs. O'Rourke*! How's the mister feeling, the kids are good? That's good. What can I show you today? Pork chops? Good, we just got some fresh ones in today. I'll go in the cooler and bring some out." They'd come in the back room holding their white-aproned crotch saying, "I'll show a pork chop you won't soon forget, you snobby bitch. Your husband is down the street in the Old Bear Lounge sleeping on the pool table. Jimmy, bring her back here, put extra sawdust on the floor and take notes!" I would laugh in wonderment, embarrassment and fascination (and wonder what intercourse was really like). The redder I got, the more outrageous they got.

"Jimmy, get up front and wait on Mrs. Skinarski's* daughter, she's about your age. She always orders Polish sausage. Unzip under your apron and slip your thing into the display case and see if she picks it out!"

I'd go out front all red-faced to talk to Donna Skinarski and I could hear them howling in the back room. They were nuts! I wonder what became of them. Sometimes I miss them. I've been meaning to ask Jim, the psychoanalyst, about the nature of their behavior towards females. There must have been some crazy shit going on in their brains, or maybe it was the sawdust.

Jim mentioned Fred Menzers' clothing shop but I want to add more. He called it a haberdashery, a word that doesn't quite fit Fred's shop. Jim might be using it to further his case for good and not so good blue-collar neighborhoods. He thinks Sabina is a cut above my first parish, Visitation, for instance, and I take issue with that. However, I will concede one point – no one ever moved from Sabina to Visitation.

That may not be going downwards, but it certainly would be going backwards.

Fred Menzer was a kindly, soft-spoken Jew approximately one-hundred-two-years old. I know he was older than my Dad. His shop had no counter, displays or cash register. Fred had developed his own system for figuring the state sales tax and seemed very comfortable in his computations. Boxes of factory-second pants, socks, shirts and underwear were everywhere but he specialized in plaid shirts. If the police ever had probable cause to put a few of our 79th Street gang in a line up, it would be difficult for the alleged victim to tell the difference between us; we all wore the same clothes bought from Freddie Menzer.

In my early years, my entire wardrobe was put together at Fred's but as I became more cosmopolitan, I expanded my horizon with the help of Mr. Frank Watson, father of Mike and Cy. He regularly took a carload of us from 79th Street down to Maxwell Street, also called "Jewtown." Mr. Watson's introduction to our Maxwell Street shopping sprees was always begun with the words "Maxwell Street. You can buy anything there from a baby's fart to a clap of thunder!" Case in point, that's where Jim's dad found the full-body bathing suit. Here Mr. Watson introduced us to Mal's shop, a much bigger version of Fred's with a huge selection of factory-second fashions. I bought most of my personal clothing there until I was well into my forties. Then I bought boxer shorts and tee shirts by the case on Maxwell Street and divided them up between my (you're way ahead of me) siblings and siblings-in-law. (What a great word!)

I became a firefighter in 1965 and a few years later while working in the firehouse one of the guys yelled out, "Mo's out in back." I went out in the alley to see who Mo was. Guess who? Fred "Mo" Menzer. I reminded him of our previous history and he remembered, "You're one of the Joyce boys." He had connected me to Jim and Jerry, not bad company. His trunk was an extension of his shop – pants, socks, tee shirts, underwear and plaid shirts – all seconds. He visited many of the one hundred firehouses on an irregular basis during the 1950's, '60's and into the '70's. When Fred died, he left a will that contributed a block of stock (Borg Warner) to the firefighter pension board's "Widows and orphans fund." To this day it is called the Walsh-Ende-Menzer-Quinn

Gift Fund. At Christmas time the fund sends a check to widows and kids. The checks total $400,000.00 each year! What a fine Christian Fred was! I'm proud to say he was a part of my growing up.

Around this time a new concept of enterprise was introduced in the country – the shopping mall. One of the first built in the United States was just thirty blocks south and west of Sabina at 95th and Western. It was called the Evergreen Plaza and it was a marvel. All the stores were in one structure! The developer was Arthur Rubloff, another fine Jew.

I can't think of the Plaza without remembering our science teacher at Leo, Mr. Blosser*. He was an elderly fellow whose mind did not connect the dots. His stay at Leo was brief because student control wasn't his strong suit. We had our own program going on in the back of his musty classroom. One day Jim and I did a scientific experiment with what we called a new form of ink. It was actually Mr. Blosser's grape juice, which he didn't miss. One of our snooty peers (similar to sibling, both words in use prior to DNA) was showing off his new, expensive fountain pen. We talked him into using our new, improved, ink. He had a negative experience, the pen was ruined, and he told Blosser that "The Joyces ruined my pen." "Who are the Joyces?" asked Blosser. This student will remain unnamed as he went on to a stellar career as an Army General and CIA officer.

In an attempt to win us over Mr. Blosser offered to get us students Christmas holiday jobs at Carson Pirie Scott department store in the new Evergreen Plaza. "Just go to Carson's employment department and ask for Harvey Fink*," he said, "And use my name." John Nugent Glenville, Jim and I took the bus after school and located Mr. Fink. Based on my experience at the butcher shop, I fully realize the pressure felt by those in retail, especially prior to the holidays. At the mention of Mr. Blosser's name Mr. Fink reacted rather badly. "#*...!#@" were just some of the words he used as he showed us to the escalator with a message for Mr. Blosser to quit sending kids out here for jobs. "The old bastard's crazy!" said Fink.

"Okay, dude, lighten up," we thought but we didn't say it because "dude" hadn't been invented at that time.

We walked around the Plaza and marveled at the grandness of it all, ending up at Morrie Mages Sporting goods, ten times the size of Bill Johnson's on 79th Street. We looked at the latest in sporting equipment and attire and Glenville bought, of all things, a boomerang. As we walked along 95th Street he was reading the directions for boomerangs. We convinced him he didn't need directions. "Boomerangs are boomerangs," we said, "You throw them and they come back. C'mon, John, throw it. It'll be fun." It was dark out but there were bright holiday lights from the stores giving him some hope that he wouldn't lose it.

With more encouragement from us, "Give it a good toss," we said. "Don't be such a chicken." John reluctantly launched the boomerang, giving it a good toss. The thing went way above the lights and into the black sky and we waited anxiously for its return. It didn't return, of course, and boy, was Glenville mad at us! (It must be making the turn at New Zealand about now heading for home where it will land right back on the boomerang tree where it all started. Or, more likely, it's still on the roof of Carson Pirie Scott.)

CHAPTER 6
Job Begets Boat

I was fourteen when 79th Street provided me my first job, the one before DeLites. It was at Mrs. Burns' Catering Service, a new business in a storefront between Ada and Throop. My friend, Chuckie Crowe (later known as Jarbie), got a job as a busboy and he put in a good word for me.

Mrs. Burns, a Swedish blue-eyed blonde built like a middle line backer, was a sweet woman, but harried by the demands of running a business. From time to time she'd snap at you, but only if you deserved it. I liked her a lot.

Les, her husband, also worked in the business but nothing bothered him. His primary job was to drive the truck to the various locations where the catering was done – VFW halls, Knights of Columbus halls, church halls, American Legion halls, Masonic Temples, Jewish Synagogues, etc. The UPS-style truck was light blue with "Mrs. Burns Catering" painted on the sides. Into the back we loaded big wooden cases of plates, cups, saucers, napkins, tablecloths and silverware. Food was always cooked on 79th Street so it, too, was loaded into the truck. Large, metal containers kept it hot. Also in the back of the truck were us busboys sitting on top of the crates. Every function was a new adventure.

Les had a sidekick named Johnny who was even more laid pack than Les. Hired to help us load and unload the truck, he mostly just supervised. On the way to and from jobs, with Les driving and Johnny riding shotgun, the two of them had a great time talking about women in a way I'd never heard before, just like Jimmy in the butcher shop. I'd thought this was because Les and Johnny were Protestants, but apparently not. The Cornell butcher shop owners were Catholic. 79th Street was, indeed, a place of learning.

One of the many benefits of my job was that I worked with some of my friends' mothers who were waitresses. Mrs. Burns, although a Protestant herself, always hired people from the almost exclusively Irish Catholic neighborhood. Because my friends' mothers were my co-workers they told me to call them by their first names, Helen, Rita, Mary and others. Naturally I did not. But I got to know them as people, not as other kids' moms, and that was educational. None, by the way, were subjects of Les and Johnny's comments. Those two knew the connection and showed they had scruples by not doing so but the other waitresses, and any other females in their sights, were fair game.

When we got to our destination and the truck was unloaded, Johnny and Les always split to the closest tavern. We wouldn't see them again until time to load back up. In those days, drinking and driving was so common that I don't believe it was against the law unless you had an "open container" in the car. Breathalyzers were yet to be invented. Mrs. Burns disliked Les and Johnny always "being gone" but she never said a word. Les, I learned, had a temper.

My first day on the job we employees were hustling around the kitchen on 79th Street getting ready for that night's affair. I whispered to Les that I had to go to the bathroom. In a voice loud enough for all to hear he said: "It's down the stairs and to the right. Here, take a magazine. It's the only peace and quiet you get around here!" Everybody laughed.

I was mortified as I slunk off with the magazine but when I returned nobody even noticed me. His joke was not about me but about working at Burns Catering. I realized, for the first time, that it's okay if people know you need to go to the bathroom for a number two.

After about six months, Mrs. Burns promoted me to head busboy and gave me a twenty-five cent per hour raise. How proud I was! The other busboys didn't resent it, which made it even better.

One of the biggest jobs we ever had was at the magnificent Medinah Temple in the Loop. It lasted well past midnight. When Les and Johnny showed back up we were beat and they were plastered. Les, without reason, tore into Chuckie Crowe, accusing him of being lazy. I came to Chuckie's defense telling Les that we were all exhausted and that he wouldn't be talking like that if he weren't so drunk.

He turned on me, letting me have it with both drunken barrels, calling me, among other things, a fucking big shot. "You're fired, big shot." He pulled me out onto the street, hailed a cab and put me in it. "Take this big shot home," he told the driver and threw some money at him. I was stunned.

A few days later Mrs. Burns called and asked me to come to the store. In front of Les she told me it was a big misunderstanding and they wanted me back. He said nothing. I did return for a short time but things between Les and me were not the same. We were uncomfortable with each other, too polite, too stilted. I told Mrs. Burns that my parents wanted me to spend more time on schoolwork and I had to quit. She said she understood. Her eyes welled up; she slipped me a $10 bill, and gave me a hug.

I saved most of the money I made working at Mrs. Burns Catering ($275) and decided to buy a boat. Although my home was in the city, my grandparents had a farm on a river, the Kankakee, sixty miles away. Ever since I was little I had dreamed of going out on the river in my own boat. I knew nothing about boats so I asked my Uncle Bob if he'd help me pick one out. He owned a boat, a 16' runabout, making him an expert.

Uncle Bob and I took my $275 to Sears in Joliet where he lived. With his guidance I bought a 12' aluminum boat, oars and a 12 horsepower Evinrude motor. The salesman said the boat shouldn't have more than a 10 hp motor but Uncle Bob didn't believe it. He borrowed a trailer from a policeman buddy and we were off to the Kankakee River. Uncle Bob was a policeman.

In the middle of the Kankakee, in front of the farm, was a large boulder. We called it Turtle Rock because from the shore it looked like a giant turtle and when the sun was shining turtles enjoyed sitting on it.

Uncle Bob and I got into the boat, me up front and him in back with the motor. This maiden voyage went smoothly enough until we decided to see Turtle Rock up close. Uncle Bob roared up to it, cut the engine too late, and banged into it.

"Shit!" he said. He leaned over the side and told me not to worry. "No harm done, Jimmy. Just a little dent. Doesn't mean a thing." He then explained the workings of the gearshift on the motor (FWD, NEU, REV) and the throttle (just twist it) and told me I was ready to go.

We stood up to change places and damned near capsized. "That's why they say 'never stand up in a boat'", Bob declared. I took control of the motor and slowly maneuvered us to shore.

Bob got out on the bank. I started out gingerly but quickly gained confidence and soon got up to full speed, and that's when I knew something was wrong. The nose of the boat went way up in the air, then slammed down on the water, then way back up again, and down again. This hadn't happened when Uncle Bob was driving. I got nervous and slowed her up, but even then the nose was too high. I couldn't see in front of me. I had to weave back and forth to get back to the farm where Uncle Bob was watching from the shore. "Here's the problem," he said. "Your boat needs two people for ballast. The motor's too big. So when you are alone you need this." He picked up a boulder the size of a breadbasket and put it in the front of the boat. "Now try it."

I took off again and when I got to full throttle the nose went up in the air, but not so high this time, and when it settled down it stayed down. I was skimming across the water with a beautiful wake behind. I had a boat. My dream came true.

Because the boat was little I could take it into shallow water. I liked to putt-putt way up into Horse Creek, a tributary of the Kankakee, then cut the engine and silently drift back to the river, delighting in the clear water under the boat and marveling at the canopy of dark green leaves above. The smells of wild flowers on the banks, freshly mowed hay from the fields nearby and river mud combined to make the perfect incense for this natural cathedral. I spent untold hours in it.

There was one disadvantage of my boat, however, and that was, as motorboats go, it was slow. Because it was little with no top or windshield, you had the feeling you were going really fast with the throttle wide open but, in reality, you weren't. Twelve-horse power isn't much.

One time I took my girlfriend from the neighborhood, Judy Walsh, for a ride. Judy, in her bathing suit, sat in the front of the boat and I manned the motor in back. Soon a speedboat pulling a skier went flying past us like we were at anchor. Both the driver of the boat and the skier ogled Judy, who was a head-turner. They swung around in front of us to show off and get their eyes full of Judy.

Then they did a complete circle around us and when they flew past us again the skier dropped one of his skis, further showing off.

Judy, being a good Catholic girl never would have admitted it, but she thoroughly enjoyed the attention. For my part I tried to look cool, all the while feeling like an inadequate little asshole in the back of my inadequate little boat.

This time the ski boat kept going way up the river, almost out of sight, but I did see them stop to let the skier into the boat. Soon they came roaring back to pick up the floating ski they'd dropped. I can't tell you how pleased I was that they didn't see the ski in time, ran right over it and cut it in half. Embarrassed, they kept going. I'd never been so happy.

My boat helped me purge Leo High School from my system. After graduation I took my physics book into the basement of our home in Chicago where my dad had his work area. I found a 2-foot by 2-foot piece of plywood about an inch thick. I placed my physics book onto the plywood and opened it so the pages splayed upward. I then nailed the four corners of the book's cover to the wood.

I borrowed my dad's car and drove down to the Kankakee. I got into my boat and went up the river about a quarter of a mile and cut the engine. Then I placed the board with the physics book nailed to it on the seat in front of me. Next I saturated the son of a bitch with lighter fluid. Then I very gently placed the wood on the surface of the water. I lit a match and the physics book burst into flames.

I restarted the motor and hurried back to the farm. I parked the boat and then sat on the bank with my .22. As my flaming physics book drifted by I started shooting at it, causing the fiery pages to fly into the air and then gently flutter down onto the water. Beautiful! I continued shooting until the book was out of range and burned to a crisp. See you later, Leo High School.

My little boat gave me oh so many hours of happiness cruising up and down the river, from Warner's Bridge to the shallows above the Wilmington Dam, whether with friends or alone with the great big stone. I am not exaggerating when I say it was the best purchase I have ever made in my life. Thank you, Mrs. Burns and 79th Street.

(Note: I would have flunked physics were if not for last minute tutoring by the super-smart gang member, Tommy Carroll. He showed me the light. I aced the final.)

SECTION III
The Guys in the Gang

———————— ✕ ————————

CHAPTER 7

The Guys in the Gang

I was lucky when it came to my most important teachers, the ones who prepared me for day-to-day life, in other words, how to get along with others. These teachers were my peers, "the guys in the gang," who were, in some ways, tougher than the nuns. When I became an adult it surprised me how many people couldn't get along with co-workers, have good friends or who simply didn't fit in. They never learned to play with the other kids, tease and be teased, learn boundaries and know which ones can be breeched. My gang would have fixed them, if they'd had the fortitude to hang in there.

Twenty-four guys over the years could rightfully call themselves "one of the guys in the gang." Most of us became friends while students at St. Sabina Grammar School; many of these friendships beginning in the first grade. We shared teachers, classrooms, baseball diamonds, basketball courts, football fields, vacant lots, streets, alleys, masses and confessionals. When we graduated we attended the same parties, spun the same bottle and kissed the same girls. Others joined the gang during our high school years. Most members were close and some of us became more like brothers than friends.

To this day we refer to ourselves as "the guys in the gang," but by today's standards the name is misleading. We did not deal drugs, fence stolen goods or extort money. True, we were not always on the right side of the law, but almost all of our escapades were misdemeanors, not felonies. Our sometimes-illegal activities were not born of greed or malice, but of a youthful desire for fun, excitement and the natural rebellion of teenagers. We were normal.

Okay, it is not normal to steal a truck and its contents, temporarily depriving a man of his livelihood. It is technically a felony. It is probably two felonies and was, in retrospect, a bad thing to do. But we did it as a joke and there were mitigating circumstances: we'd been drinking, were only sixteen, and the truck belonged to a member of the other race, our natural enemy.

So "gang" is a misnomer. We were merely a group of teenagers who hung around the street corner of 79th and Racine and, from time to time, had some fun. While it is true that in our youth almost all of us spent at least a few hours detained at a police station, none of us could be considered bad people and only one did real time. And, yes, one got shot dead but after we grew up and left the neighborhood. So that doesn't count.

There was no structure and nothing formal about gang membership. No invitation, no initiation, no meetings, no elected officials, no colors, no jackets and no secret greeting. The only unwritten rule was that all members were in the same grade in school. I doubt this rule was ever stated, nor can I recall it ever being challenged. It just worked out that way.

Our usual gathering place, we called "the hangout," was DeLites. We would meet inside and order something to eat or drink and remain there until we wore out our welcome. When Gus or Tula asked us to leave, we would re-gather on the sidewalk in front of the place. From there we'd plot and plan the day's or night's activities. Joining the gang was easy, merely show up and hang around, but staying in the gang could be difficult. We were merciless critics of human nature.

Everybody knows what a pimp is, but I can assure you no gang member ever met one on 79th Street. However, the word "pimp" was frequently used, as was the word "pimping." I do not know why. Pimping (ridiculing) is what we did to each other. Outsiders and oddballs were pimps. These words were a large part of the culture of us guys in the gang.

When Seymour Kalk said the Irish, "don't like anything new" he could not have been more accurate. Any variation from the established norm would be cause for a gang member to get pimped. Showing sensitivity would raise eyebrows; using big words would beget jeers; being addicted to cars or, God forbid, motorcycles would bring scorn, and dressing different from our usual conservative ways was sure to emote derisive laughter.

A new guy started hanging around and we liked him well enough.

One day he showed up wearing black pants with pink stitches running down the sides. This new style had become popular on the *American Bandstand* television show. He thought he was simply keeping up with the times, but we knew better. He was trying to be different.

"Hey, Frank*. Nice Pants. Are they your sister's?"

"Hey, Frank. Why didn't you tell us you were queer?"

"Hey, Frank. Just come back from Puerto Rico?"

We laughed and laughed and pimped his pants - and that was the end of him.

But the quickest and surest way to get pimped would be to brag about yourself. This was not tolerated. For instance, Bill Nelligan could not say, "Did you see the tackle I made yesterday?" But others could brag about Bill. "Did you see that tackle Nelligan made? The guy will be in the hospital for a week."

Over enthusiasm, about anything, would get you pimped. It wasn't cool. Being cool was at the essence of gang membership but, smart as I am, I cannot adequately define "cool" and I shouldn't have to.

Getting fat wasn't cool, so that could get you pimped. A kid across the alley was named Eugene, nickname "Euge." We taunted his fat brother with: "Euge's brother is huger than Euge."

You'd be pimped if you acted or talked like an adult. We took pride in *not being adult*.

Tom Lally never tied his shoes. Never. The laces dragged on the ground and were out of half their eyelets. His shoes flopped with every step he took. The backs of his shoes were crushed down like slippers. He drove us nuts. We constantly pimped him about it, accusing him of severe laziness, but Tom didn't care. Pimping doesn't work if the person doesn't care.

We were rabid sports enthusiasts. Gang members closely followed the White Sox, and were devoted to them. We hated the Cubs. We all participated in the year-round sports of baseball, basketball and football whether we were any good or not. You would not be pimped for being a poor athlete, that's something out of your control. Our pimping honed in on personality defects. On the other hand, character flaws were not pimped, rather they were laughed at, even admired – stealing a truck, for instance, or money from the poor box at church. One guy enjoyed hurling his empty beer bottles through the windshield of parked cars. Another guy shot out streetlights. No problem.

There were three unquestioned beliefs that we lived by: The Catholic religion was the only true religion; the Irish were the greatest race on Earth; those who were not from the street corner of 79th and Racine were probably pimps. Chicago's Northsiders were definitely pimps (or worse). After twenty years absence, I moved back to Chicago and Barbara and I decided to live in a condo on Lake Michigan on North Lake Shore Drive. Carpenter Joyce's dad, by now a retired fireman, said to me, "Why do you want to live up there with all those weirdos?" (On the other hand, Northsiders didn't think much of us Southsiders. To this day the City of Chicago sponsors a summer festival called, "The Taste of Chicago." It is held downtown in Grant Park. A million people show up for cheap food, most of them Southsiders. The Northsiders refer to the festival as "The Taste of White Trash.")

Some gang members were not of Irish descent: Gargola, La Rose, Neher, Overbeek and the Watson brothers. The rest of us graciously overlooked their unfortunate breeding, knowing they wished they were Irish. I was only half Irish, Mom was Scotch-Danish, but nobody held this against me. How could they? Mom ran the church.

We gang members were an eclectic bunch in other ways. Some, like Carroll and McNally were super bright, most of us were average intelligence, and none were slow. Joe La Rose had a bombastic personality while Tom McArdle, Chuck Gargola and Mike Collins were laid back. I was Mr. Salesman while Joyce Carpenter was steady and prudent. Bill Nelligan was jolly unless you pissed him off. Then he could be fierce. Cy Watson was inordinately nice; his brother, Mike, was inordinately opinionated; Tom McDonough was inordinately abrasive.

Jerry Joyce exuded confidence. His IQ is off the chart. He was a Chicago police officer, then a lawyer, then a Chicago alderman, an Illinois state senator, a college professor, a consultant to politicians seeking election or re-election and today he owns businesses. He's one of the more interesting guys in the gang. (Jerry's not related to us Jimmys.)

Bob "Spooks" Cavanaugh had a beautiful singing voice, which he used often in the taverns to get free drinks. "Sing us a song, Spooky, we'll buy you a beer." You might think this was pimpy but it wasn't because Spooks was balanced. He was a superb athlete, good with his fists, affable, and a snappy, yet conservative dresser. His shoes were always shined. He also had a wonderful sense of humor.

Nuns, priests and parents taught us that nothing in our lives was more serious than our religion, yet we learned early on that few things are funnier than those that happen in church. In the seventh grade four of us guys were attending Sunday mass. The pew in front of us had three adults in it so there was room for two more. Just before the mass started an impeccably dressed fat man took up both spaces. He had a pompous demeanor; an affect frowned upon in the neighborhood, and was carrying a new fedora with a red feather in the band. He placed the hat on the seat behind him carefully sliding it off to the side.

"Spooks" was sitting directly behind the man. He looked across at us, pointed to the hat, and grinned. We'd seen that grin before and all had the same thought, "No, Spooks, don't do it. Please don't do it!" When the priest came onto the altar everyone in church stood up and Spooks did it - slowly sliding the hat directly behind its owner.

During mass we Catholics sometimes stand and sometimes kneel but when it comes time for the sermon we all sit down. During the standing and kneeling at this mass we could do nothing but think of the hat. From time to time we'd glance at it, thinking Spooks might move it back. He didn't. Time for the sermon got closer. I tried closing my eyes to get in some prayers, but all I saw in my mind was the hat. Jimmy Callahan, standing next to me, let out a snicker and tried to make it sound like a cough. Chuckie Crowe did the same thing. I tried not to breathe. We didn't dare look at Spook knowing the grin would still be there as he pretended to pray.

The time came. As the priest ascended the ornate, marble stairs to the pulpit everyone in church sat down. The fedora was flattened. But with his bulk, and because he was wearing a heavy overcoat, the fat man didn't know it. The last thing I remember seeing was the feather as we bolted from the church. Three of us were in convulsions, but not Spooks. He just held that grin. He'd have made the greatest of straight men.

But he could also do slapstick. One Saturday afternoon four or five of us came out of the Capital movie theatre on Halsted Street. Spooks said he needed to get home soon so he took off running. We did a lot of running as kids. There were few cars in the neighborhood so we walked wherever we had to go. If we were in a hurry instead of walking, we ran. Nobody paid any attention to a kid running, unlike today.

The rest of us walked down Halsted to 79th Street and then headed west to the neighborhood. As we approached Green Street we noticed a small crowd had gathered in front of Rusnak's furniture store. As we got closer the crowd got bigger. Everyone walking past Rusnak's stopped to look in the window. The people pointed at the window and laughed. We stopped and saw, to our astonishment and delight, Spooks Cavanaugh lying on the bed in the store window. When he saw us he waved.

The store window was made up like a bedroom. To get into it you had to enter through a door inside the store. This is what Spooks did, closing that door behind him. Now that he knew we were watching, he got off the bed, stretched his arms, yawned, pulled back the covers and crawled under them laying his head on the pillow. The crowd on the street went wild. To keep the laughs coming, Spooks started tossing and turning and rearranging the pillows as though he was having a restless night.

It wasn't long before the store manager came out to check on the noise in front of his store. He looked in the window, saw Spooks, and said, "Shit!" He ran back into the store and through the bedroom door, but Spooks was ready for him. He saw the manager, through his fake closed eyes, and stood up on the other side of the bed.

"Get the hell out of here!" the manager yelled as he ran around the bed to grab him. But Spooks, a terrific athlete, simply pushed a chair in front of him, hopped across the bed, went out the bedroom door, through the main door, onto 79th Street and headed west, running like the wind. Cheers and applause followed him.

Spook Cavanaugh was not only a good straight man and gifted slapstick but he also kept his sense of humor under dire stress. When we got our drivers licenses at age sixteen our favorite activity was to get quarts of beer, find a secluded parking place; sit in the car and drink.

One night Tom McDonough borrowed his dad's car and five of us piled in. We found a deserted railroad yard near Vincennes Avenue. Tom drove to the middle of it, stopped the car and doused the lights. It was pitch black. We popped open our bottles of beer with "church keys" and began to drink. But we barely got started when Tom saw in his rearview mirror headlights coming toward us. "Hide the beer," he said in a panic, "It might be cops!"

Thirty seconds later two young Chicago police officers were on either side of the car. They opened the doors and told us to get out. We did. Then they told Tom to open the trunk. He did. It, like the inside of the car, was full of quart bottles of beer. Our hearts were pounding, foreheads and armpits sweating. Our parents would kill us.

The two cops said nothing more to us as they took all of the beer–even the open ones–and put them in a box in the squad car's trunk. When all the beer was confiscated one of them said, "Get the fuck out of here," and they drove away.

McDonough started the car as relief and disbelief swept over us. Obviously the cops just wanted our beer and had no intention of arresting us. "Holy shit! Oh my God! That was too close," were uttered by everyone except Spooks. He said nothing. As Mac was pulling onto Vincennes, Spooks reached way under his seat and pulled out a fresh quart of beer, "Ha, ha!" he said, "rookie cops."

Speaking of Spooks and cops, one night he found himself many miles from home in a far south Chicago suburb. It was snowing and he had no money for a bus so he would have to walk the many miles to his house. As he passed an all night diner he noticed a car in the parking lot with the motor running. He also noted the car door was unlocked. He could see the people at the counter with their backs to the window, hunched over their food. He got in the car, put it in gear and drove himself to within two blocks of his house on Laflin Street. He parked the car and, being a gentleman, left the keys in the ignition. Curious, he looked in the glove compartment to see who owned the car he had borrowed. There he found the badge of a south suburban police officer. The word spread across the gang that Spook had stolen a cop car. Actually it was just "a cop's car" but close enough.

We guys in the gang not only pimped each other but we also played tricks on each other. One day I showed up at the corner with my four-year-old cousin, Bobby Anderson, who was visiting from Joliet, Illinois, forty miles away. I was babysitting, which was most unusual and, therefore, pimpy.

There were about ten of us milling around the corner and I wasn't paying much attention to Bobby. He'd met some of the guys before and they were entertaining him by talking to him. What more could a four-year-old want? There was a bus stop on the corner and as a bus pulled away from the curb one of the guys said, "Jimmy, look! Bobby Anderson got on the bus!"

I looked up and saw Bobby waving at me out the back window! My shock instantly became terror. "Stop!" I yelled but the bus kept going, picking up speed.

I ran as fast as I'd ever run to the next stop, beating the bus by seconds. It pulled up to the curb, the door opened and the smiling Bobby Anderson got off, with Bill Nelligan holding his hand. I could hear the laughter on the corner a block away.

I took Bobby home then returned to the corner; I wanted to beat the shit out of Bill Nelligan, wipe up 79th Street with him, but I couldn't. Nelligan was the toughest guy in the gang. I merely made a silent vow to get him back. I haven't yet, but there's still time.

Nelligan has always been a thorn in my side. In second grade, he stole my girlfriend, Janet Brown. In sixth grade, he stole another one, Rita Collins. I didn't understand it then and I still don't. Bill Nelligan is ugly and has zero personality.

Although he was the toughest guy in the gang he was not the wildest. That distinction goes to another. But Nelligan was pretty wild, thoroughly enjoying late nights and alcoholic beverages. When his dad, the policeman Big Red, lay dying in the hospital he looked up at Bill and said, "I never thought you'd outlive me."

Mr. and Mrs. Nelligan, Bill and all the Nelligan brothers and sisters were one of the anchor families of our 79th Street neighborhood.

When we were nineteen, Billy Callaghan caught mononucleosis and wound up in Little Company of Mary Hospital at 95th and California. Four of us guys in the gang went to visit him. We brought six packs in a brown paper bag although drinking was not allowed in hospitals. You probably won't believe this but in those days smoking *was* allowed in hospitals, and everybody smoked; the visitors, nurses, doctors and even the patients. There were ashtrays on their food trays.

We were having a good time sitting around Billy's room drinking, smoking and laughing it up. The doctor came by to check on Billy and was very cordial to us. He put his smoke out in Billy's ashtray before he examined him.

But soon after the doctor left, a mean nurse showed up. Her eyes got wide when she saw all the beer cans. She told us, in the sternest of voices, to clean up and clear out. "And don't come back!" We hurriedly gathered up the cans and put them in the paper bag. Some were not empty and leaked, soaking the bottom. As we got on the elevator the bottom broke through and our beer cans started dropping to the floor – "Tink, tink, tink, tink." We could hardly pick them up for laughing. "Hey lady, can you move your foot? I gotta get that beer can."

I invited Billy Callaghan and the other guys in the gang to a John Carroll Chicago Club dance. It was at a fancy hotel in the Loop and I could get them in for free because I was in charge. Billy wanted to ask Maureen Nugent, the girl who had just moved in across the street.

"So call her and ask," I said.

"What if she says 'no'," he said.

"So what?" I said.

"I'm afraid," he said.

Billy would become one of Chicago's toughest cops but at that time he was afraid of a girl. I was exasperated.

"Okay, Billy," I said, "How about this. Does she know your voice?"

He thought for a moment and said he didn't think so. "I only said 'hi' to her once."

"No problem, then," I said. "I'll call and ask her to the dance and tell her I'm you."

"Would you do that?" he said.

"Sure. I don't care if she says 'no'."

So we got into his dad's Buick and drove to Skip's Drive-In on 87th Street. It had an outside phone booth. He gave me her number.

"I want to hear," he said as I entered the booth.

"No," I said, closing the folding door. "This is private."

I called her.

Mrs. Nugent answered the phone and I asked to speak to Maureen. "Who's calling?" she said. "Billy Callahan from across the street," I said. "Just a minute, Billy." Maureen got on the phone.

"Hi, Maureen. This is Billy Callaghan."

"Oh hi."

"My friend Jimmy Joyce's school is having a dance Saturday night. Would you like to go?"

"Sure," she said. "But I have to ask my dad. Just a minute."

Billy was pacing outside the phone booth looking at me with panicky eyes. While Maureen was asking her dad I started shaking my head and pretended to talk into the receiver in a pleading way. I raised my arm, as though dejected, and then shrugged my shoulders. "Why not?" I mouthed into the phone. I thought Billy was going to faint.

When Maureen came back she said her dad said okay but she'd have to be home by midnight. My heart leapt for Billy but I turned my back to him so he couldn't see me smile and say, "That's great I'll pick you up at 6:00." Maureen then hung up but I didn't. For twenty seconds or so I continued with the frustrated body language and then slammed down the receiver. Billy was frantic.

"She said 'no' didn't she," he said. "Why did you yell at her? Why did you hang up on her?"

I shook my head, looked at him, smiled and said, "She said 'yes,' Asshole, you have a date!"

He didn't know whether to hit me or kiss me. "Really!!??" "Really. Pick her up at 6:00."

"You prick!" he said. "You're welcome," I said.

Maureen and Billy went to the dance, got married and had six kids.

A story Billy liked to tell was when he was a senior police officer and assigned to guard and escort Princess Diana of England when she visited Chicago. At the time Diana was one of the most famous people in the world. Billy said she was charming, witty and down to earth.

As they were driving through the city, a uniform behind the wheel, Billy in the front seat and Diana and her aid in the back, Diana said, "Officer Callaghan are you married?"

"Yes, Ma'am" he said.

"Do you have any children?"

"Yes," he said proudly, "I have six."

"You have six kids!" she exclaimed. She pointed her finger at him and said, "You stay away from me!"

On Saturday mornings during Lent the other Jimmy Joyce (Carpenter) and I would meet up in front of the church. It was not mandatory to attend daily mass during Lent but was highly encouraged by nuns, brothers, parents and priests. Just before we entered through the huge wooden doors we saw fellow gang member John Glenville enter the church by the side door. We figured we'd see him inside and sit with him.

We went to a pew a few rows from the back, genuflected, made the sign of the cross, slipped into the pew and knelt down. We prayed separately and silently until the priest showed up on the altar and the mass began.

About five minutes into mass we both had the same thought: Where's Glenville? We looked around and he was nowhere to be seen. Father Riordon was saying this mass. We liked Riordon's masses because he could knock them out in twenty minutes where it normally takes thirty-five. There were no sermons, thank God, at daily mass.

When the mass was ended our curiosity was at its peak: Where's Glenville? We left the upstairs church and took the steps to the downstairs church. We opened the doors and looked inside. Nobody. But as we turned to leave we heard "tick, tick, tick…" coming from the back pew. We looked at each other and tip-toed to it. There was John, lying on the seat, sound asleep, an alarm clock at his head. At that moment it went "Brrrrng!" We went into convulsions as John leapt up into consciousness.

John was the oldest of six kids. His father was an FBI man, and an inordinately strict parent, who insisted John go to church every day. The Glenville's lived on Throop Street (next door to Janet Brown, the future Mrs. Carpenter Joyce). Their house was less than a block from the church. So John obediently went to mass everyday with his alarm clock in his pocket. He asked us not to tell the other guys, lest it get back to his father. But we told everybody in the gang; it was too good a story. And we knew it would never get back to his father. No teenager in his right mind would talk to an FBI man.

And speaking of sermons, most of the ones during Sunday mass were excruciatingly dull and repetitive and, after ten years or so, we'd heard it all. "Today's Epistle means…this Sunday's gospel is about…" Come on, Father, tell us something we don't know.

Two of the standard questions our parents asked on Sundays were, "Who said the mass?" followed by "What was the sermon about?" This was to determine if we really did attend mass. Honestly, I don't know any gang member who did not go to Sunday mass. We never considered not attending. It was as much a part of us as eating, sleeping and pimping each other. In retrospect, it's surprising our parents didn't know that.

One of our St. Sabina parish priests was Father Ulysses Galvao, a native of a Latin American country. He was a very short, very friendly little man who did not speak English. Unfortunately he thought he did, and his sermons were pure torture. He wrote them out long hand and then read them word for word, page after page, his voice rising and falling like a Shakespearean actor. He also spoke very rapidly, like they do down there, and no one in the church knew what the hell he was talking about. We'd see the old ladies leaning forward in their seats trying to catch a word or two, their best ear cocked toward the pulpit. Not a chance. But Father Galvao was a really nice guy and we all pretended to be attentive. When we got home from mass, and our parents asked the question, "Who said the mass?" if the answer was Galvao, they knew better than to ask about the sermon.

Chicago is known for having only two seasons, too hot or too cold. Once Jerry Joyce decided to count the number of "nice days" over the course of a year: not too hot, not too cold, not too windy, rainy, muggy or, the worst and most common blow-your-brains-out *overcast*. Before going to sleep at night Jerry would ask himself, "Had this been a nice day?" He counted eighteen. (Recently our son, Alex, a standup comic who now lives in Chicago said, "There's only one word to describe Chicago weather – embarrassing.")

By June of 1958 about half of us had driver's licenses and on a bright and sunny Saturday (one of the eighteen) some of us decided to get into Tom McNally's car, pick up some beer, and enjoy nature at Ryan's Woods.

Ryan's Woods contains about 270 acres between Damen and Western Avenues. It is divided approximately in half by 87th Street. An unwritten agreement had been worked out many years before between the whites and the blacks, referred to as "coloreds" at the time. They would use the north side of 87th Street and the whites the south. Both sections had large parking lots, plenty of picnic tables, ball fields, water fountains, barbecue grills, grass and trees. It was a fair deal.

Spook Cavanaugh started shaving when he was about ten years old and now could pass for twenty-five, the age stated on his fake I.D. (No pictures then. That technology was years away.) He bought a few six packs at the Old Bear Lounge, where Mr. O'Rourke slept on the pool table, and McNally drove us to the woods. We found an out-of-the way grove and settled in telling stories, drinking beer and being friends.

Some weeks before this a few of us gang members had the childish idea that we should form a singing group. We would specialize in the old-timey songs and maybe even get on the *Ed Sullivan Show*. Our theme song would be, of course, "That Old Gang of Mine." Cavanaugh, Nelligan, Billy Callahan and I were good singers. We got it into our heads we should have a bench to sit on as we harmonized. It would give us a professional look. We'd put it on the corner.

Along about 4:00 in the afternoon we knocked off the last of the beer and got back in McNally's car. As we passed the colored parking lot somebody said, "Hey! Look at that! Mac, stop!"

We looked over and couldn't believe our eyes. Sitting in the colored parking lot was a large, ancient truck, open in back with wooden slats along the sides. In it was a *bench*, just like the one we'd envisioned. Fate had struck, helped along by the Meister Brau.

There were no coloreds in the parking lot. They were all at least two hundred yards away in an open area, playing baseball and cooking on the grills. We sleuthfully ducked behind cars until we got to the truck. We planned to simply slide the bench out the back, put it on top of McNally's car and drive away. He'd go slowly and we'd keep it in place by reaching up and steadying it with our hands. But when we attempted to slide it off we realized the thing was very heavy. The back and sides were wood but the legs and frame were cast iron. "You're not putting it on top of my car," McNally said, "you'll dent the roof!"

We briefly considered carrying the bench back to the corner but quickly abandoned the idea. It weighed a ton and the corner was two miles away.

Paddy Cochrane* (notice the asterisk, the real culprit does not want his posterity to know what he did) said, "Leave it in the truck. The keys are in the ignition. I'll drive it to the corner. We'll unload it and I'll park the truck where the cops can find it."

We were somewhat stunned and highly amused by this statement. Up to this point Cochrane had been one of the more conservative guys in the gang. When we reminded him that he didn't have a drivers license he said, "So what? Neither does my father." Paddy had just become a leader of the gang.

We all knew how to drive stick shifts but only when the stick was attached to the steering column. This stick came out of the floor. "I'll figure it out," said Paddy; "Just keep an eye on the coloreds."

He turned on the ignition but forgot to put the clutch to the floor. The truck lurched forward smashing the taillights of the car in front of it. Some of the coloreds looked our way, and we prepared to bolt, but then they resumed tending to their ribs and chicken. "God, does that smell good!" someone said, "those people sure know how to eat."

Paddy fiddled with the gearshift, now knowing where "first" was and slipped it into what he thought was "reverse." It was, but he let out the clutch too fast and smashed the headlights of the car behind him. Now, the coloreds became interested again and a few men (big) started walking toward us. "Get in," Paddy yelled, "I figured it out!" We all jumped into the back of the truck except McNally who sped away.

87th Street is a major, busy artery. Luckily the westbound traffic was stopped at the light at Damen but eastbound, the way to the corner, was bunching up in front of us. Paddy sped out of the parking lot and bullied his way into the traffic. Horns blared, brakes screeched and other motorists hollered swear words. Just as the colored posse', which was now running, came out of the parking lot, traffic began moving, our getaway complete.

There are about eight red lights on 87th Street, Ashland Avenue and 79th Street between Ryan's Woods and the corner. Paddy caught every one. For us in the back of the truck it was amusing, albeit unnerving, to see the faces of people in their cars staring at us. A very young white kid driving a beat-up old truck with the name "Willy Jones" and a south Indiana Avenue address, hand painted on the door, was a dead give away that we had no business in that truck. We tried to look nonchalant and even waved at the gawkers. Spooks sat down on the bench, crossed his legs and lit a cigarette. If a cop had spotted us it would have been over.

But we made it, unloaded the bench on the corner and Paddy parked the truck in an alley between Racine and May. We all went home for supper.

We gathered again at the corner that night to try out the bench and sing a few songs. Gus didn't appreciate all the commotion this caused in front of DeLites and made us move the bench along the side of the building. No problem.

That night when some of the guys who had not gone to Ryan's Woods showed up at the corner we took them to the alley to see the truck. They couldn't believe it. Some of the guys started using it to practice floor stick-shift driving, to the end of the alley and back, using look-outs, of course. It was a full week before the cops discovered it and, hopefully, returned it to Mr. Jones.

I had a pump up air rifle, which I kept at my grandmother's farm, but one day I decided to bring it home to Chicago for reasons I cannot explain. I was showing it to one of the guys in the gang who was a bit of a techno freak, liking all things mechanical and scientific. An unusual trait for a gang member. Let's call him Roger*. "How powerful is it?" asked Roger. "The more you pump it up, the more powerful it gets. It can get like a .22," I said.

"Let's go shoot it," said Roger. "Okay," I said.

The city of Chicago had recently installed new street lights on Loomis Boulevard, one block over from my house on Ada Street. They were the latest in street lighting, mercury vapor, and were on extra tall poles. They put off much more candle-power than the traditional lights, an impressive display of new technology. "Do you think this thing could shoot out one of those new street lights on Loomis?" asked Roger. "Let's find out," I said. We walked to Loomis and nailed the first one we aimed at. And then we learned something about streetlights. You can't shoot out just one. The initial explosion, with sparks flying everywhere and then descending into the darkness like Roman candles, provides a rush that's addictive. Roger and I got half a dozen of them between 79th and 83rd.

When we were done Roger asked if he could keep the gun at his house. "Sure," I said. A few weeks later, he used the gun on a security guard, who was chasing him. He was not trying to shoot the guard, only scare him like they do in the movies, aiming way over the guy's head. But somehow he got caught and had to go to trial. The judge gave him a choice, either jail time or military time. Roger wisely joined the armed forces, and I never got my pump gun back. State's evidence.

I don't know what on earth got into me that night we shot out the lights and over the years felt a little guilty about it. Then I met an expert on teenage behavior, Veryl Rosenbaum, the author and psychoanalyst. I told her the story and she said, "Jimmy, that's easy to explain. Teenagers are the devil." I felt better.

CHAPTER 8
More Gang Activity

One of the highlights of our lives as teenagers was the day we got our drivers licenses. That was the first tangible rite of passage into our rapidly approaching adulthood symbolizing marvelous freedoms and serious responsibilities.

In 1958 sixteen was the legal driving age in Illinois. Back then there was no such thing as Driver's Education classes. We learned to drive mostly from our parents, older siblings or older guys. Side streets and big parking lots were utilized for practice. This was technically illegal, of course, you can't operate a motor vehicle without a license, but we fudged on the rules and wound up with licenses without the benefit of Driver's Ed.

I was more fortunate than most kids because of my grandparents' farm. I learned the basics of driving at age thirteen on a tractor. I was fifteen when Dad got his car and I had many hours of practice on country roads and in the little town of Wilmington. On the day of my sixteenth birthday I was ready.

Mom took me to the drivers license office on 63rd Street near Halsted. It was a storefront between a butcher shop and a "Nickel and Dime." When I showed my birth certificate to the lady behind the counter she looked at me, smiled, and said, "What took you so long?"

63rd Street is a major thoroughfare and parking was scarce. Mom found a place on a side street about two blocks from the license office. When I completed the written test I was assigned to a uniformed State of Illinois Driving Examiner who would grade me on my ability to actually drive a car. He was a grouchy old man – probably fifty or so. We walked out of the office and he said, "Where's your car, kid?"

"About two blocks that way," I answered, pointing east down 63rd.

"Go get it and bring it here. I ain't walking that far. And be quick about it. My lunch break's coming up."

I hustled down 63rd, then down the side street to the car. I then realized I would have to drive on two side streets in order to pull up in front of him, on his side of the street. Otherwise I'd be across the street, which I assumed would piss him off. I got the bright idea to take a short cut through an alley to eliminate one of the side streets. I'd never driven down an alley but saw cars do it all the time and was proud of my foresight. I pulled out of the alley and was heading to 63rd when all of a sudden a colored kid, about ten, appeared in front of the car, in the middle of the street, waving his hands signaling me to stop. I did. He came up to the window and said, "You're going the wrong way on a one-way street."

"Holy shit!" I said as beads of sweat appeared on my forehead. "Thanks, kid." (That was the first time I talked to a colored.)

I backed up as fast as I could on the street, and then backed into the alley. I now realized I would have to go another block in the alley then across 63rd Street and down two more side streets to pick up my examiner. I was on the verge of a nervous breakdown.

When I finally pulled up in front of him he got in the car and said, "Where the hell have you been?"

"I got confused," I said hoping he'd understand, but terrified he'd flunk me. But he didn't flunk me because he saw the $10 bill I had wisely placed next to me on the seat. I had heard on the corner that if you think you've screwed up the driving part of the test, put a ten spot on the seat. This will assure you pass.

The driving test took less than two minutes. "Drive around the block and drop me back off here. It's time for my lunch. And don't tell anybody we cut it short."

When I parked he filled out some papers. The money, I happily noticed, was gone. "Tell your mother you passed the test and take these papers inside," he said, and that was it.

I've often wondered what he'd have done if I'd pulled out onto 63rd Street driving the wrong way on that one-way street. That probably would cost twenty bucks. And I've been forever grateful to the colored kid. It was a nice introduction to a member of the Negro race.

(Note: The cars in the 1950's did not have air conditioning, power windows, brake lights and automatic turn signals. To signify our intentions to fellow drivers we had to open our window and use hand signals: arm straight out meant a left turn; arm out but bent straight up at the elbow meant right turn; arm out but pointed down meant we were going to stop. In January, in Chicago, this made driving unpleasant. We also didn't have power steering. Parallel parking qualified as exercise.)

Jimmy (Carpenter) and I have a special love for our fellow gang member Tom McDonough. Tom's father was generous; he let Tom borrow his car often. We guys in the gang spent untold hours riding around in his old, black Dodge drinking quarts of beer or going from bar to bar. One night Tom got way too drunk to drive so Jimmy persuaded him to give up the keys. Mac at the wheel would have been a danger to himself and others. We good Samaritans would get him safely home. Of course Jimmy and I were also drunk but not nearly as bad as Mac. Besides, Jimmy has always prided himself on being an especially good drunk driver. He still does, and I can't dispute him. He can have seventeen drinks and still drive in a straight line. (Did it just the other night.) So Jimmy drove, I sat up front and Mac passed out on the back seat. The plan was to drive Tom to his house, park the car in the garage and then Jim and I would walk to our houses.

When getting home late, and drunk, it was always prudent not to wake our parents. Jimmy pulled into the alley behind the McDonough's, turned off the lights and slowly proceded to their garage door, about six houses down. I then went into the side door and opened the big garage door. So far so good except for one thing: There was a sheet of ice covering the alley and Jim could not get the car up the slight incline into the garage. The wheels kept spinning, making way too much noise. I started pushing but to no avail. I was slipping and sliding and couldn't get enough traction. I could almost do it, but not quite. It would take two of us. Mac was too far gone to push, or even walk, but we figured he could steer. We woke him up.

"Mac, just sit behind the wheel and turn it when we tell you, okay?"

"Yeah," he grunted.

Lining up the car on the ice was difficult, but with Mac's help at the wheel we finally got it into position–almost. We took a break to catch our breath and then readied ourselves for the final push into the garage. We got it going but noticed it was heading too far left. "Turn right, Mac! Turn right!" we yelled. But it kept going straight and ran into the frame of the garage door. Thud! Mac was asleep at the wheel.

"What is going on out there!" Mr. McDonough yelled from his back porch as lights started coming on from houses on both sides of the alley.

That was it for Jim and me. The Good Samaritans split and Mac was now on his own – but at least he was safe. And Mr. McDonough was a tolerant man with a good sense of humor. Years later, after Tom graduated law school, he came home one night and proudly said, "Dad, I passed the bar!" Mr. McDonough replied, "That's the only bar you ever passed."

Mr. McArthy* was not as generous with his car as Mr. McDonough, and with good reason. Mr. McArthy's car was a brand new Buick Roadmaster, golden yellow body with dark brown trim. A gorgeous automobile, which he kept spotless. But one time he relented.

It was a fine July evening when Eddie* got the keys to the car and drove it to the corner. He was very proud of his dad's fine car, as he should have been. It was the nicest, and most expensive of all our dads' cars. He even bragged about it. (But pride didn't play well with us guys in the gang.) As it turned out it was the only car available that night and we wanted to drive around the south side drinking our quart bottles of beer with the windows down enjoying the summer breezes. Eddie would not allow that.

"If you spill any beer in my dad's car he'll know it and I'll be in trouble," he said.

So we had to be content with driving out to Ryan's Woods again, drinking the beer on picnic benches instead of in the car. We had a good time anyway, downing the beers and throwing the empty bottles into the woods. Sometimes they'd hit a rock and break. More fun.

Eddie had a midnight curfew so we polished off the beer well before that and piled back into the car. There were six of us including Eddie. The first one to be dropped off was John "Nuge" Glenville. He was seated next to the left rear window. Nuge was new to drinking beer and on the way to his house he laid his head back and went to sleep. When we got to within two blocks of his house someone said, "Hey Nuge. Wake up! You're almost home!"

Nuge opened his eyes and said, "I don't feel good." Then he said, "I'm gonna be sick," and let out a loud groan.

Eddie slammed on the brakes and yelled, "Don't puke in the car!"

The car came to a stop and we all jumped out not wanting to get puked on.

Eddie, too, leapt from the car with the intention of dragging Nuge out before the puking began, but the Buick had one of those new automatic transmissions and in his haste Eddie forgot to put the gearshift into "Park."

The car began rolling, with Eddie running along side and with Nuge still in the back. Eddie was desperately pulling on the locked back door handle. "Open the door, Nuge!" he yelled, "open the door!" Nuge was in no shape to open the door. He was throwing up. Through the rear window we could see his head rise backward and then lurch forward.

Soon Eddie became aware of two things: 1) Nuge was not going to open the door and 2) the car was going faster and faster. He decided to jump back in the driver's seat to put on the brake. He grabbed the top of his opened door and skipped and hopped along, not quite able to safely make the leap back inside. By now the car was really moving, and Nuge was still puking, so Eddie had no choice. He grabbed the steering wheel and pulled heading the Buick toward the curb, which it hit, hard, and bounced over. This slowed it up enough so Eddie could get back in. (Too bad the car didn't run into another car or, better yet, a tree – making steam come out of the radiator like in the movies.) Still, it was very humorous. "Nuge is a terrible back seat driver," someone said.

Before going home, Eddie hosed out the car and left the windows open for it to dry out. Of course it didn't dry out and his dad was most curious about the soaked interior of his Roadmaster and the misalignment of the front end. Eddie told him that John Glenville got sick on a hamburger. His father, another understanding man, didn't pursue it and that ended the episode. Most of our parents were really good about looking the other way. We were the parents of teenagers ourselves, however, before we realized that.

George Overbeek's father generously allowed "Beek" to use his car. Around Christmas time, we were cruising the neighborhood near St. Xavier's' College on 103rd Street. It was more upscale than ours and the Christmas decorations in front of the houses were often large and, we thought, grandiose - people showing off their money.

As we drove down 102nd Street we saw a front lawn display of almost life-sized plastic statues depicting the Nativity scene: the Infant Jesus, Mary, Joseph, the three Wise Men, a few shepherds and assorted animals. We couldn't resist. Beek stopped the car and two of the guys jumped out, ran across the lawn and grabbed the Wise Men. They wouldn't fit in the car until we rolled down the windows. Beek drove to St. Xav's just a few blocks away. We didn't dare get on a busy street lest the cops see the plastic heads sticking out.

When we got to the college, Cy Watson, who was now referring to our fellow passengers as "the Wise Guys," suggested we set them up on the knoll at the entrance along with a half dozen or so empty beer bottles. "It'll look like the Wise Guys had a party," he said.

(Note: Today, Carpenter Joyce's brother, Eddie, lives in the very same house where we swiped the statues fifty years ago. Eddie became President of the Chicago Board Options Exchange.)

Some of the guys in the gang began another Christmas tradition known as "The Annual Lighting of the Christmas Trees." This took place during the first week of January when the people of the neighborhood discarded their dried-up trees, placing them in the alleys to be picked up by the garbage men.

After dark the guys would wander the alleys looking for dead Christmas trees and light them on fire. It was an exciting ritual, especially if the trees were placed next to wooden garage doors. The bright red fire trucks racing to the scene with lights flashing, horns blaring and sirens wailing made it a particularly festive tradition.

My dad was very generous with his car, rarely driving it himself. He took the bus to work six days a week and on Sunday he walked to church. That was his travel life.

Our family didn't even own a car until I was fifteen. "You don't need a car in the city," was the official reason for this. (We couldn't afford one was closer to reality.) But Dad was offered a deal he couldn't pass up. Through his company, Joslyn, he learned he could purchase a brand new Oldsmobile for the same price as a Ford.

It was an Olds 88, black and white, with a red stripe between chrome strips running down the sides. It was a beautiful car, and it could fly. After I got my drivers license, I was driving the Olds with some of the guys in the gang down to my grandmother's farm. We were on alternate Route 66, between Joliet and Wilmington, a four lane divided highway. It was a Saturday morning with practically no traffic.

My left elbow was out the window and my right wrist was resting on top of the steering wheel. I was doing about 90. One of the guys asked how fast my dad's car could go and I said, "I have no idea. Let's find out." I put the accelerator to the floor and our heads snapped back. We went past 100 like it wasn't there; 110 was also gone and the max, 120, provided no obstacle.

The speedometer was a circle with a yellow needle pointing to the speed. The needle continued around the circle until it hit the zero, completing the 360 degrees. Then it went "twang," popped off its spindle and came to rest at the bottom of the glass. A thin, plastic coated wire now appeared from behind the numbers. I immediately slowed up and said, "Oh, shit!"

One of the guys in the back seat said, "*Holy* shit! You must have been doing 140!"

"What will I tell my father?" I said to myself.

"Jim," my dad said a few weeks later after he'd driven the car, "I noticed the speedometer is broken. Do you know what happened to it?"

"No, Dad, but I noticed it too."

(What do you think I should have said? "Yeah, Dad, it happened right after I hit 140 on the way down to Granny's?)

My dad had a dream that one day he would own a Cadillac, but he never felt he could afford one. I, too, had a dream that one day I'd get rich and buy my dad a Cadillac, but I never felt I could afford it until after his death.

When I could afford it, and bought one for myself, I felt guilty.

(Shrinks call that the "besting the father syndrome." Shrinks have a saying for everything.) When Mary, my sister, came to visit we were driving in my new Cadillac and I told her I felt guilty because Dad never got one. She said, "Oh, Jimmy, don't be silly. He would be so proud to know his son drives a Cadillac. You made his dream a reality." I love my sister.

But I did buy Dad his first color TV. It was a great big console from Sears. He was thrilled. (It did, of course, remain dark each year for forty days and forty nights.)

One summer weekend, eight of us gang members rented a two-bedroom cabin for the weekend at Lake Como, Wisconsin. Lake Como is about two hours north of Chicago. During our youth it was a trashy place and, therefore, cheap but it was close to the ritzy Lake Geneva where the classy girls hung out.

By four o'clock on Saturday morning most of the guys were passed out, but Spooks Cavanaugh, Tommy Carroll, Cy Watson and us Joyces were still awake. We finished up the last of the beer and then decided we were hungry. The cabin was about five miles from town so we'd need a car.

"I saw Frank's* keys on the dresser. I'll get them," said Spooks.

"Who's gonna drive?" asked Tommy.

"Me," said Spook, "I'm a good driver."

This was not true but, what the hell, we were in the country.

We started down a dirt road and Spooks was doing fine; two hands on the wheel, focused. We were proud of him. The road was straight for about a mile, but suddenly it turned sharply to the left. Spooks, concentrating on driving straight, didn't notice this detail and failed to turn. We went through a grove of saplings, over a six-foot embankment, across a wide expanse of lawn and ran into a house–BAM!–cracking the siding.

"Oh my God!" somebody said.

"I hope nobody's home!" somebody else said.

Spooks, still calm as could be, put the car in reverse and backed it up. Unfortunately, the lawn was mushy. When he tried to go forward, the wheels spun. We passengers jumped out and started pushing just as we heard. "Stop!" It was the homeowner. He was on the porch in his underwear.

Of course we weren't about to stop. The man went back inside to put clothes on and the car started moving. We got to dry land, jumped in and Spook calmly drove out of the yard using the driveway. The now dressed homeowner started chasing us on foot, yelling and swearing, but in no time Spooks lost him.

We drove into town, found a little diner, and had a nice breakfast. Then we went back to the cabin. Spooks replaced the keys on the dresser, and we went to sleep.

When Frank woke up and saw his dad's car he almost had a heart attack. Clumps of dirt, leaves, branches and other shit was hanging from the undercarriage. But that wasn't the worst part. The undercarriage was supposed to be straight but Frank's father's car had a hump in it and the doors wouldn't close.

Some of the other guys went for breakfast later in a different car, and came back to tell us that the word in town was that the sheriff was looking for a black car that ran into a house about five o'clock in the morning. We admitted to Frank what we did and asked him to keep the car hidden behind the cabin. We also promised to pay for the damages.

That night he left Lake Como under the cover of darkness. The guys riding with him held their doors shut all the way to Chicago.

Frank's dad was one of the nicest of our gang's fathers, which we always found interesting because he wasn't a Catholic. When he saw the car, he was furious but soon calmed down and paid to fix it himself.

CHAPTER 9
The Haircut

John Glenville, the boomerang buying, back seat driving, church pew sleeper was one of my favorite guys in the gang. He was a bit of a geek, loved mechanical devices, gadgets and scientific experiments. He liked to come to my house and read my dad's old *Popular Mechanics* magazines which Dad saved in the basement rafters. Shortly before he died, John enthusiastically told Carpenter Joyce about his new tool set. John was somewhat of a loner, not much of a talker and secretive, but he was a great listener. We were opposites.

John was completely accepted by everyone in the gang, but was not a regular at the corner. He'd hang out for a week or two then disappear for months. He also had a little klepto in him, took specimen jars from Blosser's science class, candy bars from the drug store, books from the library. He scored the football coach's tennis shoes right out of his locker.

But nobody liked new gadgets better than my dad, especially if they could save money. He saw an ad in the newspaper: "Cut Hair at Home and Save," it said, "Barber Quality Electric Clippers." The ad went on to explain the clippers came with plastic attachments so you couldn't screw up. Dad placed an order. His plan was to cut my brother's and my hair and one of us would cut his. He was excited and so was I. My brother was skeptical. Mom and my sister smirked.

The day after the clippers showed up I was walking home from Leo with Glenville who said he had to stop for a haircut. His mother had given him $2.00 - $1.75 for the haircut and $.25 for the barber's tip. My light came on. "Nuge (his nickname), I'll cut your hair for $1.00 and you can keep the other one for yourself."

"You don't know how to cut hair," he said.

"I do now," I said and told him about the new invention.

Nuge, a sucker for gadgets, and with the thought of having a dollar, agreed to bypass the barbershop and we went to my house. I showed him the clippers and the three attachments - long, medium and short. "You see: No way can I make a mistake. If I don't do a good job, I'll give you your money back and you can still go to the barber."

He agreed and gave me a dollar.

I got a chair from the kitchen and put it in the bathroom, facing away from the mirror, and wrapped a towel around his neck. "Okay, Nuge, hold still. I'm going to start on the back with the long attachment just to get the feel of it."

I put on the attachment, and turned on the clippers. They gave off a familiar buzzing sound, just like the barber's. It was comforting. I started at the base of his head and smoothly went right to the top, shearing off all of his hair. His white skull glared at me.

"Shit!" I said.

"What's wrong!?" said Nuge.

"Nothing. No problem. It's cutting a little closer than I thought, is all. I'm going to change attachments."

"Did you screw me up?" he anxiously asked.

"Not at all, I said. "Just relax and keep your head down."

With the medium attachment, I slowly went along next to the bald swatch and this was a little better. There was still some hair left but it was uneven – dark, light, dark, light, etc. with a few more little bald spots.

Nuge fidgeted and kept asking if I really knew what I was doing. I assured him it would be fine and that I was learning fast.

I switched to the short attachment, "This isn't making sense," I said to myself and proceeded up the other side of the bald swatch. More dark, light, dark, light but this time with some tufts. It was then I realized that the angle I was holding the clippers at was more important than the attachments.

If Nuge had seen the back of his head at that moment he would have screamed but now that I knew what I was doing I figured I could make the rest of the haircut presentable. Without any attachment I went to work behind his left ear, the hair professionally landing on the towel. He didn't know I was working without an attachment.

With the clippers in my right hand, I guided it up with the index finger of my left. This worked well until I passed behind his ear and used my guide finger to bend the ear forward. Shit. Another bald spot.

By the time I got to the right ear, things were going much better, the hairs at the bottom were shorter than those above and there were no more bald spots. It was time to tackle the front.

Nuge wore his hair at normal length with a part on the left side, but I decided a flat top would now be best because it would blend better with the bald sports on the back. I suggested a flat top to him, not telling him why, of course.

"I don't want a flat top," he said, "my mom told me to keep my hair the same style."

"But Nuge," I said, "Flat tops are the *new* style. Look at the picture on the box (a good looking Army guy). Besides, these attachments are perfect for flat tops and you'll look great – older and more with it."

"Okay, go ahead," he said, "Just don't make it too short in case my mom doesn't like it."

Flat tops, as the name implies, are supposed to be flat on top but most heads are round. Even with the attachment, which I decided to use for this critical phase, I had a hard time squaring him off; the hair on the one side of his head was higher than the other. When I'd trim it down to even it, then that side would be lower, and so on. Pretty soon I was running out of hair.

"I want to see what you're doing," he said and turned the chair around to look in the mirror.

"Shit!" he yelled, "I look lopsided. You better stop!"

"How about this, Nuge? I'll make it even all across the top. If won't be exactly flat but you'll have the same effect, you know, like a *new* Army recruit," I said.

"Oh alright. Just get it done," he said.

When I finished, it didn't look that bad. Short, yes, but darned near perfectly even. Nuge wasn't happy as he turned his head from side to side but he wasn't too upset, either. "I want to see the back," he said, "Give me that mirror." There was a hand held mirror on the back of the toilet.

"The back is fine,"

"Gimme the mirror," he demanded.

I reluctantly handed it to him. When he got it positioned properly, he screamed. "You fucker, Joyce! You've ruined me! There're a million bald spots!"

"C'mom, Nuge, relax," I said, "It's not that bad. Besides, nobody looks at the back of anybody's head, they only look at the front!"

"You're crazy!" he yelled. "Gimme my money back!"

He tore off the towel and stood up, continuing to examine the back of his head, bending this way and that. "You son-of-a-bitch, my mother's gonna kill me," he yelled.

I thought he was going to start crying. I gave him the dollar.

"Nuge," I said in a calm voice, "Just do me one favor."

"Fuck you!" he said, "What?!"

"Let's walk to the corner and hang out with the guys. I'll bet you none of them even notices. Just act natural."

He agreed because he said he was afraid to go home.

We got to the corner where five or six guys in the gang had congregated. We blended right in and no one noticed Nuge's head. After a few minutes of milling around I could tell he was feeling better. Maybe that bullshit about nobody looking at the back of someone's head was true.

Every afternoon, weather permitting, Brother Hennessy, of the drumstick, took a walk. Hennessey was a hefty man, about fifty years old, with a round face, wispy hair and beady, light blue eyes that could penetrate steel. When we'd see him coming down 79th Street toward the corner - bright white Roman collar, cassock flowing, black crepe soled shoes—we tried to become invisible. Those of us who attended Leo were terrified of him. We wanted him to pass on by without noticing us as individuals.

"Good afternoon, Brother," we'd say in unison and in return get a barely perceptible nod.

But this day was different. Hennessey slowed up when he approached, his eyes, I noticed, were focused on Glenville. He walked up behind Nuge and stopped. He was staring at the back of his head. Hennessey then put his hands behind his back and slowly walked a circle around Nuge, all the while looking at his head. Nuge's face (and head) turned beet red. My heart sunk. Twice Hennessey walked around him and then said, "GlenVILLE!" his voice rising on the name, "What happened to you? Did you cut your hair yourself? You look like a fool!" He then continued down 79th Street and Glenville fled to the barbershop. At school the next day he was essentially bald. Everybody thought he caught ringworm and felt sorry for him.

It took awhile but after his hair grew back John forgave me. He was a great guy and not one to hold a grudge. As for his mother, a really nice lady, I went out of my way to avoid her for months.

CHAPTER 10

The Guys on Granny's Farm

In 1867, my great-grandparents, on my mother's side, Niels and Christiana Wurtz, "Bestafahr" and "Bestamour" to us, emigrated from Denmark to the United States. They traveled by boat to New York City; there was no other way to get there, and then by train to Chicago. They looked around Chicago for a place to settle down and begin farming.

Chicago is an Indian name meaning, among other things, "Big, stinking swamp." After a few weeks of poking around the area and being eaten alive by mosquitoes, Niels and Christiana decided the Indians got it right. They traveled another sixty miles southwest to Wesley Township and bought land on the Kankakee River. They farmed it until they died and then my grandfather, Edward Wurtz (we called him Bapa), took over. I was twelve when he died but his wife, Mary Somers Wurtz, Granny, who'd been born in Scotland, stayed on the farm. She lived there, except in the winter, until she was in her mid-nineties. After my grandpa died, Granny rented the big house to a man named Harry Rodgers, who had a wife and three horses. Granny moved into a little cottage on the property.

Granny's cottage had a small combination living and dining room, a little bedroom, a tiny guest room and bantam sized kitchen, bathroom and laundry room. There were doilies on the furniture's arms and backs, tintypes of old folks, pictures of the Holy Family and photos of our family on walls and flat surfaces. Rugs were brocade; floor lamps and table lamps had tassels on their shades. A teakettle was poised on the stove . On a table sat a large wooden radio console, in a corner was a credenza displaying cups, saucers, plates, empty glass vases and a statue of St. Francis of Assisi. Granny's rosary beads were nestled on her bedside table along with a stack of prayer cards and a hollowed out wooden crucifix with candles inside for Extreme Unction, just in case. That's the last sacrament of the Catholic Church. It's for the sick and dying. A rubber hot water bottle lay on her bed, filled at night to warm her feet.

Out Granny's back window was the captivating river. In springtime, it ran frightfully high and fast carrying dead trees, unsecured boats, poorly built docks and the carcasses of unwary farm animals. In summer, it settled down moving along nicely, as a river should, hosting a variety of watercraft to include canoes, speed boats and fancy pontoons. In the fall, it got low and slow, autumn leaves decorating its stately passage. In winter, it froze.

When winter ended, the river got a voice, groaning and whining as ice cracked and sheered. Sometimes it went "bang!" like incoming mortar; other times "pop, pop" like small arms fire. Eventually the battle ended and reluctantly, in fits and starts, the river flowed again.

When I was a teenager, I loved to visit Granny and take along one of the guys in the gang. Once I brought Spooks and we decided to ride the horses. I led them out of the barn, tied them to a fence and put on their bridles and saddles. Spooks had never been on a horse so I gave him Susy who was better trained than Star and Tonto. We mounted up and Star and I headed for an open field, but soon I realized Spooks wasn't following. I turned around and he was nowhere in sight. I went into the barn to see Spooks still in the saddle. Susy had simply returned to her stall with Spooks on her back. He was jerking at the reins and swearing at her. She was leisurely eating hay from her trough. Susy made Spooks look like an idiot, a condition he was unaccustomed to, and he's hated horses ever since.

I had Tom McDonough on the farm with me once, and only once. He'd never been on a horse either. Trying to be cool he got up on Tonto a little too hastily, swinging himself into the saddle like he'd seen cowboys do in the movies. Tonto lurched forward and Mac flew off the other side.

Mac had never seen a BB gun. I had one in Granny's cottage. He picked it up, examined it, then aimed it at a cat outside on the lawn. Granny and I were stunned when he pulled the trigger, breaking a window. "Holy shit!" he said.

"You can say that again," said Granny.

That same day Mac and I chopped down a large (two foot diameter), dead tree on the steep bank by the river. We planned to cut it up for firewood but when it fell it started rolling down the bank. I stopped it from rolling by bracing my leg against it. Mac was on the upward side. Next to him on the ground was a heavy, pointed steel rod.

"Mac," I said, "stick that rod on this side of the tree so I can move my foot."

He quickly grabbed the rod and plunged it *through* my foot. He severed a tendon. The toe next to my big one, on the right foot, is still screwed up. The scar is there to this day.

When we were leaving the next day, my foot in a big bandage, Granny waited until Mac was out of earshot. As she handed me my crutches she said, "Jimmy, please don't bring that one back. I think he's crazy."

Mac was crazy, he was a teenager, but Granny was crazy, too. Every summer Harry Rodgers took a two-week vacation. I stayed with Granny and cared for his horses. Harry was also crazy because he told me I could use his car. I was only fourteen. Granny and I took advantage of his offer. We went into town for groceries or just to ride around. She loved to ride around.

Mom unexpectedly drove down from Chicago to see how things were going and to bring us food. When she found out, from Granny, we didn't need food because I had been driving Granny in Harry's car to town everyday, she became more upset than I had ever seen her. She was furious at me, and at Granny, too. "You know the rule!" she yelled through tears. She left us without even saying goodbye.

The rule was that I could not drive a car until I was fifteen and had to be accompanied by a licensed driver. Granny did not have a license. She drove a car once, ran over a rooster, and never got behind the wheel again.

Mom's reaction to my disobedience really upset me (boy was she mad!) but Granny calmed me down, "She'll get over it, Dear, and no harm done. You'll feel better tomorrow." I went to bed that night realizing for the first time that Granny no longer outranked my mother.

Next day Granny, all chipper, decided we needed to go to town again to get groceries.

"How are we going to get there?" I asked.

"In Harry's car," she said, "let's go."

I reluctantly got in the car. She was wearing her straw hat. Her purse was on her lap. Before I started the car I said, "You know, Granny, if we do this you can not tell Mom."

"Of course I'll tell her, Dear. I can't keep secrets from your mother."

"That's it, Granny, get out of the car."

We really did need a few items: pop, potato chips, and cookie makings so I saddled up Star and rode her to town. On the way back we passed a farm and a dozen yapping beagles came running after us. A couple of kicks and Star took off leaving the little suckers in her dust. It's one of my fondest memories.

Granny was also a liar. My grandpa had a German shepherd, Rin, named after the movie star, Rin-Tin-Tin. My memories of Rin are vague, but I do recall he was crippled. Granny told me he got that way because one night Rin swam the river, at least a football field wide, to attack a pack of wolves he'd heard howling. He killed three of them, she said, adding that the farmer across the river verified this. "The fight went on for hours." Rin was a hero in my memory until I was in my late forties when I read that the last known wolf in Illinois was killed in 1818, the year Illinois became a state, and one hundred and twenty-seven years before Granny made up the story. God I loved her.

Jarbie Crowe joined me on the farm on many occasions but only one memory survives. I'd purchased, without my parents consent, a .22 caliber rifle. This was not disobedience, I never asked if I could buy one. The .22 was a huge improvement over the BB gun and air rifle because it was deadly accurate and with it I could kill snakes. There were a lot of snakes on the banks of the Kankakee and all of them, in my mind, were poisonous water moccasins. I also shot turtles because I was a teenager.

Jarbie and I were in my boat. I'd turned off the motor and we were floating down Horse Creek, a tributary of the Kankakee that flows by the tiny town of Custer Park. Horse Creek got its name because George Armstrong Custer watered his horses in it en route to the Little Big Horn. Anyway, we heard a loud noise in the trees above us as a great blue heron landed on a limb about forty feet up. Jarbie'd never seen a heron and couldn't believe how big it was.

"Want to see it up close?" I asked.

"Yeah. How?" he said. "I'm not climbing that tree."

"No need for that."

I picked up the .22, extended my right arm like the Rifleman and fired. The beautiful bird splashed, lifelessly, into the water.

"Great shot!" said Jarbie.

"Oh shit," I said, more to myself than him, "I wish I hadn't done that." I never again shot another living thing, including a snake, until I got to Vietnam.

My first real friend was Tommy Stack. In 1945 he was two and I was three when the Stacks bought the two-flat at 8025 South Ada, next door to us. Mr. Stack was an executive at the Chicago Stock Yards. He was also a dead ringer for President Harry S. Truman. People stopped him for his autograph. Mrs. Stack did not work out of the home for two good reasons: 1) Women didn't work out of the home in those days and 2) She had eleven kids. To this day I can still name them. Want to hear me? Delores, Joey, Rita, Rosemary, Lillian, Lorraine, Jimmy, Jackie, Eddie, Frankie and Tommy. They became surrogate siblings.

(It is interesting to note that the oldest Stack boy, Joey, and the youngest, Tommy, were both highly decorated combat veterans – Joey in World War II and Tommy in Vietnam.)

You'll recall the unwritten rule of gang membership that we had to be in the same grade in school. Tommy Stack was a year behind us but we'd have made an exception for him. He was special. But he had his own group of friends: Denny Cullum, who would become a cop, Pebbles Riordan, brother of Rocky and Stoney, Ronnie Saxon, a Cub fan and Deals Griffin, a singer of songs. Tommy didn't need us.

Tommy went to the farm with me for the first time when we were about thirteen and fourteen. Granny only had one guest bed so we slept together. This was Tommy's first night away from home. He must have been nervous because sometime during the night he wet the bed. Both of us woke up soaked. He was afraid Granny'd find out. I told him she wouldn't care and, of course, she didn't. She cheerily stripped the bed, fixed us a huge breakfast and did the laundry. She was delighted to have us as company and to have something to do. Tommy fell in love with her that day.

During the winters Granny alternated staying with us in Chicago and with her other daughter, Margaret Anderson and her family, in Joliet. So over the years Granny met all of the guys in the gang and she had her favorites. Spooks Cavanaugh permanently endeared himself to her when he told her his dad loved "Gramma Joyce's homemade chili sauce." (Her name wasn't Joyce but she wasn't picky). Chuckie Crowe (Jarbie), Bill Nelligan, who'd visit her "just to talk," and the other Jimmy Joyce were also tops on her list.

Granny was short, maybe 5'2", and round. She wore print dresses, lace up black shoes and was rarely seen without an apron. Eschewing cologne or perfume, she smelled either like a chicken baking, dough rising, peeled carrots, strawberries or other wonderful things to eat.

Family stories have it that she was one tough woman to her daughters and her husband. Demanding, almost dictatorial. But when I showed up she was in her sixties, mellowed out, laid back, her days full of chuckles. Nothing bothered Granny. She called me "ma Jim" and I could do no wrong.

After I was first married, Mary and I bought a poodle puppy to her house. In the night it pooped on the floor. On her way to the bathroom Granny stepped in it. "Oh ho ho," she laughed the next morning telling us what happened, "The shite got between my toes! I had a devil of a time cleaning it out!"

"We're so sorry, Granny!"

"Don't be silly. It's not your fault and the little puppy doesn't know any better."

One of Granny's favorite stories was about coming to America on a boat at age 8. She said as soon as the boat left Scotland a school of sharks started following it. "People died on the boat and they had to throw them overboard because they'd start to smell. The sharks ate them." She said the same sharks followed the boat "all across the ocean." This, too, was probably bullshit but who cared?

Another of Granny's stories, which I doubt she told Spooks, Jarbs, Wes or Jimmy, (but who knows?) was about childbirth. "I had your mother on the farm. The pain was so terrible that I screamed and screamed. Bapa heard me all the way out in the barn. When it was over he promised me he'd never put me through that again. And he didn't." (Her other daughter, Margie, was adopted.)

When we were licensed drivers, Nelligan, Jimmy and I would often "triple date" down to the farm. We'd race up and down the river in my boat, shoot the rifle, have a bonfire, cook hot dogs and marshmallows, drink beer and kiss. Our usual dates were Janice Gorman (Nelligan's) and Judy Walsh (mine). During those years the other Jimmy played the field but secretly yearned for Janet Brown. She would have nothing to do with him and I know the feeling. In the second grade I yearned for Janet, too. Back then she was enthralled by that jerk Bill Nelligan, (but I've already told you that and it doesn't bother me anymore.) A few years later Janet and Jimmy got married.

At age ninety-six Granny had to be put into a nursing home in Joliet. My dad was deceased and mom was seventy and couldn't tend to Granny's needs. Also, Granny's mind and sight had begun to leave her. I was living in Colorado during this time but Carpenter Jimmy went to visit Granny (forty miles from his home in Chicago) on a regular basis. "Jimmy Joyce is here," the nurses would announce and he'd pull up a chair and sit next to her bed. They'd have a nice visit, all the while Granny thinking she was talking to me. Jimmy never corrected her.

A bit more about Tom McDonough, who Granny thought was crazy. Tom was not crazy. He was just different and colorful. He did not have a mean bone in his body, went out of his way to help people, cared deeply for his friends, and in those regards, was the kind of person we would all want our children to be like. Having stated that, and meaning it, Tom could also be abrasive.

One time Tom, Carpenter Jimmy and I were having lunch in the cafeteria at John Carrol University, where we were beginning freshmen. Tom, unlike Jimmy and I, was a serious student. Tom was expounding on some great socio/political reality that he had just dreamed up and Jimmy and I were only half listening. Then he said, "The proverbial thinking at that time…" Jimmy and I looked up. "Whoa, Mac, proverbial? That's a big word," we said. "What does it mean?" He started explaining it, then realized we were pimping him. He blurted out, "Figure it out for yourselves, Assholes!" and left the table. Jimmy and I howled. He then turned around and, stuttering, added, "You assholes don't belong in college!" We doubled over, as he turned red and stormed out, knowing he'd buried himself, twice! (Jimmy and I have been telling each other, "Figure it out for yourself, Asshole," for fifty years.)

If Tom thought you were wrong in what you said, he'd be quick to jump on you. Tom was, therefore, a "know-it-all" and that personality quirk made him imminently pimpable. There's no question Mac was smart - graduating near the top of his classes at John Carroll and again at Notre Dame's law school - but he *didn't* know it all and few things are funnier than when a know-it-all screws up.

It was a Sunday after mass at Cannaday's Tavern. We'd had our traditional brunch of hard-boiled eggs and beer and were drinking in earnest while watching the Sox game. Bill Callaghan had gone to a later mass and now joined us. He was wearing glasses for the first time. McDonough, who'd worn them for years, noticed.

"Where'd you get the glasses?" he asked and Billy told him.

"Let me see them," he said and Billy took them off to show him.

McDonough inspected them and said, "You got the wrong kind, Asshole."

(When we guys in the gang called each other "asshole," this was not necessarily derogatory. Often, as in this case, it implied kindredship.)

"What do you mean?" replied Callaghan.

"How much did they cost?"

"Fifty dollars."

"If you drop these things they'll break," Tom said, "Mine cost $100 and they're unbreakable."

"They don't look any different than mine," Billy said, defensively.

Tom then pointed out that Billy's glasses were made of glass and said that his were made of a new, plastic like substance. "Mine are better," he said.

"Bullshit," said Billy.

"Watch this," said Mac as he held his glasses about three feet over the bar and then dropped them.

"If you did that with yours they'd break. Mine are shatterproof," he stated with pride as he retrieved them and put them back on his face. One lens was indeed fine. The other had a million cracks in it.

"Oh fuck, my father's going to kill me!" he said to himself, but loud enough for all to hear.

"Hey Mac," one of us said, "Why don't you drop them again so both lenses look the same?"

"Why don't you shut the fuck up, Asshole," he said.

Mac spent the rest of the day drinking with one eye closed. He said he couldn't see through the smashed lens. "Everything looks like there's ten of them," he said, eventually finding humor in his stupidity. That was an endearing trait of his. He could laugh at himself. Few know-it-alls can do that. When it was time to leave, he pretended to run into the wall instead of going through the open doorway.

CHAPTER 11

McDonough Practices Law

By Jim Carpenter Joyce

I remember a hot, July Sunday when we were nineteen. After 10:45AM mass, a few of us met up in front of DeLites, which was closed on Sundays. A Sunday at noon in Chicago, hot and humid, wouldn't you think we were thinking baseball? Of course we were, so we piled into Jarbie Crowe's sedan and headed down to Bob Cannaday's tavern at 69th and Justine to watch the White Sox on TV.

I will take responsibility for the following events – not the trip but the cocktail menu – okay, maybe both. We had gotten into what I considered to be a drinking rut, beer after beer, so I proposed we do something about it. "Let's order a different drink with each round," I said as we were watching the game. All agreed that was a good idea so we pooled our money. We started with a Tom Collins, then a screwdriver, a highball, a rum and coke and on down the line to a martini. We marveled at the different essences and bouquets. We were at it for quite a while when heavy thunderstorms hit the city and postponed the ballgame.

A decision was now made to change quarters to get us closer to 79th Street and our homes. But Jarbie announced that he was too drunk to drive and that he was officially grounding his car. A wise decision, we agreed, possibly colored by an incident a week prior involving the same vehicle and said owner/operator. Because we weren't leaving, we enjoyed another round of refreshments. We thought about calling Jarbie's brother, Don, to come down and rescue us. But after another couple of martinis, an addendum was passed pertaining to the previous motion and Jarbie decided that he could, after all, function properly behind the wheel. Why should Donnie have to come to our aid? We can do this. I thought I was okay too. Bub McDoo (Tom McDonough) said, "All ahead full." Mike Watson, on the other hand, said *mongalots* or *fungoe* or some other Italian cuss word. Mike fancied himself quite the cosmopolitan swearer. He refused to ride with us and hoofed it home.

We traveled the ten blocks south to 79th Street without incident. At first, we were impressed by how smoothly Jarbie was driving, but things soon deteriorated. When Chicago experienced heavy rain in our day the bridge underpasses became flooded and impassable. (This was prior to digging the Deep Tunnel under the city.) All traffic was therefore diverted to bypass the flooded areas. Another motorist, who had the right of way, turned in front of us and Jarbie tapped the side of his car. We stopped, of course, and got out of our car to calm the offended motorist who was very agitated. We talked him into driving up the street to a pullover area. We convinced him we would arrange for payment of the damages on the spot.

We hurriedly got back in Jarbie's car and decided to make a run for it. Based on our physical condition, and not thinking clearly, and what with the clinging humidity and all, we thought this was the best course of action. The agitated motorist, also affected by the humidity and upset by the ineptness of the sewer department, was slower returning to his auto and as we sped past it, Jarbie clipped the open driver's side door and tore it off. We continued fleeing the scene, but unfortunately came up short of the Mexican border. The CPD, who'd been called by amused neighbors, caught us some eight hundred feet later. We were stunned to see such a pleasant day of baseball ruined by a summer downpour.

The paddy wagon crew was called and they brought calmness to the scene. They sized up the three of us, saw Jarbie trip and bounce his head off the front bumper, and put him in the wagon for further study. One patrolman spoke to Tom and me and said he would not arrest us, but our friend was going to the station. He wanted to know what we had to drink and I told him that we split a six-pack. He seemed skeptical, then somewhat sarcastically stated that Jarbie probably had four of the cans and that Tom and me had one can each. I liked his way of thinking.

He told us to call someone for bail money. "But wait a minute, before you leave I have to search the car and then you can go," he says. Tom, at this time, had not finished his undergrad degree, but looked into the future and saw himself practicing law. Even without the necessary advanced training, Tom was very smart, he understood the basic principles of criminal law. "Hold it officer," he said, "you can't search that car without a proper warrant." Tom was so proud of himself as he whispered to me, "There's some fireworks in the glove box and I don't want Jarbie to get in any more trouble." He was indeed bright, but he had yet to develop that certain bedside manner that one needs to survive on this planet.

Tom continued being proud of himself; I was somewhat stunned and the policeman looked like he'd been by a brick. As he straightened up his body from his illegal search position, he pointed to both of us with his left hand and pulled open the security latch on the back door of the wagon with is right hand and said, "Hop in counselor and take your client with you."

Whew, was it hot in that paddy wagon! Humid too. Tom pulled in his horns and I decided to represent the three of us pro bono. The officer told us that when we arrived at the police station, Tom should cool it, Jarbie should continue sleeping and I should disabuse myself of using Sergeant Brendan "Big Red" Nelligan as a reference unless I preferred to receive a good old-fashioned ass kicking.

Sergeant Nelligan was Bill Nelligan's father, the toughest, most no-nonsense cop on the force who worked out of the same station that we were headed to. As the officer wisely counseled, using Mr. Nelligan's name as a reference was counter-productive. Mr. Nelligan was the *last* person we'd want to know about this. Okay, already. He locked us all up and disappeared for a while. When he returned, he let Tom and me out, put his hat on the table and told us to put all of our money in it, go out the back door and forget we ever saw the place, except to raise some money to bail out Jarbie. We did as the kind man suggested. "All of our money" came to $2.75 in quarters.

There we were 8:00 PM on a Sunday night at the red light at 63rd and St. Louis and didn't have a quarter to get on the bus to get back to Cannadys, where bail money might be had. We began hitchhiking, called "thumbing" in those days, with no success. People are funny; two decent looking guys still in their Sunday mass clothes and no one would offer a lift. We noticed the paddy wagon pull out from the station. It pulled along side us and the cop said, "What the fuck are you doing now?" I explained the economic realities of our situation and he gave me four quarters so we could get out of the 8ᵗʰ District before the shift change. He was a very nice man.

We had no luck raising any money for Jarbie so we went home. I don't remember if we called Jerry Joyce or if Jarbie called him after his nap. Anyway, Jerry and his generous dad arrived at the station about midnight with bail money. As Mr. Joyce was driving him home Jarbie let both of them know that he was not pleased with the slow response regarding his detention. For my part I sure was glad to get home. It was still quite hot and my bedroom window was wide open so I climbed through it instead of using a door. I went right to sleep on my bottom bunk without waking my brother on the top bunk or my father in his bedroom. Why bother that hardworking man at that late hour? (I matured quickly after that night and was married three short years later, pleased to deed the bottom bunk to my sibling, Tom, who was next up on the seniority list.)

Footnote: The following Sunday coming out of church, after Father Mollohan's mass, a friendly face smiled at me and said, "Hey, Joyce, what's up for you and the counselor today?" It was the policeman from "8" who'd arrested us! He knew we weren't bad boys, just stupid boys, and he, and other cops like him, helped make up the neighborhood.

One fine Saturday morning in 1965 Jarbie and Tommy Carroll (TC) decided to visit Tom McDonough who had recently started law school at Notre Dame. Seeing McDonough would be fun and there was a plus – Notre Dame was playing Michigan State. They stocked Jarbie's Volkswagen with beer and whiskey and drove to South Bend. When they got to the apartment Tom and his roommates were studying. TC and Jarbie were not made welcome.

They had a few drinks anyway then said they were going to the game. "How'd you get tickets?" McDonough asked. "We'll buy them there," they said. "You assholes," said McDonough "Knute Rockne couldn't get tickets to this game. It's been sold out for five years."

Jarbie and TC found a local tavern and enjoyed the game with the local fans. Even though Notre Dame lost, the revelry was not dampened. Many hours later they returned to McDonough's for a few more drinks. At 3:00AM they decided to head back to Chicago.

Incredibly, Jarbie missed the entrance to the toll road, which is lit up like O'Hare, and wandered across the Michigan state line. He saw a sign for RT 31, a road he told TC he knew like the back of his hand. "This will take us to Chicago."

But soon he got drowsy and TC was already asleep so Jarbie wisely pulled over and went to sleep himself. A few minutes later a Michigan State Trooper banged on the window arousing the travelers. He informed them it was against the law in Michigan to sleep on the side of a highway and to "Move it!" In a stupor the beleaguered football fans continued on Rt. 31 until again the arms of Morpheus enveloped Jarbie and he passed out. The Volkswagen wandered off the road into a ditch and wound up on its side.

TC woke up with the car on top of him but just barely. A culvert supported it, his passenger side door an inch above him. It is a mystery how he got out of the car with the door closed. Jarbie, in a panic, climbed up through his door and started yelling, "TC! TC! Where are you?"

"Under the car," said TC.

Somehow Jarbie lifted it just enough for TC to crawl out of the ditch. The boys, miraculously unhurt, sat down to wait for help. It came at daybreak by way of a farmer walking down the road with two plow horses in harness. The farmer, who could not have been nicer, knew exactly what to do. He hitched the team to the VW and with no effort at all, the horses dragged it up into the road. The farmer and the boys tipped the car over onto its wheels. It started right up and the boys drove home, still upset that Notre Dame lost.

Shortly after this, TC got called up by the United States Army for duty in Vietnam. He said at the time that Vietnam would be safer than hanging around with Jarbie.

NOTE: Jarbie's real name is Charles, his family calls him Chuck. He and Irene have three daughters: Erin, a civil engineer with an MBA; Laura with a Masters in education; and Colleen a medical doctor. We sent this chapter to Jarbie for his approval to publish it "as is" or to see if he wanted us to disguise his identity. We didn't know he was dying.

When the chapter arrived at his house he was under Hospice care and mostly unconscious. His daughters opened the envelope, read the chapter and then took turns reading it aloud to their dad.

Irene said, "Chuck woke up, perked up, listened to all of it and even laughed out loud! Then he faded." (We assume this meant he approved.)

At his funeral a week later, Irene, the daughters and Chuck's many siblings were pleased that Chuck would be in the book. His oldest sister, Mitzie, said, "You Joyces got the last laugh."

Rest in peace, the Never-to-be-Forgotten Jarbie Crowe.

CHAPTER 12
All Gone

I t was a good life growing up in the St. Sabina neighborhood. Streets were safe at all hours and everybody knew everybody else (not really but it felt like it). Merchants were plentiful and varied, almost everybody was friendly and there was lots of good natured teasing from the adults to us kids and, of course, there was that unending, character building pimping among us guys in the gang.

We had a great city park, Foster, at 83rd and Loomis, with many baseball diamonds, a field house and tennis courts. The church provided the grand gymnasium for basketball, handball and roller-skating. It also provided emotional and intellectual security. We did not, as individuals, have to grapple with questions of right and wrong. Sabina was a spiritual and theological bastion where priests and nuns had all the answers. Most of the guys in the gang planned to keep living in the parish into adulthood and then raise their own kids there. (And most did, vicariously, a few miles away.) The place was, if you were parochial, idyllic. But as we left our teens and entered our twenties, all of the above would change. Coloreds were coming and they could not be stopped and don't gasp. To call a black person "colored" or "Negro" today is demeaning but I'm writing of yesterday when those terms were polite. "Black" and "African American" had not yet been coined. The National Association for the Advancement for Colored People (NAACP) was founded in 1909.)

The colored migration to Chicago had its catalyst from remnants of plantation life called "share cropping." It started five hundred miles from us, primarily in Mississippi but also from other slave states. For one hundred years after being officially freed by Lincoln, coloreds had lived in the South on the edge of poverty. But after World War II jobs became available in the North and up they came. By the tens of thousands they moved to Chicago establishing their own neighborhoods adjacent to white neighborhoods. Discernable, uncrossable boundaries were established between these neighborhoods in the form of major city streets, viaducts, railroad tracks, parks or other physical entities. Both coloreds and whites were keenly aware of those boundaries.

Then, in our day, another migratory wave occurred. This time hundreds of thousands of Southern coloreds came to Chicago. At first the newcomers landed in established colored neighborhoods, but in no time those became overcrowded. Established Northern coloreds were prejudiced against, and did not want to co-mingle with, the poor, uneducated newcomers. So Northern coloreds began, slowly at first and then relentlessly, moving into white neighborhoods. There was no place else to go.

You'll recall that the parish to our east was St. Leo. That's where the coloreds first penetrated. We in Sabina took comfort in that. "They'll never get to us; Leo's too big," we said. When coloreds first started buying houses on the fringes of Leo, Monsignor Molloy attempted to halt their advance. He esoterically put out the word at his borders that if parishioners felt they had to sell their houses they should contact him and not a Realtor. The parish would buy the house. This plan, which everybody quickly heard about, worked for a little while until Molloy ran out of money. The perimeter was irreparably breached. Sound the retreat.

But Molloy, one tough old Irishman, took another ploy even though he knew he was on his heels. Before a Sunday mass began he would walk up and down the aisles of the church. When he spotted coloreds in a pew he'd stop, put his hands behind his back and glare at them. I saw him do this one Sunday at Leo's chapel. I couldn't believe my eyes. As he glared, the colored people bowed their heads. I was never so embarrassed in my life - for the coloreds, for the other uncomfortable white worshipers, for Molloy, our religion and myself. When I went home and told my parents what I'd seen they were speechless.

I heard that the Cardinal called Molloy on the carpet for this. Molloy's defense was that the colored worshippers were not residents of the parish; in fact they weren't even Catholic. "They are just there to soften us up!" Maybe so, but ruse or not, the question is begged, what would Jesus have done if He were in Molloy's cassock? The answer would depend on who you asked.

Economics is a major dictator of human behavior and at that time nothing lowered house values faster than hearing, "A nigger just moved into the neighborhood!" Houses and apartment buildings in Leo sold like crazy. In less than two years the coloreds were knocking on St. Sabina's doors where they met our monsignor, John McMahon.

Monsignor McMahon, like everybody in Sabina, watched in awe (make that horror) the demise of St. Leo Parish. Very few coloreds are Catholics, most are Baptists, so church attendance plummeted. That meant scant collection money to keep up the plant. *Sayonara* old St. Leo.

Although Monsignor McMahon was also an Irishman, he was not a tough guy like Molloy. McMahon was kindly. One could make the case that he was a better Christian (not Catholic) than Molloy and instead of glaring at the newcomers, he welcomed them. He sincerely believed (I knew him, he really did) that his parishioners would not abandon Sabina and would welcome, or at least be cordial to, the newcomers who bought houses in the parish. He knew that Sabina had a more cohesive culture than Leo and that his parishioners were tighter knit. So McMahon offered the olive branch to colored people and welcomed them to church. This posture infuriated many parishioners who accused him of "selling out to the niggers." These same people sold their houses as fast as possible, taking whatever they could get, and split to the suburbs or to parishes on the farthest reaches of the south side of the city.

As it turned out, Monsignor McMahon overestimated the graciousness of his parishioners. In no time flat they all took off. Once it began, the swiftness of the transition from white to black was astounding. Sabina fell faster than Leo. Our 79th Street, home to butchers, bakers, grocery stores, taverns, and other cozy businesses was decimated. Storefronts were boarded up, trash was strewn – it looked Third World.

Gus closed DeLites and got his real estate license hoping to cash in on all the selling. It didn't work. He never got a listing or made a sale. He was a Greek, good with food, but if you wanted to list real estate in an Irish neighborhood, you needed to be an Irishman. Besides, Gus was not a Catholic and didn't live in the parish so he was not "one of us." Tula took a job selling high-end furniture in the Loop.

When people first began selling to coloreds (the sooner you sold out the more money you'd get) they would quietly go through a Realtor, but they'd insist no "For Sale" sign appear on the lawn. When the house sold, always to coloreds, of course, the moving vans showed up in the middle of the night so the sellers could avoid their neighbors' wrath. Every house that sold caused the value of the remaining houses to drop. Soon, however, there was no more secrecy and no more game playing. Panic set in, for sale signs were everywhere. The St. Sabina that we knew was gone forever.

During this white flight, I was in the Army. After my discharge I married and settled in Georgia. Each time I'd go home to visit Mom and Dad I saw the change. Soon all the faces on our block were black except for theirs and an elderly lady, Frances Wagner, who lived three doors down. Mom and Dad refused to move for racial reasons believing that to do so would be a sin. They became friends with their new neighbors and were the godparents of at least one of their kids. "These are fine people just trying to better themselves," my folks said. And, indeed, the houses and little yards were perfectly maintained. Only 79th Street looked like shit. Today, forty years later, much of it still does.

Mom was always a do-gooder and Dad, who worked all the time, encouraged her activities. When the neighborhood began to change, in an attempt to stop the white flight, and with the encouragement of Monsignor McMahon, Mom invited coloreds she'd met at various functions to our home, along with some white people from the parish. They'd eat, greet and talk. Mom did this to show the whites that coloreds were normal people and that our differences were few compared to all we had in common. We could certainly share a neighborhood. This sounds ridiculous today, but back then many whites had never had a social conversation with a colored and vice versa. It was a nice try, but a futile one. I invited one of my most prejudiced friends to one of the gatherings. Afterwards he admitted that the colored people were intelligent, friendly and nice. "But I still ain't livin' next door to a nigger," he said.

About this time my sister, Mary, had her first child, Leone. Mary and Floyd asked their good friend, Russ Marshall, to be her godfather. Russ was colored, but I don't think their request was racially motivated. Russ was a retired mailman, a solid Catholic and a good guy. Many described him as "saintly." But when people heard he was colored eyebrows went way up. It just seemed wrong.

When Dad retired, he and Mom decided to move to the family farm on the Kankakee River and live with Granny. Because they were in no hurry and very frugal, Dad bought a Pontiac station wagon and planned to move their belongings to the farm on a piece meal basis. They decided not to put the house on the market until the move was complete. I calculated this would take about thirty-five years.

Unfortunately, Dad had the heart attack and died. Mom was devastated and lonely and decided to move to the farm right away to be with her mother. She put the house on the market merely by telling the neighbors it was for sale. They found her a buyer. Because the neighborhood had completely changed, real estate prices had stabilized and begun to rise. Mom got $19,000 for the house in 1972. It was bought in 1941 for $6,000. Not a great return, but not that bad either, all things considered.

I have seen and heard much prejudice in my life, both in the North and the South. As an adult, I've lived more years in the South than the North and two expressions I've heard often seem to summarize the white inhabitant's feelings towards African Americans. In the South: "I would never mistreat one," implying a lesser species. In the North: "I hate niggers," implying equality. And I've never witnessed such overt hatred as the day Rainbow Beach was integrated. Chicago has a number of good, sandy beaches along Lake Michigan. Rainbow Beach is the farthest south, stretching from 75th Street to about 79th Street. It was the last city beach to be integrated and it happened a few years before Leo and St. Sabina were overrun. I was there.

The word was out that coloreds were coming to Rainbow Beach. It was a Sunday in July. Uniformed cops were lined up every twenty feet or so on the pavement leading to the sand. On the sand, intermingled with sunbathers, were many other cops in bathing suits wearing tee shirts to cover their guns. Squad cars were all over the place. Captains and Chiefs were all over their radios. It was tense.

But as the day progressed there was no sign of colored people. About the time we began assuming they'd changed their plans, someone shouted, "Here comes the niggers!" Sure enough, a few young coloreds, including a girl, got out of a car and started walking toward the beach. The cops surrounded them providing protection, and the epithets began, "Go home you fucking niggers! You filthy niggers don't belong here! We're going to kill you niggers!" And so on.

The coloreds walked down to the water and into it up to their knees. The venomous screams continued and got louder as more people realized what was happening. I do believe if the cops hadn't been there the young coloreds *would* have been killed. They were only in the water a few moments. They turned back, walked to their car and drove away – squad cars following. Rainbow Beach had been integrated.

Many years after the Sabina we grew up in had completely changed. I was visiting Chicago and met a guy I knew from years before. We were discussing the old days in Sabina and he said, "You should see what the niggers have done to the church. They've got fucking bongo drums on the altar. It's enough to make you puke." This I had to see.

I told Carpenter Jimmy what I'd heard and he was curious also. Jim knows everybody and arranged to get us into the church the next afternoon. Sure enough there were bongo drums in the sanctuary and reed instruments of African origin leaning against the altar. Leopard skins were draped over the communion rail. It was indeed stunning, but certainly not enough to make you puke. The church itself hadn't changed one bit. The marble, carved wood and stained glass were still exquisite, prettier than I'd remembered. Then I thought of "Father Kelly," and his insane sermon on the YMCA, and I had to smile. If Kelly'd seen the leopard skins he would not have puked, he'd have dropped dead. We continued touring and saw on the back wall of the vestibule of the downstairs church a number of photographs depicting St. Sabina's history. In one of them was my mom. It made me proud.

To this day, I return to Chicago a few times a year to visit family and friends. Often I exit the Dan Ryan Expressway at 79th Street and head west for nostalgic purposes. I drive around the parish and then park in front of our house at 8027 Ada. I sit there, remembering. I feel at peace. Then I drive down the alley and park behind the house. The front and the back have their own set of memories. A few years ago I told a Chicago friend that I do this. He said, "Jim, you gotta be out of your mind. That neighborhood has the highest crime rate in the city."

But I still do it anyway and I always will. Sabina, and all that it used to be, defined me.

Monsignor McMahon retired shortly after the neighborhood changed but remained in the parish, living at the rectory. His replacement, Father Pehler, invited him to do so. It was a nice gesture. When Father Pehler suddenly died of a heart attack, his assistant, Father Michael Pfleger, extended the invitation to McMahon. Some years later I happened to be in Chicago on business when Monsignor McMahon died. Mom drove up from the farm and she and I went to the funeral. The upstairs church was almost full and almost all the faces were black except for Mom, Jim Clark, a retired cop who'd been a parishioner before the exodus, Dorothy Morrin, a retired spinster teacher, and me. Dorothy, too, stayed in the neighborhood after the change until she was mugged on 79th Street walking to the store. She wound up in a nursing home and died.

Today, in 2011, St. Sabina is thriving as a parish because of the guile, energy and forcefulness of personality of Father Pfleger, who's still the pastor after thirty years. To learn more about St. Sabina today read the fine book *Radical Disciple*, by Robert McClory. It tells, among other things, how Pfleger has had Cardinal Archbishops of Chicago talking to themselves.

CHAPTER 13

All Gone (Another Take)

By Carpenter Joyce

E ven today, 2011, almost every discussion with friends about our early years on 79th Street repeatedly turns toward the activities centered around Saint Sabina church, school or gym. Even non-Catholics or those "fallen away" talked about their memories of Saint Sabina. (However, I didn't know many non-Catholics.)

There were many adult activities involving the Church and women and men's clubs and societies that brought our parents to the Church or the priests brought the activities to our homes. We all remember spending many evenings on our knees in our living rooms reciting the decades of the rosary. "Block Rosaries," the "Pilgrim Virgin" and "the Blue Army" were examples of outreach programs probably designed by the marketing department from headquarters in Rome. The Holy Name Society and Saint Vincent DePaul Society were the organizations for men and were used for social activities as well as fundraising for the poor.

Saint Sabina School was packed with kids and taught by Sinsinawa Dominican nuns. There were upwards of twelve hundred kids enrolled in the school and as many as twenty-five nuns living in the convent. At that time there were very few lay teachers helping these wonderful Sisters. I knew them well; two of my dad's sisters were Dominican nuns. The school hosted lots of activities mostly centered in the gym.

The gym was the centerpiece of the neighborhood for young people growing up near 79th Street. I'll attempt to do justice to the Community Center, the proper name for the gym at that time. The basketball floor was parquet wood, placed on end, similar to the Boston Celtic's, "Boston Gahden," local pronunciation. The gym had a handball court which was unheard of in a parish gym at that time. It was well used by the city's seminarians because Quigly Seminary made the boys go to school on Saturday but was off on Thursday. Who knows what the strategy was on that decision? Female avoidance?

Grade school P.E. classes were extensive. Men's CYO leagues were played there. The Saint Sabina A.A.U. basketball tournament was legend. Where else could one watch college all-Americans play in your local gym? Great stuff! The annual roller skating "variety show" packed the place with young skaters displaying their considerable talents in exotic costumes made by volunteer mothers. It seemed that the gym was occupied twenty-four hours a day, seven days a week! Sunday night dances for high school aged kids began in 1939. The gym was packed with young men and women swaying to the big band sounds of the day.

Across the street from the gym was the Lateran Club. This building was used for social gatherings when other church venues were booked. One function I recall was the meetings of the "Over 21 Club." The Sunday night dances were for the younger set but the Church had a sense that they needed to keep the connection with their young adults so this club was established. At that time many couples were married by the time they reached 22-25 years of age. Thus the nickname for the Over 21 Club became the "Last Chance Club."

The term "social networking" may seem to be a new term but as I've described previously Saint Sabina had a pretty good idea and working model that provided most of the spiritual and social needs of its parishioners. The design was established and executed by some very capable leaders who had a finger on the pulse of the community.

This is a brief description of the importance of Saint Sabina Parish in the lives of thousands of residents of that community. It was a good place during a good time. Perhaps with this glimpse of local history you understand the disappointment and sadness on the part of many former "Sabina" people. Some thought that this great place would go on forever. We often thought of one day bringing our own kids to DeLites to meet Gus and Tula and maybe play with the sugar shakers until ejected. I often admired how the "older guys" showed up at Chris Quinn's tavern on Saturday afternoon with their kids. The guys would enjoy a few 7oz. glasses of Schlitz on tap while the kids had a Coke and some peanuts. Life was good! Little did we know that there was a growing population of blue collar families looking forward to those same things that we enjoyed as they searched for better housing and schools. That population was located just to the east of us, wanting to move away from conditions not conductive to child rearing.

As African-American families purchased homes on the east side of the parish rumors flew all over the neighborhood about crime, fires by arson and losses on home values. Unfortunately the rumors were more than rumors. The shooting of Frank Kelley in 1965 right in front of the gym seemed to be the "beginning of the end." The "change" was coming in rapid fashion. "Panic peddlers" moved in, realtors who had no real estate stake in the neighborhood but change was good for business. They helped to spread fear, and fleeing whites were ripe for any stories that were circulating.

Whites attended Church looking for hope and direction. But the leadership they were accustomed to had no practical advice. Spiritually and ethically, of course, the priests preached a welcoming message. But whites knew the history of changing neighborhoods in Chicago and there were no examples of successful integration in neighborhoods similar to ours.

The change seemed to come overnight. No one wanted to be the last on the block to sell; the price would be too low. The pace of the white exodus was astonishing. The murder of Frank Kelley in August 1965 was a significant date in the white flight. Of equal shock to the guys in the gang was a series of closings of "institutions" that played significant roles, places that marked time in our lives. The dates amazed me as I did my research. It happened all at once! DeLites (restaurant and ice cream parlor and premier hangout) closed in April 1966. Chris Quinn's Tavern (premier hangout as we matured) closed April 1966. The Saint Sabina A.A.U. tournament began in the 1940's–ended in 1966. The Saint Sabina Sunday Night Dance (started in 1939) ended in 1966.

Many now refer to the end of our era in St. Sabina as "the day the music died." This is a euphemism for "when the blacks moved in and we moved out."

The neighborhood today remains a blue-collar community and Saint Sabina Church, school and gym remain the center of the community's activities, as it always has. Whether the residents are Catholic or not (most are not) has no real meaning. They have needs similar to the ones we had and Saint Sabina continues to meet those needs.

An interesting note, at least to me, is how time weaves many characters into our lives. Much of what I have just described took place in the 1960s. In 1964 Cassius Clay (Mohammed Ali) became the heavyweight champion of the world. Fast forward forty-five years to May 15, 2010 when Michael Joyce, son of Jeremiah Joyce, married Jamillah Ali, daughter of Mohammed Ali. On October 16, 2011 Jake Daniel Ali Joyce arrived, weighing in at 8 pounds 2 ounces. No, the wedding was not held at St. Sabina, but it does go to show all of us that anything is possible in this world.

Appendix 1
The Guys in the Gang with their eventual occupations

Name	Occupation
William Callaghan	Chief of Intelligence–Chicago Police Department
James Callahan	Don't know, after Vietnam he went to Kansas
Thomas Carroll	Group Underwriting Manager
Robert Cavanaugh	Sales executive – United States Steel
Michael Collins	School engineer – Chicago Public Schools
Charles Crowe	Lieutenant – Chicago Fire Department
Charles Gargola	Business owner
John Glenville	Stevedore
James "Ada" Joyce	Psychoanalyst, business owner, author
James "Carpenter" Joyce	Commissioner – Chicago Fire Department
Jeremiah "Jerry" Joyce	State Senator, entrepreneur, attorney
Thomas Lally	Business owner
Joseph La Rose	Business owner
Thomas McArdle	Engineer – Chicago Fire Department
Thomas McDonough	Attorney
Daniel McAvoy	General Contractor (Arizona)
Thomas McNally	Engineer
Arthur Mosher	College Professor
Ronald Neher	UPS driver
William Nelligan	Police officer – Chicago Police Department
George Overbeek	United States Navy
Charles Reilly	Trucking industry executive
Cyril Watson**	Judge, attorney
Michael Watson**	Engineer, business owner

**Brothers

Our dads' occupations were also varied. Joyce Carpenter's dad was on the fire department, my dad and Mr. McDonough were electricians. McNally's, Nelligan's, and Billy Callaghan's fathers were policemen. Jerry Joyce's dad was a CPA and Mr. Cavanaugh drove a beer truck. Mr. Glenville was a FBI man. Mr. Carroll was a railroad man. Other dads owned businesses: Watson a butcher shop, McAvoy a clothing store, LaRose a grocery store and Callahan a metal fabricating shop.

Appendix 2
A Photo Gallery

Carpenter Joyce with Ed Joyce

My younger brother, Ed, and I decided an assortment of photos of neighborhood landmarks might be an interesting supplement to the narrative.

I drove and Ed worked the camera. I had my memories of my teen years on 79th Street and Ed had his. Ed's experiences included much more racial tension than mine, he is ten years younger. My family moved from 7636 S. Carpenter to 7836 S. Loomis while I was away at colleges, in the Army and then married. Mom and Dad wanted my siblings to finish at Saint Sabina before the inevitable move further south and west while still staying in the city limits. Dad was a Chicago firefighter and had to live in the city.

I had a list of addresses, some of which I actually remembered from the 1950s. My memory proved to be quite reliable as we drove the streets and shot over one hundred photos. While parked in front of Ada Joyce's house I heard a voice ask, "Why are you taking pictures of my house?" I quickly introduced Ed and myself and explained our mission. We met Ruby and Norman Clark who have lived in the Wagner house for forty-two years. Mr. Clark wanted to know if we were part of the Joyce family who lived next door to him. He stated that he "loved the Joyces" and told us what a smart man Mr. Joyce was. "Did you know that Mr. Joyce moved his stuff out of that house by himself with a block and tackle? He gave me two boxes of Lionel trains that I kept for fifteen years and then put them out in the alley and they were picked up right away." I told Mr. Clark that I had six boxes of Mr. Joyce's bent nails. The Clark's invited us into their home and could not have been any nicer. It seems it isn't much different in the neighborhood in 2011 than it was in the 1950s and 60s, just depends on whom you meet and how you meet, and so much of the neighborhood looks the same.

(For more photos see: jamestjoyce@aol.com.)

Bill Nelligan, 7955 S. Laflin

Billy Callaghan, 7717 S. Aberdeen

Bob Cavanaugh, 8208 S. Lofflin St.

James "Carpenter" Joyce, 7636 S. Carpenter St.

Charles Crow, 8030 S. Ada St.

Charlie Gargola, 8145 S. Elizabeth St.

Cy & Mike Watson, 7723 S. Aberdeen St.

Dan McAvoy, 8121 S. Ada St.

George Overbeek, 8201 Throop St.

James "Ada" Joyce, 8027 S. Ada St.

Janet Brown Joyce, 7719 S. Throop St.

Jeremiah Joyce, 8245 S. Elizabeth St.

Jim Callahan, 7917 S. Ada St.

Joe LaRose, 7838 S. Loomis Blvd.

John Glenville, 7715 S. Throop St.

Mike & Rita (McDonough) Collins, 1322 W. 77th St.

Grandmother Joyce ~ Carpenter, 7836 S. Loomis Blvd.

Ron Neher, 8241 S. Elizabeth St.

Edwina Kroll House, 102nd & Central Park
scene of "Three Wisemen"

Tom Carroll, 7924 S. Loomis Blvd.

111

Tom Lally, 8131 S. Ada St.

Tom Mc Ardle, 7634 S. Morgan St.

Tom McDonough, 8118 S. Elizabeth St.

Tom McNally, 10401 S. Hamlin St.

Tom Stack, 8025 S. Ada St.

SECTION IV
JCU and the US Army

CHAPTER 14

Of Monkey and Boys

After Leo High School I attended John Carroll University (1960-1964) near Cleveland. Students were all male, all white and all Catholic. There were two distinct groups, the daily commuter from the Cleveland area, "day-hops," and those of us from someplace else. Chicago, Detroit, Pittsburgh, New York state and small Ohio towns provided the bulk of us. We out-of-towners lived in dormitories on the beautiful campus in University Heights, where we were subject to many rules: Lights out at 11:00; no visitors to our rooms after 8:00; no music after 9:00; never any loud noises; a curfew every night including weekends; no girls allowed in the building and don't even think about alcohol. It was not unlike a federal prison.

Jesuits run John Carroll, an order of priests who specialize in teaching at the college level. They considered dormitory living a privilege. I had that privilege in the building called Pacelli Hall, until the end of my sophomore year when the Jesuits threw me out. I was placed on "academic probation" because my GPA had fallen below 2.0. I was allowed one more semester to get it back up to 2.0. If I didn't, they would expel me from the school completely.

There were other ways to get tossed off campus. For instance Al Rutledge (we called him "Moe," I don't know why) got a letter over the summer from the dormitory prefect, a Jesuit named Father Joseph O. Schell, who was a stickler if there ever was one. It stated, "You have an attitude incongruous with good dormitory living." Out you go, Moe. Recently I asked another guy why he had to live off campus. He said he did not remember and added that he'd told many lies during that time of his life. "I wonder what I told my folks?" he mused. One Saturday night, when most guys were out of the dorm until curfew, Fr. Schell searched our rooms including going through closets. He found a little firecracker in Dave McClenahan's coat pocket. Dave had forgotten it was there, a leftover from the previous 4th of July in Pittsburgh. Schell called him to his office. "I know your kind, McClenahan. You start trouble then sit back and watch." See you later, Dave. (Today Dave is a senior partner in K&L Gates, one of the largest law firms in the world.)

So we dummies, misfits, and liars were left to our own devices to find a place to live for junior year. No problem. We may have been liars and lousy students, but we quickly learned how to rent an apartment. Four of us, Rutledge, Eddie Christie, Bob Arber and I banded together and found a dandy place in Cleveland Heights. It was a third floor walk-up about four miles from campus, making it an easy hitchhike down the glamorous Fairmont Boulevard through Shaker Heights. As good luck would have it, four of our friends found the same kind of apartment *right next door*. (John Breen, Bob Mirguet, Jim Heavey and that troublemaker, McClenahan) We now had our own dorm complex but without any rules. We were on our own with lights on, music playing, and friends of both sexes coming and going as they pleased. Our parties lasted all night. The first thing we did was stock up a bar.

Jesuit logic had it that if a student couldn't make adequate grades in the controlled environment of dormitory living then his chances of graduating were practically nil if left to live freely. Happily, the Jesuits were wrong. Seven of the eight of us graduated two years later – a few of us even making the honor-roll our senior year.

None of us had ever had such freedom and we reveled in it. The four of us at 2089 Coventry quickly decided we needed a pet to make our house a home. Eddie and I wanted a dog. Arber and Rutledge, who were more creative, wanted a monkey. We bought a monkey. Eddie and I agreed when we realized it would be a good enticement to pick up girls. "Want to come to the apartment to see our monkey?"

Not only did that tactic not work, but we soon realized monkeys make terrible pets. They're no fun if left in a cage, but when they're out being cute, climbing curtains and jumping across the furniture, they also shit and piss on everything. They bite without warning and they masturbate freely, often and without shame.

Oley, that was the monkey's name, loved grapes. Show him one from wherever he was perched and he'd be in front of you in a flash with his hand out. He'd take the grape in his tiny fingers, peel it with his needle teeth; spit the skin on the floor and chew the pulp. Then he'd scamper back up to his favorite spot, a curtain rod. You should have seen the curtains.

Oley hated his cage. Getting him into it was difficult and dangerous. Not even a grape would tempt him; he was too smart. You had to grab him and stuff him inside. When you did you were gonna get bit. We finally bought heavy, reinforced welders gloves.

One time Bobby Mirguet from next door came to visit. He loved animals and was enthralled by cute, little Oley. I warned Bobby about the biting but he didn't pay any attention to me. He got on the floor with Oley and they were playing "chase." Bobby'd throw a grape and they'd race to get it. Oley always won, of course, and they were having a great time. Then Bobby made the mistake of trying to pick Oley up to cuddle him. Oley chomped down on Bobby's finger. Blood spurted out.

"Joyce! He bit me!" he yelled, looking at me with disbelief.

"I told you so, Bobby."

One night we had a big party planned with some thirty people expected. In the rush to get ready we forgot about Oley. Just before the guests were to arrive Bob Arber said, "The monkey's still out." We didn't have time to go through the ritual of catching him so I lured him to the door of my bedroom and threw a grape into it. He flew after it and I closed the door.

The party was a great success; nobody got bit, and when I went to bed many hours later Oley was up on my curtain rod sound asleep. I got into bed and put my head on the pillow. It was soaked. Oley had pissed on it, getting his revenge, I guess, for missing the party. I threw the pillow on the floor and went to sleep.

I slept without a pillow for a week until one afternoon in the cafeteria I overheard a guy at the next table say, "Did you hear what Eddie Christie did to Joyce?" He said we'd had a big party at our apartment and during it Eddie snuck into my bedroom and poured a glass of water on my pillow. "Joyce thought the monkey pissed on it. Eddie said he's been sleeping without a pillow ever since."

With the Thanksgiving break approaching, the problem of Oley loomed. None of us would take him home and we sure couldn't leave him alone in the apartment. We decided, unanimously, to sell him. We put an ad in the *Cleveland Plain Dealer*. A lady answered it. "I've always wanted a monkey," she said on the phone, "but my husband wouldn't let me. But he just died and I am going to use his insurance money to buy your monkey. Is he cute?"

"Cutest thing you've ever seen," Eddie assured her.

Eddie and I got Oley into his cage, one last time, and put it into the back seat of Eddie's car. The address the lady gave was a converted, one room garage, off an alley, in a run down neighborhood on Cleveland's east side. It took us forever to find it. It was snowing like crazy.

When we knocked on the door, we heard the barking of many dogs. When the lady opened the door at least ten of them ran past us into the snowy night. She invited us in. The rest of the dogs were milling around. There were also dozens of cats and dozens of birds in cages. It was an unbelievable sight. When the dogs saw Oley they went berserk. He clung to the top of his cage. We were afraid he'd have a heart attack.

The lady took the cage out of Eddie's hands and put it on a bureau, "His place of honor," she said. She shushed the dogs, put her fingers through the wires of the cage and stroked Oley's head, telling him it would be okay. He didn't bite her. We were watching a miracle.

The lady paid us the asking price of forty dollars, which is what we'd paid for Oley. Eddie gave her ten of it back. "This is to help pay for his food," he said. "He likes grapes."

I've known many unforgettable characters and Eddie was one of them. He looked like Alfred Hitchcock – big belly, double chin, ski jump nose, and receding hairline. At twenty years of age he could have passed for forty.

One night we had a party at our apartment that lasted into the wee hours. At 3:00 in the morning there were only a few of us still awake. We were sitting in the living room telling stories when I heard a squeaking sound. I'd not heard that sound before and thought I may be hallucinating. I concentrated and, sure enough, every few seconds "squeak."

I looked over at Eddie, who was sitting next to me on the couch chain smoking. It seemed like whenever he breathed in I'd hear the squeak. "Eddie, quit breathing," I said. "Why?" he said. "Because I think you're squeaking." He held his breath. Everyone else quit talking. "Squeak."

"Oh shit!" I yelled. "There's something under the couch!" And with that a large rat ran out. Eddie and I jumped up onto the back of the couch. We couldn't believe our eyes.

Our roommate, Bob Arber, was an artist. He had created a large mural on canvas in a wooden frame. It sat on the floor and reached almost to the ceiling. The rat ran behind it.

A giant of a guy named George Bednar who was on the Notre Dame football team was a guest, a friend of Heavey from next door. Unlike the rest of us, he was not afraid of rats. He went into the kitchen, found a broom, and started poking it behind the mural. The rat ran out the other side, and then stopped. As Bednar ran over to step on it, it darted back behind the work of art. This happened three times. Bednar, an offensive lineman, wasn't quick enough to get across the painting.

"One of you guys take the broom and start shoving it behind this thing. I'll wait 'til it comes out again and step on it."

"Fuck you," we said.

So in frustration Bednar, who was in his bare feet, and who did not have an appreciation for art, started kicking the bottom of the mural, splintering the frame and tearing the canvas. Soon all squeaking stopped. He slid the mural sideways and picked up the dead rat by the tail. "What do you want me to do with it?" he asked. Eddie and I almost fainted.

When we told our landlord, Mr. Lee, about the rat he didn't believe us until we showed him the body in the back yard. The poor man was horrified. "I keep up building perfectly clean," he said. "How could this be?" All we could do was shrug.

Mr. Lee, an Eastern European, stood about 6'6" tall and weighed maybe 300 pounds. He had a wife and two little girls. They were Orthodox Jews. On Saturdays their apartment, one floor below us, remained dark and not a sound was heard.

One time I got strep throat. I was really sick and running a high fever. It was a Saturday night and my roommates went out partying. Somehow Mr. Lee heard I was sick. That night he came to check on me. I was lying in bed half delirious. When he saw how sick I was he said he'd be back with Mrs. Lee. They returned a short time later with a bowl of chicken soup. She propped up my pillows and fed me. The fever broke, I went to sleep, and in the morning I was fine. Mr. & Mrs. Lee, Freddie Menzer, the Kalks and Schwartzes. Early on, I learned to like Jews.

The boys next door had a big party, which ended in a scandalous mystery. Their landlady, Mrs. Gorchester, another Jew, was the nicest of people and treated the boys like sons. The day of the party she'd baked a cherry pie for her own family and put it on her windowsill to cool. They lived on the second floor so to get to the party on the third floor you had to pass her kitchen window. While the party was just getting going, Mrs. G. noticed her pie was missing. She came charging up the stairs. "Who stole my cherry pie!" she yelled. "As nice as I have been to you and your friends, how could you do this?"

The boys felt horrible, we all did, and we told her we didn't take it and didn't know who did. We searched the apartment. There was no pie. The party ended early and it took a day of apologizing and appeasing by the boys before Mrs. G's fury finally died down.

In the middle of the night it came to me that Eddie never made it to the party. I went to his bedroom and quietly opened the door. He was sleeping by the light of his TV, which he never turned off. He was covered in cherry juice from his chin to his shorts. The empty pie tin stuck out from under the bed.

"You rotten bastard!"

He sat up. "What do you mean?" he said. "You stole Mrs. G's cherry pie," I said. "She's pissed at everybody!"

"No I didn't," he said.

When he was finally lucid, he was ashamed and remorseful. He promised he'd buy Mrs. G two pies and leave them at her doorstep. He pleaded with me not to tell anybody and I didn't until a class reunion twenty-five years later. Then I simply stood up and said, "I have an announcement. Eddie stole the cherry pie." Everyone roared.

Eddie and I became the best of friends in college. Once he invited me to spend a weekend at his home in the upscale Bloomfield Hills area near Detroit. His dad was a famous physician, the first to deliver quadruplets by Caesarean Section. They wrote him up in *Time* magazine. The Christie's home, furnishings and surroundings were opulent and I was in awe. Once my folks visited Detroit and Eddie's parents took them out to dinner. On the table of the elegant restaurant were matchbooks embossed with the words, "Welcome guests of Dr. and Mrs. Christie." My dad never got over it.

A few times Eddie stayed at my house, a small bungalow on Chicago's south side. He told me years later that he envied the environment I grew up in; the tight knit neighborhood that was St. Sabina parish and the friendliness of our neighborhood taverns. So envious was he that, a few years after he left John Carroll, he moved to Chicago to have more of that experience.

Eddie was more sophisticated than me. Once, on a weeknight, he told me to put on a suit and tie. "Why?" "We're going drinking for free," he said. We got into his Opel and went to a fancy hotel bar where traveling businessmen hung out. He sat down next to one, ordered a drink and struck up a conversation. The man proceeded to buy us drinks for the rest of the night. "Notice I kept asking him questions?" he said. "People love to talk, especially about themselves. They like to give young people advice. They are lonely. It never fails."

One night, late, Eddie and I were going home in the Opel. I noticed the car was slowly veering to the right and heading toward a parked car. I thought Eddie was just goofing off, but when I looked over he was sound asleep. I grabbed the steering wheel just in time to avoid a crash. This woke him up. "Wow. You just saved my life!" he said. That's probably true. This was in the days before seat belts. Thereafter, he liked to tell people that Jim Joyce saved his life. It never dawned on him that I saved my own life, too.

When I went to Leo High School, Mom had one request, "Jimmy, please join the glee club." When I got to Leo, I checked around and discovered that most glee club members were pimps. So I did try out but flunked the test on purpose by singing the scales out of tune. Mom knew there was something fishy about me flunking a singing test but she didn't pursue it.

When I went to John Carroll, Mom had the same request, "Jimmy, please join the glee club." When I checked around, I discovered that some of the coolest guys on campus, including football players and the President of the Chicago Club, were members. I joined the glee club. Eddie was also a member, which is where we first met.

Eddie had a strong, marvelous bass voice. I was an okay baritone.

The highlights of the glee club were the trips we took to sing joint concerts with Catholic girls' colleges around the Midwest. In the past, these trips were known for their raucousness even on the buses. Guys would drink all the way to Toledo, Fort Wayne, Chicago and so on. When they arrived, many were smashed. There had been numerous complaints over the years and by the time Eddie and I were in our junior year, drinking on the buses was strongly discouraged. To reinforce this discouragement, they now ordered buses without bathrooms. But Eddie was not easily discouraged. He brought aboard a big, plastic ice bucket, plastic cups, a fifth of vodka and a quart of orange juice. Screwdrivers for the ride.

All went well for a couple hours until we both had to go to the bathroom. A dilemma Eddie'd already solved. "The ice is almost gone. We'll just piss in the bucket and throw it out the window," he said.

When we finished, the bucket was almost full. Eddie opened the window. What happened next is hard to describe and even harder to believe. Our seats were in the back of the bus, which was doing about 70mph on Interstate 80 heading for St. Mary's college in Terra Haute, Indiana. Trailing us was the second glee club bus. Eddie let the piss fly, bucket and all. The wind sucked the piss from the bucket and around to the back of the bus. It became a vaporous mass of tiny bubbles floating in suspension over the highway. Defying gravity, it just hung there until bus number two ran into it. The driver had to turn on his windshield wipers.

In the front seat of the second bus was our glee club director, Mr. Jack Hearn, a really nice man. Guys in that bus said when the piss hit the bus all Mr. Hearn did was shake his head.

Eddie and I drank an astounding amount of alcohol together. We were always in unison, glass for glass, smoke for smoke and story for story. He's as good a drinking buddy as I ever had. He never monopolized the conversation, was always interested in what I had to say and his stories were always interesting to me. Neither of us got sloppy. Some of the best times we had were in winter when Cleveland was frozen solid and the winds off Lake Erie were fierce. I'd cut my classes and Eddie'd bring out a bottle of Southern Comfort and a six-pack of Squirt. We would drink and talk all day.

Eddie developed an aversion to attending class. It was obvious he was flunking himself out of school. He said he was bored silly and wanted to do something real. It is a testament to his intelligence that he lasted at Carroll as long as he did. When Eddie heard something he never forgot it, but to pass tests you had to hear it first and that meant attending class. Ed was gone at the end of our junior year.

Over twenty years went by before I saw him again. I heard he was back in Detroit working for the federal government. I flew up to see him. We met at a restaurant and when the waiter appeared, I ordered a Scotch and soda. Eddie ordered "just tonic water." I thought he was putting me on.

"You're not gonna have a drink, Eddie?"

"I can't. I'm CIA."

"Whoa. I knew you worked for the government but I didn't know you were with the Agency!"

He said he was with the Department of Commerce, International Trade Division, and not the Agency.

"But you just said CIA."

"Jimmy, that's Catholic, Irish, Alcoholic. I've been sober for seven years. Best thing I've ever done for my family and me. Booz was destroying me."

For many people, drinking is an elixir allowing perspective to enter consciousness. It promotes honesty, soothes the nerves, takes the edge off problems and clears minutia from the mind. To others it is poison as they use it to try to wipe out *everything* from their minds, so they must quit or loose all. The wise ones, like Eddie, quit. I am in awe of their willpower.

Two of my life long friendships began with drinking; the first was Jim Heavey. Although he lived in the apartment next door, he and I were not friends. I thought of Heavey as boring. Also, he intimidated me. I'd heard of him back in Chicago where he was an outstanding football player at DePaul High School on the north side. Now, at Carroll, he'd become an icon by setting four national punt return records in his sophomore year. (One still stands today, fifty years later.)

One night during junior year we found ourselves at Cosmo's Tavern sitting next to each other at the bar. None of the other guys were there. We were both a little uncomfortable, but after a couple of beers we warmed to each other, even admitting that, until just now, we thought of *each other* as boring. "With a few beers in you, Joyce, you're a pretty nice guy," he observed.

"And you, Heavey, actually have a good personality when you're drinking. You're not a stuck-up asshole like I thought."

We bonded that night and decided that some day we'd start our own brewery. The name of the beer would be "Personality." Our slogan would be "Drink one and get one." We marketing geniuses would have made a fortune.

From Chicago, in the middle of our annual two-week semester break, we had to travel back to Carroll for one night to register for the spring semester. This trip was always in January. Four of us, including Heavey, were in somebody's car, I have forgotten whose. Just before we got off the Ohio Turnpike near Cleveland we had a blow-out. It was freezing. Fingers numb and faces frozen, we fumbled with the jack and the spare and finally got it changed.

Not twenty minutes later, driving through a Cleveland suburb, another tire blew out. We couldn't believe it. Fortunately, we were near a gas station and had both tires repaired.

The next day on the way home, shortly after getting on the Turnpike, Heavey opened his window, letting ice-cold air fill the car. He pointed his finger into the sky and said, "I defy God to give us another flat tire!" Thirty seconds later, Bam! We wanted to kill Jim Heavey.

Our house on Ada Street had three bedrooms. Mom and Dad's was in the rear off the kitchen. Their window looked out over the tiny back yard, the garage and the alley. My sister Mary's room was near the front of the house off the small dining room. Her window looked at the brick wall of the Stack's house. My brother Bob and I shared the middle bedroom, off the bathroom. Our view was the same as Mary's.

Bob, eight years older than me, was extraordinarily religious. One summer when he was home from the seminary he drew three almost life-size pictures on three of the bedroom walls. He used crayons. One was of the Crucifixion complete with lots of red blood, the horrible crown of thorns and the cruel nails the size of railroad spikes hammered through Jesus' wrists and feet. Those Romans were vicious bastards. Another picture was the Agony in the Garden. Bob, a good artist, captured Jesus' anguish perfectly. Lastly there was the Ascension of the

Blessed Virgin into Heaven – Mary in her blue gown rising on the white cloud – her face the essence of sweetness and sorrow.

One night Jim Heavey came to our house to spend the night. Jim was a northsider but not a pimp. He chatted with my folks a while, then he and I headed to 79ᵗʰ Street to go drinking with the guys in the gang. We started at Chris Quinn's and then hit a number of other taverns in the neighborhood. When we returned to the house it was very late. I didn't want to wake my folks (Bob and Mary were gone) so I guided Heavey into my bedroom without turning on the lights. I had him touch the side of the bed and showed him the pillow. He lay down and passed out. I did the same in the other bed.

When the sun came up and light came in the window, Heavey started waking up. He had a crushing headache, his mouth tasted like pulverized shit, his throat was raw and his lips were paste. And, try as he might, he couldn't remember where he was.

Slowly he opened his eyes. He saw the holy pictures on the walls and bolted upright.

"Wah!" he yelled, waking me.

"Heave," I said, "what's wrong?" He was ashen.

"Holy shit, Joyce! You should have told me about the pictures! I thought I was dead!"

My roommate, Al (Moe) Rutledge and I were always cordial, but there was a distance between us. We were polite but didn't click. Frankly, we didn't like each other. On the last day of our senior year, when all exams were finished we wound up together in Mike's bar. "I'll buy you a drink," Moe said, "What would you like?"

I said, "whatever," and he suggested we have beers with shots of Peppermint Schnapps. "Something festive to celebrate the end of our college days," he said. (Maybe that's why I didn't like him. He had style.)

In no time Al and I told each other what incredible assholes we thought each other was as we proceeded to get bombed. It was a wonderful conversation repairing two years worth of silent complaints. Our friendship continues to this day 47 years later. And to this day, when I see a bottle of Peppermint Schnapps, I get a queasy feeling. I will never, *ever* drink that shit again. (Recently, I reminded Moe of that day.

He said, "I'll never drink that shit again either and, by the way, although we remain pals after all these years, you are still an asshole.")

One of my few claims to fame was becoming President of the John Carroll University Chicago Club. This was a social club for Chicago guys who attended Carroll. Our reason for existing was to have two parties each year back in Chicago, one at Christmas and one in the summer. The parties were held at fancy hotels in the Loop. They were raucous, wild and unruly. When they ended hotel management usually told us not to come back.

One Christmas we rented a ballroom at the upscale Conrad Hilton on Michigan Avenue. There was a large potted plant in the lobby. As the party was ending one of our members, in plain view of all, climbed into it, dropped his pants, and took a dump. Check off the Conrad Hilton.

CHAPTER FIFTEEN

One Oh Five

Almost all college students were broke and I was no exception. My parents, with the help of my sister, Mary, paid my room, board and tuition. For spending money, I was on my own. I took odd jobs: tended bar, babysat, cut grass, shoveled show and, one time, painted a house with Carpenter Joyce. I also had money from full-time summer jobs, but it was never enough. I was always scrounging.

One of my classmates, a born entrepreneur, had dozens of ideas for making money. His name was Henry*, but everybody called him Shylock. I liked Shylock because he was always in a good mood, but I didn't completely trust him. One day in the cafeteria he sat next to me and in his cackling, conspiratorial voice told me he had a new idea, "That could make you a lot of dough." My first question was, "what will it cost me?"

He said, "Nothing." He was not offended by the question. He took me to his dorm room and opened a large suitcase. In it were hundreds of beautiful silver and gold watches. "Try this on," he said, handing me one that said Bulova.

"Shy, I can't afford a watch, especially a Bulova. I thought you said this wasn't going to cost me anything." I said, irritated. He cackled. (He is the only person I ever met who truly did cackle.)

"Look closer, Jim, it's not a Bulova it's a Buliva. A fake. You can have it on consignment for $3. If you sell it for more than that you keep the difference. Just pay me the $3." He said I could take as many as I wanted and he'd trust me to pay him or return them. "And here's the best part. Although they're fakes they work great. I personally guarantee them for five years." How could I go wrong? I was already hatching a plan to make some money.

When Eddie Christie was asked to leave John Carroll, Arbs, Rutledge and I got another roommate to replace him, Gus Fehrenbacher from Manhattan, Illinois, a small, farm town near Joliet. His dad was the town's dentist.

(Dr. Cotter taught Shakespeare at JCU. He had a speech impediment which he overcame by saying "it was" when he got tongue-tied. Long words were tough for Dr. Cotter so he called Gus, "Mr. Fehren it-was bacher".)

When I got home with the watches, I showed them to Gus and he was very interested in Shylock's deal. Instantly we were both on the same marketing wavelength - One O Five!

Cleveland's toughest neighborhood was on the east side of the city, bisected by 105h Street. When all other bars in the city were closed you could always find some open on One O Five. On Saturday nights Gus and I would frequently go there. It was in an all black neighborhood but Gus and I were not prejudiced. Usually we were the only white guys present, as conspicuous as ducks in a desert, but the blacks treated us just fine. We were never harassed, threatened or made to feel unwelcome.

The only irritation was from local entrepreneurs who worked the bars selling stolen watches. We'd be sitting at the bar and they'd sidle up to us and pull up their shirtsleeves. On their arms were half a dozen watches. "They're hot" they'd say. "Give you a great price." We'd say "No thank you," and they'd move on. Everybody in the bar was approached not just us white guys.

Gus and I both figured that never in history have white boys gone into black bars trying to sell hot watches. They wouldn't dare: we couldn't miss. In a darkened bar who would see the difference between Buliva and Bulova? Besides, we were not going to be greedy, only marking up the watches a little bit over Shylock's consignment price. Plus I had his guarantee that they'd work for at least five years. That very night, a Friday, Gus and I headed to One O Five. We had watches up to our elbows.

Our success was immediate and gratifying. We almost sold out, getting ten dollars a piece for Shylock's three-dollar watches. We quit working at 2am and decided to have breakfast at a restaurant next door to the last bar we'd hit. While we were eating a local guy came up to us. "Are you the white boys selling watches?" We were the only white boys within miles. "Lemme see what you got." Gus rolled up his sleeve. He had two left, Elgan's. The guy bought 'em.

Gus and I were ecstatic. We could hardly wait to see Shylock, pay his consignment fee, and replenish our inventory. Shylock, too, was ecstatic and when we told him where we sold his watches he declared us "marketing geniuses."

"You're sure these watches really work? Will they really last five years?" we asked.

"You have my personal guarantee," he said.

Gus and I were back on 105th St. the next Friday night. Again, business was great. Around midnight a gorgeous woman, Sharon, came up to us. She asked us to tell her the truth about these watches we were selling. Sharon, a VIP on 105th Street, owned numerous nightclubs and taverns, including the one we were now working. People treated her with respect.

We answered honestly, "We don't know if they are stolen. The guy we get them from guarantees them for five years. Also, the brand names are misleading." We showed her the misspelling, "But he guarantees the inner workings are top quality." She said she liked our honest answer and invited us to her birthday party on the following Friday night. She gave us her home address, which was only two blocks from the tavern. She asked who our supplier was and we told her his name was Shylock. She said she never heard of him, but we could invite him and other college students. "It would be fun to have some white boys there," she said.

Gus and I told Shylock of the invitation, but he said he couldn't make it, much as he'd like to, because he was going home to New York for the weekend. He showed us a magnificent gold woman's watch to consider for Sharon's birthday present. "My cost is $20, and you can have it for $15," he told us, as a token of his appreciation for our business. We bought it. He put it in a beautiful satin lined gift box. We all agreed she'd love it. We invited other friends to Sharon's party but none took us up on the offer. A few told us we were crazy.

We found Sharon's house, a stone mansion, and parked a block down the street. There were already fifty people there, all of them black, standing around drinking and nibbling hors d'ouvers. Everyone was dressed up, including me and Gus, in suits and ties. Sharon greeted us with kisses on the cheek. We gave her the box and she squealed with delight when she opened it. The watch perfectly matched her gold dress and she immediately put it on. She took us all around the party introducing us to her friends and showing off the watch. Her guests, businessmen, politicians, sports figures and media people, were impressed. Gus and I were a hit.

Booze was flowing and Sharon told us to mingle and have fun while she played hostess. After a few drinks we became comfortable being the only white guys. We were looking forward to meeting the famous Jim Brown, of the Cleveland Browns, who was supposed to attend. He was a hero to us.

In about half an hour Sharon approached us. "My watch quit running," she said handing it to me. There was an edge to her voice. "Damn," I said, "we forgot to wind it." I set the correct time and wound it. It began ticking. "Oh thank you!" she said, "I thought there was something wrong with it" and she eased back into the crowd.

"Hey, Gus, didn't you wind it earlier?" I asked in a low voice. "Yeah," he said, "About two hours ago. Maybe I didn't wind it tight enough."

Another hour or so went by and the noise level was way up there as the booze did its thing. I decided to get close to Sharon, without her noticing which was easy to do with all the people, and check on the watch. By now Sharon was blitzed, laughing, yelling and hugging her many guests. I caught a glimpse of the watch and not only had it stopped running but one of the hands had fallen to the bottom of the glass, not unlike the speedometer in my dad's car. I went back to Gus and said, "We gotta get the hell outta here. Her watch is broken."

We found a side door, which led out to a darkened gangway. We slunk along the side of the house toward the sidewalk and peeked around the corner to see if the coast was clear. It was. We walked to Gus's car as fast as we could without running and sped away – never to return to 105th Street.

I learned a lot of stuff in college outside classrooms. I spent a night at Gus's house in tiny Manhattan and we went drinking with his friends in one of the few bars in town. About midnight they said, "Let's go. Time to ride the rails!" We were in two cars, my dad's and one of the other guys.

"Where we going, Gus? What's 'ride the rails,' another tavern?" I asked.

"Just follow Rodney," Gus laughed. "This is fun."

We drove down a country road to a railroad crossing, but instead of crossing it Rodney maneuvered his car sideways so that its wheels were on the railroad tracks. He then headed down the tracks. "Holy shit!" I said. "You want to do it?" said Gus. Without too much hesitation I said, "Why not?"

I lined up my dad's '88 Oldsmobile. Gus made sure all four wheels were perfect. "Okay," he said "give it a little gas but whatever you do Do Not Touch the Steering Wheel." We headed back to town where the next crossing was. "What if a train comes, Gus?" "We'd be fucked," he laughed. "But the next one isn't due for an hour." So we rode the rails back to town and returned to the bar. A night of small town fun. And what if Dad's car had slipped off the rails? I don't want to think about it.

I thoroughly enjoyed my time at John Carroll, especially meeting future, life long friends. And lest you get the wrong idea, it wasn't all drinking and partying. We did a lot of that, for sure, but almost exclusively on weekends. From Sunday afternoon until after classes Friday we had our noses in books. Carroll was a tough school. Of the more than 700 freshmen who started with us less than 300 graduated four years later.

CHAPTER 16

Another Car Caper Gone Wrong

(by Carpenter Joyce)

Our teachers at John Carroll in Cleveland didn't know our streets in Chicago so to keep us straight Ada was Joyce 76 and I was Joyce 77. 76 and 77 were the last digits of our school assigned IBM numbers.

Ada and I shared two classes, Creative Writing and Spanish. Our Spanish teacher, Miss Ramirez, was a diminutive Colombian who, like Father Galvao, only thought she spoke English. Jim and I sat next to each other and goofed off through her classes until she finally separated us. "76, you sit in back. 77 you stay here." McDonough was right. We didn't belong in college.

When our parents met Miss Ramirez she told them, with a smile, she had to "disseepleendem separat." They had no idea what she was saying and politely smiled along with her, making for a perfect parent teacher meeting.

Many of my great ideas came from ordinary circumstances. Age and maturity also influenced me over the origin and implementation of such ideas. Or, rather, lack of age and maturity helped in the origin and implementation of those great, and sometimes not so great, ideas.

As any mature reader knows, things don't just happen in a vacuum. There is a lifetime of experience that forms an individual. In hindsight the actions of a seventeen year old are somewhat predictable, especially to a sixty-eight year old reminiscing about his earliest college experiences of 1960. I must fess up at this point that I was the seventeen-year-old college student who played a significant role in the caper described in the next few pages.

As you've followed the antics of the "guys in the gang" you'll recognize Ada Joyce, Carpenter Joyce (me) and Bub McDoo (Tom

McDonough) as repeat offenders. Ada didn't really receive his full benefits in this story. His investment of $17.00 was wasted because as everyone knows the value of an automobile drops dramatically as soon as one drives it away from the showroom. He did get to ride around Fairmont Circle for a week but the anticipated trip home to Chicago never materialized for him due to a John Carroll University Glee Club gig that weekend of September 28th, 29th, and 30th, 1960. He considered himself lucky, but he was short sighted.

Bub McDoo and I were the lucky ones. We got to experience a most memorable college highlight. I intend to put my memory to paper while I still have a memory! Remember reader, this is my recollection of the events of that week. Bub was a true partner in the crime but Ada just remains a "person of interest" in the dusty crime annals of Steuben County, Indiana. Bub McDoo won't have any input into this narrative due to his early, unfortunate demise in October 2000. Bub was a wonderful, generous and very bright guy with a propensity for getting caught in every caper in which he participated. The selection and purchase of a used car and the ensuing ride to Chicago was no exception.

I mentioned previously that this anecdote was one of many college experiences. I had so many college experiences mainly because I went to so many colleges. Nine. I only wish I was as mature when I started as I was when I finished. I started at JCU, toured local community colleges, Northern Illinois University (twice), Chicago State University, Governors State University and Harvard. I finished with an honorary Ph.D. from Saint Xavier University where I was a commencement speaker. What a wonderful trip through academia full of great experiences!

Maturity, or lack there of, remains a main ingredient in so many of the escapades I remember. I might have made something of myself if I'd understood this quote fifty years ago: "Anticipation of consequences is a marker of intelligence." I believe that may have come from the brilliant architect of New York's Central Park, Joe Pepitone, and isn't it the truth!

Let me set the stage and you'll soon see that the decisions we made, in retrospect, made almost perfect sense. I was the oldest of seven kids. At seventeen I had never been away from home for any length of time. When I got to college in Cleveland after about a month I was feeling a little lonely. I was in the beginning of a budding romance back in Chicago that ended in a long and fruitful marriage. My girlfriend, Janet, asked if I could be home for the 25th wedding anniversary party for her parents. What a good idea!

Tom McDonough was also dating Rita, who would eventually become his wife, and she asked if he would be home around the same time to celebrate his eighteenth birthday. What a good idea! None of us had any money so round trip train or bus fare from Cleveland was out of the question. I was able to pick up odd jobs from the Student Center job office so that I could enjoy a cold beer or martini from time to time at The Frog Bar but that was it. But, about this time I got lucky and landed a job painting a house. I cut Ada in on the deal. (It took him a little while to get up to speed, but he was okay because he has a lot of smart brains.) The homeowner went with the low bidder on the project and we settled on seventy-five dollars, he bought the paint and brushes. We were in the chips!

J.C.U. had strict rules against freshmen owning cars, but I lived off campus so I had a place to hide one. It made so much sense to buy a car for trips home to Chicago with the holidays on the horizon. Wouldn't our parents be proud of our thoughtfulness in saving precious transportation dollars? Gas was only 29 cents a gallon. Ray Charles could see that now was the time to buy! We put a limit of fifty dollars on the purchase price and set out to find the best place to shop. It was right in front of us – Circle Drugs on Fairmont Circle right there in front of the campus. We stood at the stop sign with dollar bills between our fingers like a beer vendor at Comiskey Park. Any car that looked like a beater with lots of miles on it was hawked. "Sell us your car, time to get rid of the junk" was our sales pitch. It worked almost immediately. A gentleman passed ownership of his 1950 Ford for $50.00. What a deal! Too bad he removed the plates.

I stashed the car at my off campus house and we made plans for our trip to Chicago to see our girlfriends. A couple of small bumps in the road appeared, however, that would have been apparent had we listened to Joe Pepitone. In Ohio you had to be eighteen years of age to hold title to an automobile. Uh Oh! Could we get temporary license plates – no! The DMV surely wasn't very considerate and our trip was just days away. I made an executive decision and hitchhiked to the nearest Sears,

Roebuck and Co. For three dollars I bought a screwdriver (Craftsman) and pliers.

We were then able to secure temporary plates from the faculty parking lot of a Cleveland public high school. The security guard, we noticed, was portly and most likely too mature to catch us. (The plates would have been returned the following Wednesday after Mrs. Ramirez's Spanish 101 class. No fooling!)

The much-anticipated departure finally came early on Friday September 30, 1960. I drove the first leg at moderate speed because of the misappropriated license plates, the cloudy title and the possibility, if not likelihood, that a ten year old car with 100,000 miles on it would be temperamental. All went well on the Ohio Turnpike until Bub wanted to drive. He didn't possess the internal governor that I used while executing risky exercises. He got that Ford up to 85mph attracting the attention of an Ohio State Trooper. He clocked us and issued a warning ticket and told us that we could go but he was going to check us out because we couldn't produce registration. Bub outfoxed him by getting off the turnpike at the next exit and taking the country roads. After stopping for gas and a six-pack of Carlings Black Label 3.2 beer we continued on, our plan working perfectly. Soon we were out of Ohio. We finished the beer as we crossed the border into Indiana and looked for an entrance to the Indiana Toll Road.

Joe Pepitone reared his ugly consequence head once again. As Mac, again, hit 85 the Ford overheated and the motor seized. But no real problem for two bright guys in the early stages of a Jesuit education. We abandoned the car, took the stolen plates off, climbed the fence into a farmer's field and buried them. We then walked about five hundred yards to the nearest road. We would hitchhike to Chicago. But guess what? The first car to come along was the Indiana State Police. Damn! The cop appeared to be very angry as he clomped through the field with us in search of the license plates. It was my first time in handcuffs as we drove through Angola, Indiana to the Steuben County jail.

The trooper and various jail officials accused us of a lot of things and scared the life out of us as they discussed a weekend in jail before a Monday hearing with a judge and questioning by the FBI for taking a stolen car across a state line. Their scare tactics worked. I figured that my college career was over before the leaves fell in University Heights.

Thinking of my father's reaction also scared me - if he found out. My initial plan was to return to Ohio, clean out my off-campus room, and join the Army. But that idea was dashed when I received a phone call at the jail from Father Joseph Muenzer, Dean of Students at John Carroll. He said the police had called him and that he had talked to my father and Mr. McDonough and that they would be in Angola by Saturday and that he, Father Muenzer, would deal with me when I got back to school.

Bub McDoo was not in a cell anywhere near mine and I inquired as to his whereabouts. He was celebrating his eighteenth birthday in the adult cellblock and I was in a cell in another wing. Bub and I were brought together for questioning and the police were able to "sweat" the truth out of us. We sang like canaries and were returned to our quarters with a baloney sandwich, an apple and a carton of milk for dinner. The rest of the day and the night seemed like a week. No chair, no TV, only a steel bunk without a pillow and no Egyptian 300 thread count bed sheets. The almost constant crying and screaming from a female voice in a distant cell made sleep difficult. I wonder if that tortured voice wasn't a recording they use to scare young people straight. If so, it worked!

Day two in the big house started with breakfast served through an opening in the bars – two little boxes of Cheerios, milk and a banana. I expected the FBI after breakfast but they must be off on Saturdays. Lunch was again baloney and fruit and a soft drink and I didn't waste any of it. At that time our fathers showed up along with the arresting officer and we all went to a magistrate's office. We got a brief lecture and the trooper then suggested, with a smile, that the FBI be cancelled and that he would reduce the charges to a misdemeanor with a fifty-dollar fine. What a relief for my dad and me. He told me later that the police told him that he would need five hundred dollars cash just for bail. He didn't have that much money and had to borrow it from his sister, Aunt Mary.

The ride home to Chicago was agonizingly long with comments about how lucky we'd be if they let us back in school. After we dropped the McDonoughs' at their house, my dad parked the car before we got to our house and said what I did was stupid. I was not to mention it to my siblings, as they were anxious to see me and receive me as a returning hero. I was the first one of our seven to be gone from home for any length of time and my homecoming was special. My dad never mentioned the incident again. Back home I asked my mom if she had any baloney but she said no, that's only for lunch, tonight we're having round steak. I was able to have a good time at Janet's parents' party but was up early the next morning to get on the train back to Cleveland for an uncertain homecoming get together with Father Muenzer. We first met with Ada in his dorm room for a thorough debriefing, and to get our stories straight. We told him not to lie. Muenzer knew it all.

I dreaded facing Father Muenzer but apparently he had experienced knuckleheads before in his role as Dean of Students. No hollering, no screaming, maybe a bit of sarcasm as he probed for answers to explain our decisions. He quickly got off the subject and asked me if I planned to attend the annual Military Ball to be held in late October. I said no that I hadn't given it much thought. Father Muenzer then said that as a result of my stupid activities of the previous week my punishment would be that I was not to participate in the Military Ball! Next question: Is your family coming for Parent's Weekend on the same weekend as the Ball? I wasn't sure how to answer that. I had spent money my parents didn't have and was concerned that they'd still feel obligated to come even though they might not be able to afford it. Father Muenzer then said that my uncle, Father Pat Clear S.J. (also a Jesuit and Muenzer's friend) would be disappointed to find out that the Joyces from Chicago didn't get to see John Carroll's beautiful campus. He then told me that he made a reservation at his favorite hotel for a three-room suite for my family. I couldn't believe this guy!

Two weeks later eight Joyces arrived and checked into a classic, old Cleveland hotel that was a little past its prime. But it was roomy and Muenzer got us a deeply discounted rate. What a great weekend that was! I was so proud to show my family the campus and my apartment. I introduced my parents to Father Muenzer and it seemed as though they already knew each other. My dad even asked if he could see the famous Fairmont Circle.

As I look back on that brief episode of my life I smile as I think about how lucky I was, and am. Older people are wiser than younger ones, aren't they? The ones that I met in the fall of 1960 certainly were! Beginning with the Indiana State Trooper, the jail keeper, the judge, Father Muenzer and my dad, they all seemed to know the score as if they'd done it before. I'd like to tell you that the lessons I learned in 1960 put me on the straight and narrow, but I can't. I was wiser after that time but remained somewhat adventurous. Today I can now feel maturity creeping up on me, but I'm making every effort to fight it off.

Joe Pepitone? From a classic *Seinfield* episode, or, as Bub would say, "Figure it out for yourselves, Assholes."

CHAPTER 17

All Grown Up

The official orders came in the mail. I was to report to Ft. Eustis, VA, on January 5, 1965. My adult life would begin. I told my boss that my last day as a cab driver would be December 15th. He could've cared less. "Enjoy the Army," he said. This word got to the gruff-talking, but soft-hearted lady who was the radio dispatcher. She told me to try to be around 87th and Aberdeen at 2:00 the afternoon of the 15th. I was, and she gave me a plum, a trip to O'Hare, about $20.00 on the meter plus tip. The perfect ending to my career in a Chicago taxi.

My college buddy, Bill Smith, received the same set of orders so we drove to Ft. Eustis together in his car. On the way we stopped in Youngstown to visit a classmate, Mike Herald. His dad took us drinking. He kept saying, "Everything will be fine boys. Everything will be fine." These were comforting words to us soon to be full-time Army guys.

Next, Smitty and I swung by New York City where his girlfriend was leaving for Europe on the Queen Mary. Smith and I had never been to New York and the only hotel we'd heard of was the Waldorf Astoria so that's where we made our reservation. We walked through the elegant lobby wearing blue jeans. People looked down their noses at us, making us self-conscious. Then we remembered seeing a sign on the way into New York that said a rodeo was in town. So we started walking bow legged, pretending we were cowboys, giggling all the way and fooling no one.

When we got into our room we ordered room service, a six-pack of Bud. It showed up on a silver tray, the cans neatly stacked in an ice bucket. Smith was lounging on the bed in his underwear. The waiter, undaunted and with a flourish, poured a beer into a champagne flute, walked around the bed and handed it to him. We were favorably impressed and agreed that this was the way to start adult life. Next day we got to board the Queen Mary with Smith's girl friend and her parents. The only thing I remember was the polished wood deck. It positively gleamed and I recall thinking that this is what they mean by First Class.

Two days later we found Ft. Eustis, reported for duty and that was the end of first class. Our first nine weeks on active duty were Officers Basic Training. Sleep deprivation, calisthenics before day break, crawling through mud, sleeping on the ground, and polishing boots and belt buckles 'til they gleamed like the Queen Mary's deck. Inspections, forced marches, latrine duty, k.p., weapons cleaning, severe verbal abuse, and of course, running, running, running and always in formation. The Army loves nothing better than to see troops running in formation. When it was over, we were in great physical shape but our IQ's plummeted. The Army is generally prejudiced against smart people when they are in basic training, and it is particularly prejudiced against "individuals." Get in line, soldier!

But when basic ended life for us new officers got good, really good. Instead of living in barracks, sleeping in bunk beds and taking a crap with no partitions between commodes, we who were bachelors were assigned to nice motel-like rooms. Married guys were given real houses with lawns. Food in the mess halls was free, plentiful and delicious, or you could go off base to a restaurant. When we were not on duty, which was usually 8 to 5, five days a week, we could do whatever we wanted as long as we showed up for work. There was no curfew. Just like civilians. At Eustis we dated the co-eds at William and Mary College in nearby Williamsburg and spent untold hours at the Fort Storey officers' club on Virginia Beach. And we had money! Officers' pay, coupled with the many benefits, was more than adequate.

There is an analogy between going away to college and going into the Army. In both you meet people from different places and backgrounds. That is broadening. John Carroll is a Catholic school so although I met guys from New York, Dayton and Pittsburgh, we all shared the same religion. In the Army I met, and got to know well, guys from Texas, California, Louisiana and many other states. Most were not Catholics. Some weren't even Caucasian. Now we're talking broadening.

Dale Stiles from Malvern, Arkansas was a broadening person. He knew all about making moonshine, and he played the guitar. He sang ballads better than Glen Campbell, had a way with women that was astounding, and he drove a Jaguar. Dale was also a great salesman. He talked me into buying the Jaguar before he shipped out to Europe. At first I was skeptical, Jaguars had a history of being maintenance nightmares, but he convinced me, saying he'd "Never had a minute's trouble with it." This was the first car I ever owned and she was a beauty – an XK150 fire engine red. People stared at it when I drove by. Life was getting better by the minute.

Shortly after I bought Dale's car, Bill Smith and I took it to Washington, DC to visit a friend of his, Ernie Dehnert, who was attending Georgetown. It was a fun weekend and the Jag performed as advertised, with nary a glitch. On I-95 I briefly took it up over 100mph just to see. It hugged the highway and hummed along with loads of power to spare. "I'll bet she'll do 140," I said. "Let's not find out," said Smith.

When we got back to Ft. Eustis I parked in the lot in front of our bachelor officer's quarters and turned it off. We got out. As we took our bags from the trunk Bill said, "Joyce, I think the car is still running." I put my hand to the hood and sure enough the engine was purring along. "But I have the key in my pocket, " I said. "This is impossible." At that moment the car wobbled, went "Bang!" and then hissed. A puff of white smoke came out of the grill. The engine stopped. "Oh shit, I need to ask Dale about this."

"He left for Europe yesterday," Smith said.

For the next few days the car worked great. Turn it on; turn it off; no problem. What happened after the D.C. trip was probably an anomaly, I decided.

That next weekend my mom and dad came to visit. I told them they'd have to rent a car because my new one was too small. "Oh surely we can squeeze in, Jimmy," Mom said. "Not a chance, Mom," I said. They landed at Norfolk and followed me to Fort Eustis and parked their rental next to my Jag. When we exited our cars, mine continued to run. "Aren't you going to turn it off?" asked dad. "I did, but sometimes it continues to run for awhile." Dad knew a lot about cars. "I never heard of that," he said. "Pop the hood."

He peered inside at the humongous engine crammed into the small space and that's when the Jag shuddered, banged, hissed and puffed out the smoke. Dad closed the hood and shook his head. "Strange" was all he said.

That night I took Mom and Dad to dinner at the Officer's Club. Officer's Clubs are pretty swanky. Before dinner I had whiskey and ginger, my first drink in front of them, and after dinner I lit up a smoke, my first smoke in front of them. When the check came I charged it to my account. I was beginning to feel grown up – an officer and a gentleman was I.

A few months later I drove the Jag to U.S. Army Flight School, my new assignment, at Fort Rucker, Alabama. The car did fine except for the driver's side window. One day it would not roll up. I was told a part had to be ordered. "How long will it take?" I asked the mechanic in Enterprise, Alabama. "Don't know," he said. "All Jaguar parts come from London." For two months I drove around with plastic wrap in the window. People pointed. Then a taillight went out, followed by a headlight and other troubles I have forgotten. The Jag also needed to be driven fast, its engine demanded 80mph, and that's hard to do on two-lane south Alabama roads. Once, late at night, I took it up to 80mph in third gear just to "blow it out." An Alabama state trooper pulled me over. He did not ticket me, however, because I was at Rucker and no doubt bound for Vietnam. Alabama troopers were good about that. He said he just wanted to know, "How fast does this thing go?" I told him I didn't know yet. I finally traded the Jag for a Chevy convertible. Never did find out how fast it could go.

(Dale: If you read this please know I do not regret buying your car. It's been a conversation piece for many years.)

Another guy I would not have met at John Carroll was a mean spirited, bigoted frat boy who thought he was someone to be revered. He came from one of the South's more prominent families. One day in the officer's club a bunch of us were hanging out and the bigot decided he would explain to those of us who were Yankees why slaves were better off in slavery than they were back in Africa. I listened with amusement, wondering, "Who is this asshole?" He was on a roll and segued from Nigras to Catholics. He explained some of the erroneous theological tenets of the Church and its various, rules and traditions.

His tone was condescending and dictatorial. I got pissed. I let him wind down and said, "You are absolutely full of shit, 'Charles'*. You've no idea what you're talking about. I am a Catholic and you have it all wrong." Everybody perked up. I then proceeded to explain my religion to the group. Charles hated me for embarrassing him and from time to time he tried to trip me up in our flight training. A classmate told me that once, when I made a particularity ugly landing, Charles pointed it out to a cadre. "Look at that landing Joyce just made!" But when the cadre looked up, my plane had quit bouncing, and was rolling smoothly down the runway. "What's wrong with that?" said the cadre. "He was bouncing!" said Charles. "Any landing you can walk away from is a good one," said the cadre. Even cadre hated tattle tales. It turned out nobody liked Charles (what was to like?) but were intimidated by his family's status. In time he became an invisible member of our class.

Until the Army, I didn't have Protestants as friends. Such was the cloistered environment of St. Sabina and John Carroll. In the Army I met Jerry Jackson from Texas, Joe Hodges from Mississippi, Bill Montgomery from Idaho, Roger Fraser from New Jersey, Palmer Haines from Texas, and so many dozens more who, although Protestant, were the essence of decency. I would ask myself, "How could they have gotten that way without the benefit of being taught by priests and nuns?" The Army was indeed a broadening experience.

My first assignment after officer's basic (now I was a real officer) was assisting a Lieutenant Colonel who was escorting a dozen or so foreign military officers showing them certain aspects of U.S. Army training. As we gathered in front of a two story barracks a telephone started ringing on the second floor. I asked the colonel if he wanted me to run up and answer it. "Of course not, Lieutenant," he said, "if it's important they'll send a car."

I liked being an officer in the Army and considered making it a career. Working with bright, dedicated, world traveled people was enriching and the pay, benefits and retirement plan were exceptional. The only down side was war. The Army, from time to time, goes to war. I went once and did not want to do it again. Because I was a helicopter pilot, I would have had to do it again. So when my three-year obligation was over I got out.

The Army and John Carroll are intertwined in my memory. It was at John Carroll that I first wore the uniform, where I learned to march in formation, carry a rifle and study the principles of war. John Carroll is where I learned to properly salute, whom to salute and when to salute. It was at John Carroll where my mom pinned on my 2nd lieutenant's bars.

On November 22, 1963 a sergeant interrupted our military science class being taught by a captain. "Excuse me sir, but you should know the President of the United States has been shot." When the class ended twenty minutes later, the sergeant was in the hallway with tears streaming down his face. He choked out the words, "He's dead."

As we walked across the quadrangle the flag was being pulled down to half-mast. I was in uniform and should have stopped and come to attention. But nobody else did so I kept walking. A life regret.

Forty years later McFarland and Company published my book, *Pucker Factor 10*. The commander of the ROTC program at John Carroll, Colonel Henry Russell*, heard about it and called me at home in North Carolina. He asked if I would give this year's address at the awards banquet for graduating cadets and their families. He said he didn't have the budget for an honorarium, but would pay all my expenses. I told him it would be an honor to speak and I'd pay my own way.

He then said, "Mr. Joyce, I only ask one thing. Please don't scare them. Most of them will be going to war soon (Iraq or Afghanistan), but they still have time to drop out."

"Roger, Colonel." I laughed. "I'll try not to be too honest."

"Thank you," he said.

I must admit I was nervous as I looked over the group of beautiful faces, both men and women, in their dress blue uniforms, seated next to their proud moms and dads. Of course I was nervous because I had to give a speech, but I was also nervous for them. Many would soon have experiences in war that would color the rest of their lives even if they weren't active participants.

Just being around combat could be awful. For instance, you watch a helicopter set down in a dry rice paddy surrounded by earthen dikes. A young soldier runs across the top of the raised dike to get to the chopper. He doesn't duck low enough. The rotor blade takes his head off. Or, you are a doctor in a MASH helplessly watching your patient bleed out while crying for his mama. Collateral damage to the psyche that never goes away.

In the speech I quoted John 15:13 giving John a little edit, "Man hath no greater love than to lay down his life for his friends," I said, then added, "Or to attempt to do so. If you get lucky, and don't die, it is a source of pride and solace forever." I told them that saving lives was a soldier's great honor and that taking lives, to save others, was easy enough to live with. I told the cadets that as I reflected over my life, one of my proudest acts were to have served my country in uniform. And then I gave them a tip: "If you get the chance, a shot or two of vodka, just before battle, is a good idea." (I noticed Colonel Russell stifle a smile.)

I explained to the cadets that the Vietnam War had defined my generation. It affected every young male, those who went and those who didn't, and that few people in the country were more than one degree of separation away from a casualty. I told them that over the years I'd met many men who'd dodged the war and that some paid a life long price for that decision - in guilt.

The talk ended and I was still standing behind the podium as a very large man in a suit and tie rapidly approached. His face was somber, menacing, I thought he might take a swing at me. But he stopped and said, "I am one of those people you just talked about. I dodged the draft and have been paying for it ever since." His lips quivered and his eyes welled up. He took my hand, thanked me for serving, and hurriedly left the room.

Section V

Jobs

CHAPTER 18

Of Mouse and Salesman

I don't remember his name so I'll call him "Frank." We were only together for one day and that was fifty years ago. Frank was the most successful salesman for the Holland Furnace Company. For that one day he was my assigned mentor who would teach me the ropes.

This was a summer job, but unlike bus boying and dish washing, it was an adult job, my first. I found it in the *Tribune*. The job, as the recruiter described it, sounded easy. I would go door-to-door in a nice middle class neighborhood and offer a free inspection of a home's heating system. If I found the system needed cleaning, I would then attempt to sell that service for a very reasonable fee. Holland had big vacuum trucks that could suck out all the soot, dust and debris in the flues and ductwork. It parked on the street in front of the house and it took less than half an hour to completely clean a system. The furnace and its ancillary tentacles would then be much more efficient and much less of a fire hazard. Half of the modest fee would be my commission.

And the deal sweetened. If during the cleaning it was discovered the furnace was so old and inefficient a new furnace, costing thousands, was called for, that's where the money was. All I had to do was get the door open for the real salesmen, the hard-core closers. If they sold a furnace, I'd get a big commission.

I met Frank on the corner of 111th and Michigan, the Roseland area. He was driving a big white Pontiac. Frank was a large man. He wore a rumpled gray suit, scuffed brown shoes and pale blue socks. His stained tie did not reach his belt, stopping half way down his big stomach. He had a sheepish grin between his dimpled jowls. His eyes were twinkly. His handshake was soft and meaty. He wore a narrow brimmed fedora with no feather. There was nothing ostentatious about Frank. You could trust him.

In those days husbands went to work and wives stayed home. We walked up to the front door of the first home on the block with Frank in front and me behind. "Just listen and watch, kid." When the lady answered the door Frank removed his fedora and held it to his chest.

"Good morning, ma'am. I'm Frank with the Safety Division. We are in your neighborhood today to offer free furnace inspections. As you know furnaces can be fire hazards. This will only take a minute or two. Please show me where your furnace is. And, oh, this here is Jim. He's in training. A nice young man." We were in.

As the lady led us to the furnace, always in the basement, Frank asked how old her furnace was – she wasn't sure. He asked if it had ever been cleaned – she didn't think so.

"They should be cleaned every five years," Frank told her, "For safety sakes. You'd be surprised the stuff that can build up in the ducts over the years and cause a fire."

When we got to the furnace, he removed his huge suit coat and handed it to the lady.

"Would you hold this please?" He then rolled up his right sleeve, opened the furnace door, and reached way up inside. "Uh–oh," he said, "What?" she said.

"Look at this" he said. There was a dead mouse in his hand.

The lady shrieked. "I think you should get the system cleaned," he said with deep concern. A sale was made.

We left the house with contract in hand. Frank walked past the next two houses and approached the third. "What about those two?" I asked. "Nah. Sometimes they talk over the back fence." Frank said.

At the third house and at the sixth house the same scene played out. I then realized that Frank had planted the dead mouse, deftly putting it in his pocket, after each sale. I was appalled. "Frank, is that right, what you're doing with the dead mouse?" He looked at me with true surprise. "Kid, we're making sales ain't we? That's all that counts."

I was not then, nor am I today, totally free of the sin of greed. But that was too far over the line. I would never resort to such trickery.

The next day I was on my own with no Frank and no mouse. After a fruitless morning of rejections, I finally was allowed into a house. The lady had heard furnaces could be dangerous and should be cleaned. I was filling out the little contract when her husband came out of the bedroom in his underwear.

"What's going on?" He said in a mean voice.

"We are going to get the furnace cleaned," she said. "It's not expensive at all."

"What company you with buddy?" he asked.

"Holland Furnace," I said proudly.

"Get the hell out of my house!" he yelled. "You crook!"

With minimal research I learned the company had a pattern of dismantling furnaces during their cleaning and then refusing to put them back together, claiming they were beyond repair. Then they put the pressure on to sell a new one. This marketing scheme worked really well in the winter. Numerous articles had been in the newspapers about it and dozens of lawsuits had been filed, including one by my own Aunt Kathy.

I quit.

CHAPTER 19
The Worst Job of All

After the embarrassing stint with Holland Furnace I got a job at the American Can Company at 61st and Western. My first assignment was working the Prestone Anti-Freeze double-seamer line, the worst job in the place. I was on the second shift 3 to 11pm. If you don't want a life work 3 to 11pm.

The double-seamer line consists of four large double seamer machines that affix the bottoms to the cans as they pass rapidly by on a conveyer belt. Bend down and take a large handful of metal bottoms from a wooden crate and place them neatly into the first feeder, which was head high. Go to the next one and do it again. Then the next and the next, until you're back to number one which was, by then, almost empty. It was mind numbing. The perfect job for robots, but they had yet to be perfected.

God help you if you let a feeder run out of bottoms to affix. Hundreds of cans would be mashed together and it would take an hour to clean up the mess. It only happened to me once. The foreman was enraged; he got paid on production. He called me, in disgust, a fucking college kid. "You're worthless!" he screamed.

He had to scream to be heard. The Prestone Anti-Freeze line was the loudest, in the loudest factory on earth. Talking was impossible, so we used hand signals. Two fingers to the mouth meant a smoke break - ten minutes, two per shift. Hand-to-mouth with chew motion meant go the lunch, thirty minutes. Hands up in air meant "bring me more crates of tops - I'm running out." Hand up in air with blood on it meant "I cut myself and need a Band-Aid." That was the extent of our communication.

Bad as the job was, there was still some fun to be had and things to learn. On my smoke breaks and during lunch I met many career factory workers. I learned that just because a woman has tattoos this does not make her dumb or unkind. I learned that men without high school diplomas can perform the most complicated of tasks, fixing the antiquated, monster machines when they broke down, for instance, which they did on a regular basis. Almost all the full-time factory workers were nice to this college boy and had no hard feelings that I would one day be "superior" to them. They accepted me as a co-worker.

Harry Fitch is the only fellow factory worker whose name I now recall. Harry, in his 50s, had been at American Can for thirty years. When he gained enough seniority, he asked to get off the line, "it's too fucking boring" and became a janitor, "where I got some freedom to myself." He was a diminutive man, 5'4", perhaps, and full of energy. He took a liking to me. Whenever I had a break, Harry would sit next to me and complain about management. Harry hated all managers.

Harry's favorite expression was cocksucker, which he pronounced "cahsuhker" the emphasis on the cah. Harry had no teeth. All managers were cahsuhkers and so were many fellow workers. Almost every sentence Harry spoke had cahsuhker in it. Perhaps the worst cahsuhker of all was the head janitor, Harry's immediate supervisor, who was even shorter than Harry, under 5' for sure. He had a sour expression on his face at all times. "The cahsuhker ain't never smiled," said Harry.

One day as I was working the double-seamers, I looked across the floor to see Harry and his boss carrying a hose. The boss had the front end and Harry, about six feet behind, had the other end. When Harry saw me he smiled and waved, then put his end of the hose in front of his pants. The other workers saw this and howled. I couldn't hear them, of course, but I saw them, laughing, waving and pointing at Harry. Harry waved to all and pointed at his boss's back while making funny faces. He started walking bow-legged. The cahsuhker never had a clue.

One of the dumbest, most embarrassing things I've ever done was at American Can. One of the assembly lines was for little pepper cans. The tops and bottoms were in the same large wooden boxes used on the Prestone Anti-Freeze line but, because these tops and bottoms were tiny, each box held 10,000 pieces. The boxes were stacked six high, ten feet in the air. I was told to get the hydraulic, hand-held, forklift and transfer a stack of boxes closer to the line.

I put the forklift arms under the load and lifted it up. What I didn't know was that right behind it, and touching it, was another stack of boxes. I put the arms too far under my load, so when I cranked it up to raise it off the floor, I tipped over the one behind it. As loud as that factory was it still sounded like a bomb went off as all ten feet of boxes hit the floor. People ducked and ran. Tops and bottoms of 60,000 pepper cans were now scattered everywhere. "Pick 'em up, asshole," the foreman said. It took me and two other guys the entire shift.

On my last week of work before returning to school, I was assigned to actually work on the pepper can line. At first I was happy for the assignment. It was so much easier than the Prestone line. I got to sit on a stool and simply place little tops with holes in them onto the cans as they went by. A machine, a little double-seamer, then pressed them tight. This job was normally done by women, the thought being they could better handle the tedium, and their hands were smaller and better suited for this somewhat delicate task.

Soon the tedium got to me. The line of cans was endless and fast. At lunch I told a fellow summer employee that I was about to lose my mind on the pepper can line. He said he understood, he'd worked it before, and told me what to do.

He said that if I "accidentally" dropped one of the little tops down into the can, instead of placing it on top, when it got to the machine, it would jam it. The cans behind it would then start stacking and compressing until they built enough pressure to explode into the air. Then he said all I had to do was turn off the machine and clean up the mess. "That'll give you about a twenty minute break from line work."

I asked if that wouldn't piss off the foreman and he said, "Of course. But he won't be too pissed, it happens all the time." In the middle of my next shift I tried it. It worked great.

Incredibly, the American Can Company invited me to return the following summer, which I did. Although the job was god-awful, the money was great and it provided all the resolve I needed to get a college degree.

CHAPTER 20

Best Job I Ever Had

I didn't know what I wanted to be after I graduated from Carroll. I majored in English literature and minored in history. This qualified me to be a teacher and teaching seemed to be a logical occupation. My mother had been a teacher and my brother, sister and their spouses were teachers. To get certified to teach in the Chicago Public School System I needed more education courses. However, due to my ROTC commission, I had a three-year commitment to the Army looming. A dilemma.

I decided to see if I could stall the Army and get the education courses completed prior to going on active duty. The Pentagon said it was no problem; told me to take a year if I needed it. I then enrolled at Loyola in downtown Chicago. The courses at Loyola were repetitive of the ones I'd taken at John Carroll even though the course descriptions were different. Bureaucrats must have written the teaching curriculum, and the teachers were ridiculous. "This is how you use an opaque projector most efficiently," they'd say in earnest, taking an entire class to explain it. How much can they teach, I wondered, about how to teach? I was bored silly.

I could have lived with that boredom but my classmates, who would be life-long peers, presented a bigger problem. Most of them were boring, too. In no time, I decided teaching was not for me. I called the Army back and asked to go on active duty as soon as possible. They said "Okay, but now we can't get you in until next January." That was six months away. Now what do I do?

I applied for some sales jobs but when the companies learned of my commitment to the Army they, naturally, would not hire me. "After three years in the Army you'll forget all your training here. Besides, who's to say you'll come back to us?" Tough to argue with that.

Finally, one company, Campbell Soup, did hire me. The interviewer liked the fact that I was a handball player. That was his favorite sport and he had a hard time finding someone to play with. He even showed me the company car I'd be driving, a big Chevrolet. I was to start the next day. For six hours I was ecstatic, but then the phone rang. His superiors nixed the hire because of the Army commitment. He was terribly sorry. I went from ecstatic to crestfallen.

By now my brother and sister were married and gone so that left Mom, Dad and me, the unemployed twenty-two year old college graduate, living in the house. It would be a long six months if I didn't get a job. In desperation, I again opened the want ads in the *Tribune*, this time scaling down my aspirations from sales to *anything*. An ad caught my eye, "Taxi cab drivers wanted. Full or part time." I hustled over to the cab company and was hired on the spot.

Driving a cab was the best job I ever had. As soon as I left the barn in the morning I was in charge, the CEO of my own mini enterprise. I could stop for breakfast, lunch, afternoon pie and coffee, whatever. Park at the lake and take a walk. I could work eight hours or twenty; the company didn't care. From my "office window" the view was constantly changing and I was meeting different people all day long. Most days I arrived at the barn at 74th and Ashland Ave around 8:00 in the morning. I'd be sure to be home by five o'clock. At six Spooky Cavanaugh would call, "Yo Jim!" from the sidewalk and we'd walk to the handball court at the Sabina gym. (He'd never ring the bell. That was for adults.) We'd play for an hour, take showers, and then sit at the bar at Chris Quinn's Tavern drinking beer. Then we'd walk home. This was Monday through Thursday–I never worked weekends. Weekends were reserved for fun trips to Lake Delevan, Wisconsin or Grand Beach, Michigan. It was the perfect job at the perfect time. Way better than selling soup.

Well, I should say *almost* perfect. There were a few drawbacks to driving a cab; the main one was the cops. Cops don't like cabbies. Cabbies are horn-blowing swervers and red-light runners who nose through crowds of pedestrians, never yielding the right of way. In my first three months of driving a cab I got three tickets: Not yielding the right of way to pedestrians at the corner of LaSalle and Madison; running a red light at 63rd and California; speeding on Lake Shore

Drive. All three were moving violations, which meant an automatic revocation of my driver's license.

When I returned to the barn after the third ticket I was beside myself with worry. What would I tell my parents? How could I continue to work? How would I get to Grand Beach?

One of the old timers who had befriended me pulled into the barn. When he got out of the cab I walked with him to the office and told him what happened, ending with, "I'm screwed, Ed."

"No you're not, kid," he said, and gave me a business card with just a phone number on it. "Call this number and they'll tell you what to do. And tell them it was me said to call. I'll get credit."

I called the number and told a man's voice that Ed said to call and related my problem. The voice listened then said, "Put $60.00 cash in a plain white envelope. In the morning at ten o'clock sharp be at (a hotel on Clark Street, I've forgotten which one). Use the house phone in the lobby and dial this room number. Then go to the elevator and wait."

I did as instructed. When the elevator opened a man stepped out. "You Joyce?" he asked. I nodded. He took the white envelope from my hand and gave me a manila envelope. He got back on the elevator and the door closed. The transaction took less than ten seconds. In the manila envelope were my driver's license and the unprocessed speeding ticket. I was back on the streets.

Aside from being the favorite target of traffic cops, another negative of cab driving is the drunken fare. (Passengers are called fares.) Most are not a problem, especially during daylight hours. These are professional drunks who are mannerly and usually good tippers. But on a few occasions I worked nights, just for the experience, and then I encountered amateur drunks. Two come to mind. The first was in his forties, well dressed, even dapper – a thin mustache, suit, tie, trench coat and hat. I picked him up in the Loop about ten o'clock. He practically fell into the back seat. He mumbled the address we'd be going to on the far south side and passed out. I'd heard on the company's radio that the Dan Ryan was backed up from an accident near Comiskey Park. I took Michigan Avenue to bypass it.

The drunk remained comatose until I got to 55th St. and headed over to the Ryan. I'd practically forgotten about him. Then in the rear-view mirror I saw a flash and heard a guttural "fuh." I turned around to see him trying to light a cigarette.

He couldn't get the lighted match to the end of the cigarette. His head was going up and down, as the flame in his fingers went back and forth. He never came close. The flame went out when it got to his fingers. "Fuh!" he said again and threw the match and cigarette on the floor. He went back to sleep.

I exited the Dan Ryan at 95th Street and headed west toward the Beverly area. As I crossed Vincennes, I noticed another flash from the back seat. I turned around to see my passenger with a match sticking out of his mouth. He was attempting to light it like it was a cigarette. "Stop!" I yelled but too late. This time he found his mouth and a flame shot up and over his nose. "God Damn It!" he yelled as he slapped out the flame.

His home was a large residence on Longwood Drive. I pulled into his driveway and he got out. The fire had sobered him up a bit and he was able to walk to my open window. His face was charred. "How much?" he said. "$10.75," I said. He fumbled two twenties out of his wallet and said something about being sorry for the mess in the back seat. He staggered to his front door. Somebody opened it and I split.

I picked up another drunk one night. He, too, fell asleep but stayed asleep until we got to his house. I said, "Sir, we're here!" He woke up and threw up on my back, all over the floor, and on the seat.

Naturally, that was my last fare of the night. I drove back to the barn as fast as I could, all the windows open, running red lights and stop signs. Even the most hard-hearted cop would forgive me when he smelled my situation.

When I pulled in to the barn, I told the maintenance guy what happened. "Pull over by that hose," he said. He followed me, opened the four doors, and hosed out the inside of the cab. Every square inch of it. "No problem, kid, this happens a lot. Did he get any on you?" "Just a little." I said. He hosed me off, too. "Good night," he said.

I was called to a tavern at 79th and Damen one mid-afternoon. A well-dressed man came out and got in the cab. He had bourbon breath but he was not drunk. He told me to take him to Presbyterian St. Lukes Hospital. In his hand he carried a brown bag made circular by twisting it around a bottle. When he got in the cab I greeted him with a "How you doing?" He did not respond.

We rode in silence for many minutes. I looked in the mirror and tears were running down his cheeks. He saw me look at him.

"This bottle is for my best friend," he said. "He's dying. It will ease his pain." Shaken, surprised and not knowing how to respond I quietly asked if the doctors would object to him giving booze to a patient.

"They won't give a shit. There's nothing more they can do. I'm a doctor myself."

Certainly the scariest fare I ever had was a woman going into labor. "Lady gonna have a baby, Southside!" said the anxious dispatcher. She stated the pick-up address. I was the closest in the fleet so I called back and said I'd take it. I pulled up to the apartment. Two ladies, one very pregnant, were standing at the curb waiting for me.

The non-pregnant said, "Drive fast the baby's comin'!"

"Okay," I said "Little Company of Mary is just a couple blocks."

"No, no. It's gotta be Cook County!" she yelled as the pregnant woman moaned.

"Cook County is over ten miles away," I yelled back, "What's wrong with Little Company or Christ?" (Christ Community Hospital.)

"They cost money," she yelled over the moans of her friend.

Oh, shit.

I flew down Western Avenue as best I could, but we were coming up on rush hour so I couldn't blow through red lights. The lady's moans got louder as did her friend's demands that I hurry. Sweat ran down my forehead and my palms were soaked. I frantically looked for a squad car to escort me but when you need a cop... (Sorry.)

We weren't even halfway there when the moans turned to screams. "I think the baby's coming now!" yells the friend.

"Should I pull over? I read about delivering babies!" I yelled back.

"Not now! Just keep going! I'll tell you when to pull over!"

I called the dispatcher and told her the problem. She said she'd have Cook waiting for us with a stretcher. "But if you have to deliver the baby be sure you don't drop it. And don't worry about the chord. They'll cut it at the hospital."

I started running red lights, despite the traffic, using the horn like a siren. Miraculously we made it, orderlies in the driveway taking charge.

I drove away with the lady screaming and my heart still pounding. I never even thought about collecting the fare.

While driving a cab, I learned a little about the dark side of human nature. I was on the Kennedy Expressway taking a thirty-something lady to the northwest side. A car came up fast behind me then cut into the lane on my right. I heard a slight, very slight, "tuh."

"That car just hit us," the lady said.

"Well he sure didn't do any damage, I felt nothing."

"But he did hit us and now my back is starting to hurt," she said.

I thought she was making a joke so I laughed and asked if she thought it was one of those whiplashes you read about.

"I'm serious," she said and started copying the information from the vehicles' identification plate.

"I know where there's a doctor's office up ahead. Take me there." She told me the address and I saw red.

"Lady," I said, "if you file a lawsuit I will swear to God that it is bogus. You are making me sick. I've read about people like you but didn't know for sure they really existed."

We pulled up to the doctor's office. I collected the fare and repeated my warning. She didn't tip me. When I returned to the barn I alerted the boss. We thoroughly examined the rear bumper. There was a small smudge on the bumper but no dent. By the time I'd left for the Army, we'd not heard back from the woman.

CHAPTER 21

GDC

Thanks to the Army I had a Commercial Pilot's License – multi-engine, instrument, fixed wing (land) and rotary wing. For those who wish to be pilots that is a license to be envied. I figured I'd make a living as a pilot when I got out of the Army.

A definition of flying is, "Hours and hours of boredom interspersed by moments of sheer terror." In my experience that is true, especially when flying airplanes. I did not want to be bored by my job ninety-nine point nine percent of the time. Helicopters, on the other hand, with flights of relatively short duration and their ability to land almost anywhere, are a lot more fun. But pay for chopper pilots was far less than with the airlines. (The terror part is present with both.) Another life dilemma.

In a tent in the Vietnam Delta one night, I was discussing this dilemma with a warrant officer friend, Gary Driggers, from Cincinnati. I told him I didn't want to be "just a pilot" but didn't know what else to do. "It would be a shame to waste all this training," I said, "but I want to do more than just fly."

Gary said he knew a man in Daleville, Alabama, named Lou Herring, who worked with the General Development Corporation, who might provide a solution. He said Lou was always looking for pilots who were also good salesman. Lou owned a DC-3 and flew customers to Florida to sell them property. Some time later when I returned to Ft. Rucker, my final Army assignment, I contacted Mr. Herring. The wheels of my adult working life started rolling down the runway.

Lou had a storefront office on Daleville's Main Street. Daleville's Main Street looked exactly as you would imagine - non descript with no redeeming features. There was not a building more than two stories. The main drag was a series of pawnshops, thrift shops and gas stations. The residential part of town was mostly trailer parks. But that didn't matter. Lou Herring had me wild-eyed that day when he told me the amount of money that could be made selling Florida lots to military people .

"But I won't sell anything that I don't believe in," I honestly said, wanting oh so badly to believe him. "Come see the property next weekend. I'm taking a group down to Florida in my DC-3. I'll save you a seat."

"What will it cost?" I asked.

"Nothing, I *want* you to be sold on the property. Then I think you can sell a bunch of it. Be at the Dothan airport at 8:00 next Saturday morning."

General Development Corporation was based in Miami. It had three developments (future cities) in the works: Port Charlotte on the west coast near Ft. Meyers; Port St. Lucie on the east coast near Ft. Pierce, and Port Malabar, also on the east coast near Melbourne. "GDC" used independent sales franchises to sell its properties. Lou had been awarded the states of Alabama and Georgia.

The next Saturday I flew with the group of prospects to see Port Malabar. Lou invited me to join him in the cockpit as his co-pilot. As we flew down the center of the state, he showed me the "frost line," where the orange groves began, a diagonal that goes from Daytona to Tampa. He pointed out the massive development under way near Orlando, "That's Walt Disney's new project – 27,000 acres." A few minutes later and off to the left, was The Kennedy Space Center at Cape Canaveral. I was wowed. I'd never seen the "real" Florida before, only the Panhandle.

We landed in Melbourne and were driven in vans to Port Malabar just a few miles away. The new development was beautiful with a classy clubhouse, lush eighteen-hole golf course, and attractive model homes. There were future plans for schools, churches, shopping centers, more golf courses and so on. General Development had already dedicated land for those purposes. I was sold.

Lou's marketing plan was simple: Invite prospects either through direct mail or boiler-room, (aka telemarketing) to a free dinner at The Daleville Inn, a motel with a restaurant. After dinner, show them a movie of the developments. GDC had hired celebrities to narrate the movies: Gordon McRae, Anita Bryant, Merv Griffin and others.

Ideally the dinner guests would be bachelors or a married couple. Just the husband without the spouse was discouraged because when the pressure to purchase (sign on the dotted line) was at its strongest the prospect had the perfect out. "I've gotta check with my wife." Married attendees without their spouses were referred to as "one legged deals." No way to sell them. Other unlikely purchasers were black people. There were no blacks in the promotional movies - playing golf, playing cards, fishing or frolicking in the pools. Blacks, therefore, never bought. Although there *were* black families in the communities, General Development left them out of the movies. If our white customers saw blacks living in their eventual hometown they would think, "There goes the neighborhood before we even get there."

I turned out to be a gifted salesman, selling so many lots that Lou got nervous. "What if Jim leaves me and goes to another franchise?" he thought. So he made me his partner and gave me control of day-to-day operations. He moved his family from Alabama to Florida and bought a run-down resort, near Port Malabar, on the Atlantic Ocean. The setting was gorgeous but the buildings had been neglected for decades. Lou's goal was to refurbish it. The place had a main building with a restaurant, ten duplex cabins for guests, and a pool, all overlooking the beach. Cape Kennedy was only twenty miles north. When a rocket went into space, Lou's resort was a great place to watch, especially at night. On our promotional trips we housed our clients at Lou's resort. (Note: A year or so later Lou and I did break up - suing each other over money (of course). When the suit was settled, I wound up with the GDC franchise. He kept the resort.)

Any business that markets its goods or services through commissioned-only salesmen has a very high turnover of salesmen. There was an adage in our business that anyone can sell a piece of property to a few friends and family members, but after that things get tough. Constant recruiting was necessary. Most of my salesmen were moonlighting military officers. They'd come to a dinner party, buy a lot, go see the development in the DC-3, get all fired up, buy another lot or two, and sell their close friends and their folks back in Ohio. Then they'd burn out, or be sent to another duty assignment. So the dinner parties were not only the way we sold the property, but also how we recruited salesmen.

Some hard-core closers, professional salesmen, worked for me. There were four of them, older guys who'd been around. They'd sold aluminum siding and other impulse items including encyclopedias, bibles, used cars, furnace cleaning services, etc. They were greedy, ruthless, and sometimes unscrupulous and always broke. "Hey, Jim, I've got the shorts this week. How about a little draw 'til payday?" "You got it, Jack." They were great producers so I knew they'd be good for it.

They were also creative. Throughout the developments there were a series of drainage ditches that were plainly visible on the colorful plat maps that we spread out on the tables after dinner. The salesmen sometimes elevated these ditches to the status of "canal" thus making the lots that backed up to them "waterfront property." I heard of one closer in New Jersey who went even farther. He told his customers that twice a day a 7-11 Store, mounted on a barge, would float past their lot. "If you want it to stop just hang a flag out. General Development has thought of everything," he'd explain.

One of my closers "Earl" had a trick he played when he felt he was losing his prospects. He'd start to cry. Of course the people noticed and asked him what was wrong. He'd compose himself enough to tell about the time he accidentally rolled over his three-year-old son while backing his car out of the driveway. "He died in my arms," the closer would weep. This often turned the clients around and they'd buy a lot out of sympathy.

I thought Earl's story was true, and so did the other salesmen until the night he brought his wife to a dinner party. The salesmen were encouraged to bring their wives because women were more honest than men, so the thinking went. There was a comfort level established when purchasing something from a couple. One of the other salesmen gave his condolences to the closer's wife on the loss of her child. She had no idea what he was talking about. "You didn't lose a son?" he asked. "Hell no, me and Earl never had kids. He never wanted any."

Another of my closers also played on clients' sympathies when he felt he needed an extra edge. He didn't go so far as accidentally killing his child; he merely started stuttering. It is all but impossible not to buy something from someone who is stuttering. He had the act down perfectly and made a lot of money.

Perhaps my best closer, at least for a time, was the oldest guy, fifties, who came to me directly from a monastery in Florida. Although not an official monk he'd lived and worked with them for five years. "I'd made so many mistakes in life I decided to drop out for awhile. Now I need a job, I'm broke." Ed was a Florida native and had at one time been a real estate broker there. "I know every inch of the state," he said. I hired him. Why not? It was a commission only job.

Cocktails were served before dinner but I noticed that Ed never had one. "Club soda is fine." He was making sales almost every night and soon was able to move from his rooming house into a nice trailer. He bought new clothes. But after a few months I noticed Ed did take a drink, "just a touch of vodka to keep the soda company," and before long it was "make it a strong double." A few nights later the worst happened. In the middle of the movie there was a crash. On went the lights and there was Ed, passed out on the floor.

The next day I went to Ed's trailer to have a talk. I was 27 and Ed was 57. It was awkward. I knew I should fire him but really did not want to. Before I got there, I decided to give him another chance. But he wouldn't let me. "I don't want another chance. I'm a drunk. I'm going back to the monastery. I called the abbot this morning. He has a bed for me."

Being a Florida land salesman carried a stigma. There had been so many scams over so many years that when I told people what I did for a living some thought I was joking. When I convinced them it was true (and attempted to sell them a lot) they'd inevitably ask how far under water it was.

GDC was listed on the New York Stock Exchange and its officers and board members were some of the country's most high profile and respected businessmen. When I was with GDC the company's president and CEO was Charles Kelstadt, the recently retired president of Sears. He was Mr. Integrity, who, we were told, coined the phrase "the customer is always right."

Kelstadt gave a talk at a company convention to an audience that included three hundred of us hard-charging closers in the audience. He wound up his talk by telling us that he'd heard reports of salesmen making exaggerations about the properties and their investment potential. "Remember," he said, "whenever you tell a lie, a black mark goes on your soul and it stays there forever." Three hundred closers squirmed.

The GDC marketing concept was actually quite sound. While still fairly young, people could buy a home site in Florida with very little money down and make small monthly payments at a low interest rate. By the time they retired they would own their future home site. This truly did make sense. The ethical problems arose for us salesmen when we encouraged people to buy a lot "just for investment." Or when we encouraged people to, "buy one lot for yourself and more to sell later." We would then graph out the rise in real estate prices in Florida. It all made sense on paper and was very appealing to our trusting customers sitting at a dinner party in the cozy Dalesville Inn.

"But I'm not buying anything until I see it first," the wise prospect would say. "I can drive to Port Malabar in eight hours."

"Of course you can," we'd say, "but here's a better option: Sign up tonight and we'll fly you down there for free in our company plane, a DC-3. We'll throw in a night in the Bahamas. If you don't like Port Malabar we will refund your money." We gave them a certificate stating so.

In all of my trips to Florida with customers, it was rare indeed that anyone asked for their money back. Most people bought more lots after touring the property. But if they did want a refund we gave it to them.

Meanwhile my first wife, Mary, and I moved to Columbus, Georgia and opened another office to work Fort Benning. We were making a lot of money. We bought a home on beautiful Lake Oliver in the upscale Green Island Hills area. Our house was on seven acres of (real) waterfront property. We also had a boathouse with a guest apartment above it. Our "neighbors" (we could hardly see their houses) did not have eleven kids: they were millionaires with two kids. This blue collar raised Yankee, and his Alabama wife, were completely accepted into Green Island Hills society. We were invited to join the exclusive country club and the even more exclusive Supper Club. Our house at 210 Cascade Road was a fabulous place to live. You should have seen the humongous magnolias and other mature trees. The place was special. I was twenty-nine.

But my conscience was bothering me. From time to time someone wanted to resell the lot(s) they had bought. But there was no market for these lots and wouldn't be for many years. We were selling a very long-term investment but that reality was not part of our sales pitch.

You recall that my JCU buddy, Bill Smith, was the son of John Smith, the well-known president of The Inland Steel Company. Presidents and CEO's of big corporations know each other and Smitty's dad was a friend of Charles Kelstadt. Using that connection, and as a franchise holder of General Development, I was able to schedule a lunch with Mr. Kelstadt whose office was in the new Sears Tower in Chicago. Although he was retired, he maintained an office there. I wanted to see if this man, who believed in sin, knew what his salesmen were saying to make GDC so successful on the NYSE.

Mary and I went to Chicago to meet the old man. He could not have been more cordial. He also could not have been more out of it regarding the way the properties were being sold. "A salesman should never sell anyone a home site unless the buyer plans to build his own home on it. To sell these lots as investments is a disservice. It is wrong. There's too many of them."

(Shit!) I was afraid he'd say that. I reluctantly did the math. GDC owned over 300,000 acres. Each acre held four lots. That's a lot of lots. I had to get out of the business. The property could not be sold in sufficient volume to make a living without leaving the truth behind.

(Note: Everyone I know who bought property from GDC did make some money on their investment, including my mom and dad, but that took many years and at nowhere near the profits we had projected.)

CHAPTER 22
Innisbrook

When my conscience finally caught up with me, I gave up my franchise with GDC. I decided to write for a living. But with a twist. I wrote letters to children under the pen name, Granny Grasshopper. Granny smoked a corncob pipe and lived in the South Georgia woods. My plan was to sell this letter-writing service to grandparents. Each month I would mail the letter/story to kids making sure their grandparents got the credit for it.

"Dear (insert kid's name) my friend (insert grandparents name) asked me to write to you from my cabin in the woods. Love, Granny Grasshopper." I stole the idea from the Fruit of the Month Club. In the apartment over our boathouse I composed the letter/stories. I wrote twelve, had them hand scripted and illustrated (they were beautiful), and went into business.

Sales were brisk, until I ran out of family and friends. Ads in national magazines cost a lot of money and I was again forced to do some math. I delayed doing this because I was having so much fun. I asked myself, "How many letter services would I have to sell to make a lot of money?"

Answer: "Way too many. You could never do it on your own."

I obtained the copyright to the name "Granny Grasshopper" and I took it, along with my brilliant marketing idea, to the Hallmark Card people in Kansas City. I planned to sell it to them and collect the royalties. The nice lady at Hallmark was charmed by Granny and thought my idea "cute": she offered me $150. Period. Ouch.

Next, I became a Shaklee Products distributor, which didn't last long. Shaklee sells its multitude of products in the Amway model whereby a million dollars can be made. I did some more math and decided it was true. A million dollars could be made by one in a million people. It was time to get a real job.

My brother-in-law, Larry Morris, was recently hired as the sales manager of Innisbrook, the fancy golf resort in Tarpon Springs, Florida. We rented our house on Lake Oliver, planning to return some day. We bought a house in Clearwater and I went to work for Larry selling condos. Although it was 8am to 5pm, six days a week, I loved it. How could I not?

The condos were sold primarily as investments. They were lousy investments, but the millionaires who bought them could care less. We sat with them in a "closing room" and went over the numbers. "You should buy today because very soon there'll be a price increase," we'd say. The husband didn't give a damn; he just wanted access to the three magnificent golf courses. The wife was far more interested in the furnishings and décor she could choose. It was a vanity purchase for the clients, making our jobs real easy. Innisbrook was, and still is, a magnificent facility.

There were three of us salesmen. We took turns getting "ups." We knew as soon as we saw the customers walking toward the sales office whether they were potential buyers, or not. If they were dressed like golfers, they were prime. If they were dressed like locals from Tarpon Springs or New Port Richy there was no way they could afford the place. Once I got stuck with an elderly little lady, plainly dressed. I knew I'd be wasting my time, I but had to be courteous. We sat down in a closing room and as I started in with the pitch she stopped me. "I will buy a three bedroom unit today, but only if you assure me that my name will not be on any list. I want total privacy." I assured her. She paid with a check. Her name? Nope, I promised, but it's one well known by those in the upper crust.

Ronnie Wallschlager was a salesman whose previous job was hosing elephant shit out of cages for the Ringling Brothers Circus in Sarasota. He had no real estate or any other sales experience, but Larry saw potential in Ronnie and gave him a chance. The other salesman was Greg Anderson, who was only one year older than Ronnie but a seasoned sales veteran.

When Ronnie got his first "up" he was a nervous wreck. They were prime prospects, dressed like golfers and looking rich. He took them into the closing room, a converted bedroom of the condo we used as a sales office. The prospects sat a table with their backs to the window. When Ronnie closed the door, Greg went out the front door and crept along the side of the building. When he got to the window where Ronnie was working, he crouched down. Then, with his back to the window, he jumped. Ronnie had started in on his recently memorized pitch, nervously writing numbers on a piece of paper, when he saw a movement outside the window. He looked up and it was gone. He continued, but then saw it again and realized it was Greg, jumping up and down.

Ronnie's nervousness was replaced by anger at what Greg was doing to him, but as Greg continued jumping, Ronnie saw the humor in it. He felt the giggles coming on. He awkwardly asked the people if they'd trade places with him, trying desperately to stifle a laugh. They did, but a few moments later the lady said, "Excuse me, sir, but I think I just saw someone jump outside the window." Ronnie, now out of control, said, "I'll go check," and bolted from the room. Larry was in the hallway in hysterics. I don't remember if that couple bought or not. Business was so good at that time it didn't matter.

Larry believed in happy employees. When things slowed down, especially in the summer, we spent lots of time on the golf courses, tennis courts and fishing the numerous lakes. We ate free lunches every day at the Copperhead clubhouse, whatever we wanted from the menu. Larry would take us in his Lincoln. As he passed the driving range he'd always slow up until he saw a guy on his back swing then he'd blow his horn and the guy would shank the shot.

The condo sales department was the envy of the place and the clerical and administration people resented us. It infuriated them that while they were stuck at their desks they'd look out their window and see us riding around in golf carts with our potential customers. Once the head administration guy said something about "the goof-off condo salesmen" to Harvey Jones, Innisbrook's founder and president. Harvey said, "you are guaranteed a paycheck every week, Bill. Those goof-offs you're talking about don't earn a penny unless they make sales. Want to trade places with them?"

Harvey's daughter, Candy, married John Fahey at Innisbrook. The place had only officially opened a few days before. Harvey went all out for Candy's wedding. She was his oldest and favorite child. (He had nine of them.) It was a posh affair and a great way for Harvey to show off his new resort. Maybe even get some customers. Guests were seated under a canopy, set up by the first tee of the Island Golf Course. They had a beautiful view of the lake. But just as all were seated, and the food was being served, the automatic sprinklers came on. Before the maintenance people figured out how to turn them off, everyone, and everything, was soaked. Earlier that day a guest's toy poodle was walking along one of the lakes sniffing at the weeds. An alligator picked it off.

"How was your day, Harvey?"

When Innisbrook got rolling it was a super success. Harvey, originally a home builder from Toledo, and his partner, Stan Wadsworth from Lockport, Illinois, decided to do it again in Colorado. They built Tamaron Resort, which was even more magnificent than Innisbrook. It is located between the coolest town in the state, Durango, ten miles to the south and the Purgatory Ski Area, ten miles to the north. Bordered on the west by the Hermosa Cliffs and on the east by Missionary Ridge, it is breathtakingly beautiful. I decided to transfer to Tamaron. Stan Wadsworth had moved out there to take charge. Harvey stayed in Florida.

Durango was not well known at the time, nor was Purgatory, but Harvey Jones and Stan Wadsworth believed in the old adage: "If you build it they will come." They didn't. We salesmen had to go out and get them and I targeted Phoenix. When I garnered enough leads from that area, generated by ads in ski and golf magazines, I flew to Phoenix and stayed at the upscale Arizona Biltmore where I hosted a reception with free drinks (top shelf), hors de oeuvres and a slide presentation about the resort. With me was a beautiful girl who worked at Tamaron and who'd been a bunny in the Phoenix Playboy Club. She was an asset, charming the men and chatting up the women as she served them. Her knowledge of both Phoenix and Tamaron was valuable. It was a tasteful presentation suitable for rich people.

My pitch to our potential customers was straightforward and simple. Fly to Durango at our expense. Stay at Tamaron for three days and two nights as our guest including meals and drinks. Check the place out on your own. No salesman will approach you unless you ask to see one.

After one of my presentations, a strikingly handsome middle-aged man came up to me. He had a full head of beautiful white hair and a bronze tan. His clothes and demeanor said "money." With him was his equally attractive wife.

"My name is Bill Mennen, this is Audrey. Does my name mean anything to you?" he said.

"Only in that you filled out a lead card," I said.

"Have you ever heard of the Mennen Deodorant Company?"

"Sure."

"I own it."

"Holly cow," I unprofessionally said. "Nice to meet you!"

He then told me that my deal to see Tamaron at no expense was too good to believe. "What if we spend our money to fly up there and don't buy a condo? Am I supposed to believe you will still reimburse us?" he said.

"How about this, Mr. Mennen," I said, thinking fast and reaching for my wallet, "Here's my credit card. Buy your tickets with it. When you check in at Tamaron, leave it at the front desk. And, I promise, you'll never see me unless you ask for me. I'll be at the sales office."

That's a deal," said the multi-millionaire as he put my Visa card in his pocket.

When I got back to Tamaron, I spread the word. When the Mennen's showed up I had employees all over the property reporting in: "They're playing tennis. He's on the golf course. They're eating lunch in the dining room," and so on. At the end of the second day, Mr. Mennen called. "Jim, this place is all you said it was. Let's talk." My heart leapt.

Bill and Audrey bought three condos, one for themselves and one each for their children. He wrote a check. Of all the sales I've ever made, that was the most gratifying. And the Mennens, wonderful people, said they'd tell all their friends about Tamaron. "We'll sell the place out for you, Jim." Unfortunately, this didn't happen. I was about to get fired. I stupidly blew the whistle that there was something wrong at Tamaron.

Innisbrook was the friendliest of places with cheerfulness abounding. Tamaron was cold, stiff, and snooty. The employees lived in fear of their jobs and were frequently berated. The problem was the general manager that Stan had hired to run hotel operations. Condo sales were not under his jurisdiction. His name was "Helmut*", a German guy with a heavy accent. He was a stickler, a screamer, a control freak, and a perfectionist. (He was also arrogant, of course.)

Innisbrook and Tamaron were owned by Golf Hosts, Int'l, Inc. with Harvey and Stan as the principals but neither, by themselves, had the majority of stock. There were other, lesser stockholders. In 1974 the U.S. economy took a nosedive and both resorts were dramatically affected. A power struggle ensued between Stan and Harvey, two very different personalities, and Harvey won. He relieved the Tamaron condo sales manager and gave me the job. I was very pleased. This meant big bucks. I decided to take my promotion a step further and wrote Harvey a "confidential" letter regarding the Gestapo-like attitude on the hotel side at Tamaron. It was a long letter for "his eyes only." I really let Stan and Helmut have it. Harvey, of course, couldn't wait to read the damning letter to Stan.

I was the condominium sales manager of Tamaron for about three weeks when the power struggle re-emerged between Harvey and Stan and, this time, Stan won. He sent one of his flunkies to my office with instructions to escort me off the property and to tell me I was "barred from Tamaron for life." I was pissed for a while that Stan didn't fire me in person but then realized that was hypocritical. I've fired people over the phone and, one time, by Western Union Telegram.

Ironically, and comically, thirty-five years later one of my companies does business with one of Stan's companies. He has no idea and, realistically, he probably doesn't even remember me. I was a little fish in the Innisbrook and Tamaron pond.

I've written numerous irate letters like the one to Harvey but thanks to Stan, I gained the wisdom to put them aside for a few days and then throw them away. I burned one bridge, and that was a doozy. I never burned another, at least not with a letter.

In essence, the difference between Tamaron and Innisbrook was this. Both resorts had little buildings, guard shacks, at their entrances. The one at Innisbrook was used to welcome people and give directions. The one at Tamaron was used to cross-examine anyone who dared enter.

I knew one of the guards at Tamaron. He said one night it was snowing like crazy and he saw movement coming toward the shack. He stepped out to get a better look. It was a mountain lion. "I jumped back inside, and waved him right on through," he said. "Screw Helmut!"

One of my most memorable nights was at Tamaron. Greg, the jumper, had also transferred there and sold a condo to the famous baseball figure, Billy Martin. Billy and his then wife, Heather, came to close on their unit and Greg asked me if I wanted to join them for dinner. Martin at the time was managing the Texas Rangers. Heather went to bed about ten o'clock and Billy, Greg and I went to the bar. We stayed there until the sun came up (literally), Billy regaling us with stories from his famously colorful past, especially those from his time as a Yankee. Mickey Mantle and Whitey Ford were still his best friends. He would be joining Mantle for bird hunting in Georgia after leaving Tamaron. Being with Billy Martin was like listening to a baseball card talk. He was a great storyteller, and a very nice man.

Getting fired from Tamaron was a bit of a bummer, but I was not too upset. I was planning to quit in a few months anyway. I'd decided to become a psychoanalyst.

In 2007 my book *Use Eagles If Necessary* (A Psychoanalyst's Stories), was published so I've written enough on that topic. But a quick note here about psychoanalysis and psychotherapy for those who don't read the book, and with apologies to Carpenter Joyce.

There are numerous varieties of each of these disciplines but all must have the following dynamics to be worthwhile: Patients and shrinks must like each other. Patients must have total trust in their emotional mentors so they can be brutally and embarrassingly honest about their life experiences, fantasies, desires, regrets and screw ups. Therapists must be secure enough in their own skin to keep their comments to a minimum so the patients can learn from themselves. Without those dynamics, psychoanalysis and psychotherapy are mostly, if not completely, a waste of time and money but when these elements are present, miracles can take place.

Lastly, both parties must be aware that they'll be together for a long time.

Reprogramming the unconscious mind can take years and that's enough about this topic.

CHAPTER 23

The Glenrock Company

Mary and I divorced in 1976. In 1978 I married Barbara and we moved from Durango in 1980. My psychoanalytic practice had slowed up; they always do in recessions, when real problems often trump the less serious neuroses. I was burned out anyway. We decided a big change was in order. Even in good times lay psychoanalysts don't make a lot of money. I knew what it was like to make real money and I wanted it again. I figured I'd paid my dues to my fellow man, so we headed "home," my home, Chicago.

My first job was working on the "Richard Daley for State's Attorney" campaign. Guys in the gang member, Jerry Joyce, got me appointed as the coordinator of the south suburbs, an area never before won by a Democrat. I didn't know Daley and asked a fellow campaign worker, Gene Campion, a lawyer and future judge, if Rich was a better public speaker than his father, who was horrible behind a microphone. Gene laughed and said, "Rich makes his father sound like Demosthenes."

When the original Mayor Daley spoke in public he blubbered, spouted, mixed metaphors, chopped up sentences and generally sounded confused. The people of The Great City of Chicago (his favorite expression) loved him for that. He was without pretense - one of them. He was also a fabulous mayor and political organizer. John F. Kennedy would agree. Daley's machine handed him the presidency.

And Gene was right about Mayor Daley's namesake, Rich. He was a chip off the old block. Listening to him talk in public hurt your ears – his mind two steps ahead of his mouth – but Chicagoans didn't care, in fact they liked it. Smooth talkers were not to be trusted.

I never met the father, but had occasion to be with Rich during the campaign. He was friendly; focused; no nonsense. And like his dad he was a very effective administrator and eventual mayor of The Great City

175

of Chicago. Daley beat the incumbent, Bernard Carey, thanks in part to a last minute editorial by Mike Royko in the *Sun Times* blasting Carey. We papered Cook County with copies of it. The night of the election was one of the most exciting of our lives. The win was a squeaker. They were still counting votes at two o'clock when I went to bed. At four, Barbara woke me up, "We won!" (And I am pleased to write that Rich carried the south suburbs.)

When you have a key position in a political campaign you expect some reward if your candidate wins, usually in the form of a job. Unfortunately, Daley won a lawyer's job, State's Attorney, and I was not a lawyer. I *was* offered a job guarding a safe however, "Jim, you can read all day" I was told, but I passed on it. Another campaign worker, who was smarter than me, grabbed it.

So the euphoria of Daley's victory was short-lived for us and I floundered. I tried selling real estate in upscale Lincoln Park for a while, but the recession lingered and nobody was buying anything. I interviewed for a half-dozen sales jobs and finally landed one selling concrete. It was a stable paycheck, but I yearned for more. Then along came the Glenrock Company.

Four of us bought the Glenrock Company: Mike Watson, a childhood friend and member of the gang, who was an engineer specializing in waterproofing systems. He loaned me the money for my share. He was also the only partner who understood the business and its products. The other two were Jerry Joyce, then a state senator; and Bill Daley an attorney and Rich Daley's brother. Bill would years later become the Secretary of Commerce in the Clinton administration and today he is The White House Chief of Staff for President Obama.

I was the front man for the purchase of Glenrock. It took me about nine months to convince the original owner, Gene Finegan, to sell me the company, which he'd founded twenty-seven years before. (My partners, for various good reasons, were "silent.") When the deal was finally done, I happily quit the concrete company and became Glenrock's president.

Up to this point, my claim to fame as a businessman was my extraordinary ability to sell. Unfortunately, The Glenrock Company was in the construction chemical industry, a technical field, and those products cannot be "sold." If a contractor doesn't have an immediate need, he would be nuts to buy them. When he does need them he asks the obvious question, "What's your price?"

Getting personally close to customers was important so they'd tell you what price they had been given by competitors (called "last look") when it came time to buy. I was good at that. But that's taking orders, not selling. Also, there was nothing "technical" about me. The products themselves, many dozens of them, bored me silly. Who cares about a silicone sealant, a polyurethane coating, a concrete bonding agent, a latex caulk, an acrylic sealer or an epoxy? Actually, lots of people care, Glenrock customers, for instance. I just couldn't get interested in the products.

(We partners sometimes hired our kids for summer work, mostly in the warehouse, but occasionally to answer the phones. One of them, who was very smart, would take a call and he'd have no idea what the customer was asking about, what with all the technical jargon, so he'd simply hang up the phone and go to the bathroom. He knew when the guy called back someone else would get the call. "We must have been disconnected," the customer would say.)

Technically, I should not have had to be technically aware as the company's president. Glenrock had many competent, experienced employees. Watson, who joined us later, brought thirty years experience in the industry. My job should have been primarily 1) Expanding our customer base – I did that and 2) Assuring the company was on sound financial footing. Although sales almost doubled in the four years I was there it was never financially sound. I spent those years primarily juggling bankers and trying to stay off "credit hold" by suppliers. In both instances, I told a lot of lies. It was a nightmare. The day I walked in as the "new owner," Lois, the lady comptroller of many years, said, "I hope you brought a lot of money with you; we're broke."

Two days later all the employees decided to quit because they'd heard I had Mafia connections from the concrete company I'd worked for, Prairie Materials. Only a two o'clock in the morning phone call from Barbara to Lois at home stopped them from quitting. She convinced Lois that Prairie had nothing to do with the purchase of Glenrock and, by the way, Prairie had nothing to do with the Mafia. Barbara staved off disaster.

Once every quarter we would have a board of directors meeting at Daley's law office in the Loop. I dreaded them, as I never had good news. I would go over financial statements with my partners and they'd quiz me until I ran out of bullshit, and then they'd let me off the hook. They were nice guys. Then we'd go have dinner at a fancy restaurant. (Bill Daley always ordered the lamb chops and one night he gave me a bite. I was hooked.) After one of the dinners, I gave the company credit card to the waitress. It was declined. Jerry had to pay. I was forever in a state of embarrassment at the Glenrock Company.

In hindsight it is now obvious that as the president of Glenrock, I was an example of: In over his head; biting off more than he could chew; Peter principled; out of his league. Essentially, I didn't know how much I didn't know. My problems as Glenrock's president were further exacerbated by the following:

First, I was not computer savvy. In 1983 real computers were just coming into their own. At the time we bought the Glenrock Company it was undergoing a "computer conversion" transitioning from the antiquated punch card type to the kind that puts data on terminal screens and, if you want, prints it out on paper. Months after he started it became obvious that the computer programmer who began under Finegan would never get the job done, I appealed to our newly appointed CPA firm to find another programmer. They said they knew a good one who would work at reasonable rates. His name was Ron* and, at first, he appeared to be fine. Real data was starting to be produced. Early on he discovered that frugal Finegan had purchased a bootleg computer program that was way too large for our system. "That's been part of the problem," said Ron. "The company it was designed for is fifty times bigger than you. It's a street lighting company called Joslyn Manufacturing, but I think I can make it work." (Joslyn was the company my dad had worked for. One heck of a coincidence.)

Second, Ron seemed to be doing okay jerry-rigging the Joslyn software until he started drinking on the job and the numbers quit coming. Turned out that he had problems with booze and other things but the CPA firm claimed ignorance of that part of his history. One day he showed up with face scratches and a black eye. His boyfriend caught him cheating. Eventually I had to fire Ron, abandon the entire system, and start all over with a new computer that came with appropriate software and a factory trained installer. Finally, after more than a year, and over $100,000 wasted, I was getting accurate numbers. They weren't pretty but at least they were accurate.

Third, I'd had no previous experience with a company that carried inventory. Inventory, if not purchased judiciously, a skill learned from experience, will eat cash at an alarming rate. Thus, the purchasing agent plays a critical roll. Unfortunately the previous purchasing agent had recently quit Glenrock and started his own company, directly competing with us. He set up shop less than a mile away. He not only took his experience he also took a key employee, a former key employee and lots of customers. He was also given most of our product lines by our major suppliers.

Fourth, we did not purchase the company wisely. The price was fine but the terms were killers. Payments should have been spread out over many years instead of just a few. Every month I was late paying Finegan. He'd call and whine and I'd cajole, smooth talk and lie. Every month this conversation drove him, and me, nuts but I had to keep suppliers relatively current lest they cut us off. Finegan had to be paid, and he was, but he was not my priority.

Fifth, I spent too much money entertaining customers and potential customers. Sox games, Bulls games, Hawks games, Bears games, even Cub's games. Innumerable games of golf were played with customers at the private Itasca Country Club where I'd gotten a membership. I also threw expensive Christmas parties that, while tasteful, elaborate and appreciated were not necessary to enhance sales. I should have learned something from the project superintendent caulking the windows of the new Northwestern Terminal Building in the Loop. He'd be spending tons of money with us on GE Sealants. He was an American Indian and when we first called on him he said, "I don't need, or want, any of that fancy entertaining shit. Just get me a microwave for my trailer." I did, of course, but would have spent much more to keep his loyalty to Glenrock.

Another Indian, this one from India, was an engineer, Atul Aluwalia*. He was a senior partner with a firm that rehabitated concrete parking decks. He was a friend of a friend of mine, the contractor, Doug Loos*. Doug offered to introduce me. "Atul loves all sports," he said. "Take him to a Cub game and you'll be his friend."

At this time Glenrock was about to get an *exclusive* line on a really fascinating, revolutionary, concrete deck silicone sealer. It would be our first exclusive line. Although the product was clear it had properties that inhibited ultra violet degradation similar to an aliphatic polyurethane. It was not exothropic, contained no diluents, had a workable viscosity of thirty-seven centipois and after it cured (only three hours) you couldn't smell it. It was 87% solids. Everybody was really excited, as you can imagine. But it needed to be specified by engineers to be sold and Atul could do that. Glenrock, I reasoned, would make a killing on the product because we'd have no competition. There was no equal to it on the market.

So I took Atul and Doug to a Cub game. The Cubs weren't bad that year and had a chance for the playoffs. During the game Atul said, "I'd give anything to take my son to a play-off game." I said, "Atul, you got it. If the Cubs make the playoffs, two tickets are yours compliments of Glenrock." He was thrilled.

Well, the Cubs did make the playoffs and I called my partners and told them I needed two tickets. I knew with their vast connections in Chicago that would not be a problem. It was a problem. Apparently their influence did not extend north of Madison Street where Cub territory begins. So I asked one of my salesmen, Eddie Dinucci, if he could get me tickets. Eddie had some shady connections. He came through…at $400 per ticket (keeping a little something for himself, no doubt). And to make matters worse the new sealer that was going to make us rich? It didn't pass its final testing by the state of Illinois.

It seemed like everything I did at Glenrock was wrong. When it was decided the company would be better off without me, I was at once relieved to be free of the burden - and ashamed that I had failed.

Although my years at Glenrock were angst filled, I did get an education in real business, in general, and the construction supply business, in particular. It was now time to put that education to work on my own terms, with my own company and without the strangling debt. There'd be no more board of directors meetings, thank God, and the lamb chops would come again soon enough.

CHAPTER 24

Green Mountain International, Inc.

There was only one product that I was exposed to at Glenrock that interested me. It was a polyurethane liquid that stopped water leaks. This was relatively new technology and I found it sexy. It did something, rather than just sit there like a caulk. When the liquid product came into contact with water, it reacted in seconds and then began expanding. It expanded *20 times* its original volume to become a dense closed-cell foam that stopped the water. What I also liked about it was that only two companies made it, the giant, 3M, and a company from Europe. Both products had flaws and I figured I could discover how to make a better one, with a little help. Then I'd form my company making and selling just that one thing. Where to start? Indiana. That's where Terry Hodges lived. I'd never met him but knew he was a big user of chemical grout.

I called Terry out of the blue and introduced myself. He agreed to have lunch with me the next day at the Denny's Restaurant off I-80 in Gary. I told him my plan. He was enthusiastic. He was currently employed by a large contracting firm out of Pittsburgh, which, he felt, was exploiting him. Before the lunch was over we shook hands as "partners in progress" in this venture. All we needed was a product to sell. After my initial bravado this was now a concern to me, but not to him. "No problem," he said. "I know a company that can make it for us. It's in Maryland."

(A more optimistic person I have never met. If someone told Terry that both wings of the plane were engulfed in flames he'd take a sip of his beer and say, "No problem. The pilots have remote control fire extinguishers.")

I called the people in Maryland and they were confident that they could indeed make what I had described, but they said it would take time, with lots of trial and error. During this time, I scrambled like crazy to make money. Jim and Walter, now teenagers, had moved up from Alabama to live with us. I had three jobs. Selling concrete repair products for Specco Industries, working in sales promotion for Tom and Ted Chakos, who owned a construction company, and trying to peddle real estate for John Nettleton in Addison. I was forty-five years old.

Every month or so the Maryland company sent Terry and me a small (one pint) sample of their latest attempt to make our product. With anticipation and fear we played with each sample. The first few were disasters, expanding just fine but then collapsing back on themselves. I began to lose hope. Terry didn't, of course, and eventually, as Maryland re-jigged the formula, those collapses got less and less and finally, seven months later, the product expanded and held its shape. We were euphoric. Terry quit the big contracting company and started his own contracting business stopping water leaks. He would be our first customer and, for almost a year, our *only* customer. I had to learn the product and its varied applications so I could sell it to other contractors. To me, a daunting task. I had to learn technical terms such as hydrophobic and hydrophilic, and chemical terms like MDI, TDI, DINP, pre-polymers. And I had to understand the test procedures for the product and its various formulas: compressive, tensile, elongation, flexural, viscosity and so on. And I had to learn how to use it, in other words, where to drill the holes in concrete (as well as where not to drill them) to inject the product so it would do its magical expansion act. I did not grow up in the construction business so, unlike Terry, I could not see through concrete walls, floors or ceilings. Nor could I see under the ground. I needed to learn how to insert pipes into the ground, at what depths, at what intervals, and decide which product to inject through them, and at what rate. "Read the soil borings reports," said Terry. (What's that?) Eventually I learned enough to solo.

It didn't take Terry long to get his first job with our new product. It was in October 1987. I put four five-gallon pails of our new invention in the trunk of my Chevy Caprice, three more pails in the back seat and two more up front with me and drove from Chicago to Highland, Indiana. Terry met me there.

In the 1920s, on the highest hill in Highland, Indiana, (not that high) the man who invented Aloe Vera oil for commercial use built himself a castle. After he passed away the castle changed hands often, eventually ending up in the hands of the state.

Over time, the state gave up on maintaining it and it lay dormant for decades. In 1987 a private individual from Argentina bought it and began re-furbishing it for himself and his family to live in. Below grade walls and floors were actively leaking, the basement was a swamp.

Terry was confident the product would work because our "cup samples" were perfect, but he'd never tried it on a real job site. I was not so sure and with much trepidation I unloaded the car, watched Terry drill holes, place packers, stir the catalyst into the polyurethane and start pumping. And, sure enough, the water slowed, slowed, slowed and stopped! In its place was dense, yellow foam. We had a business. We named it Green Mountain Incorporated.

I followed Terry from job to job all over the Midwest seeing this miraculous product stopping all manner of leaks from trickles to gushers. And the fix was permanent. Once I asked Terry how he decided how much to bid on jobs. He said, "I don't bid on them I bet on them." "You what?" I said.

"I tell the guy, I'll bet you $10,000 I can stop your leaks. If I don't, don't pay me."

At this time chemical grouting was relatively new to the United States and very few engineers were aware of it. They had to be educated to specify the product. Engineers are reluctant to try anything new; they are anal by necessity. A tough sell. The best way to sell them was to take them to jobs in progress. As the water stopped their jaws dropped.

We asked our wives, Barbara and Brenda, to be the company's stockholders and officers because "WBE's" (Women's Business Enterprises) are given concessions on certain government jobs. But they were not token owners; they took their jobs seriously, Barbara as president and Brenda as secretary. Both worked from their homes, ours in Illinois and Brenda's in Indiana. Company headquarters consisted of a desk in the northwest corner of our living room. In a few months it relocated; it took over the dining room.

At this time Terry's contracting company, T.R. Hodges, Inc., landed a job with Turner Construction Co., one of the world's largest contractors. Turner was building the United Airlines Terminal at O'Hare. The slurry walls (basement) leaked like sieves. Terry told Turner he'd be using

Green Mountain's polyurethane. He told them Green Mountain was a WBE, which pleased Turner, as it would satisfy part of their quota for minority participation under City of Chicago rules. There'd been a lot of fraud; people with companies posing as WBE's. Turner said they'd be sending someone to our corporate headquarters to check us out the next day. Shit. Too late to get a real office.

The Turner representative, a thirty-something woman, rang the doorbell of the house. I took her through the living room into the dining room where Barbara was working. She could hear the kids playing downstairs. I was waiting for the lady to split. But Barbara engaged her with talk of hydrophobic and hydrophilic, the most efficient injection port to use on a slurry wall and other techno speak. The lady was impressed. Barbara passed muster and we got the job at O'Hare, over one thousand gallons, which was huge at the time. Then Terry got another Turner job, the Prudential II building in the Loop, almost two thousand gallons. We were now a *real* company, we felt, and time to move out of the house.

Alex and Zack were still small and Barbara did not want to be an absent, working mother so instead of renting an office we re-furbished a small building on our property which had previously served as a chicken coop. Barbara and I were "walking home from work," one evening, a distance of about 50 feet, when two squirrels ran in front of us. "Traffic is heavy tonight," she said.

But after the O'Hare and Prudential jobs, business all but came to a stop and we were getting low on funds. The polyurethane grout business is an "as needed" business, few companies keep inventory and there are only so many leaking structures that need to be fixed. I was considering a part-time job when Terry landed a monster project in Indiana. He pumped over 6,000 gallons around a leaking pit at a steel company. Finally, we could breathe. The steel company was affiliated with the Joslyn Manufacturing Company. (Coincidence, again.)

With money in the bank Terry and I could now promote Green Mountain. We flew from coast to coast and across both borders seeking out other chemical grouting contractors who were using our competitors' products. We converted many of them. Green Mountain became a player in this field, but chemical grouting with polyurethanes is a small field. We had to go national to establish a market that would sustain us month after month and year after year. And we did.

When Terry and I were on the road we stayed in the same motel room to save money, but we splurged on food. We both enjoyed prime rib and ate it all over the country. The best prime rib, we both agreed, was at the upscale restaurant in the Providence, Rhode Island airport. FYI.

Traylor Brothers, a large, national infrastructure company, was building a tunnel in Milwaukee. I'd heard they had water problems and called to see if I could get an appointment with the job supervisor. "Hell yes," he said, "Get up here. We got a leak we need to stop." I put on my best suit and drove to Milwaukee alone, without Terry. When I walked into his construction trailer he said, "Are your boots in your car?" "I don't have boots; do I need them?" I said. "Yes," he said and handed me a pair that came up to my knees. "Put these on. And wear this hard hat." It had a miner's light on it. I had no idea what I'd gotten into.

We walked outside and I looked for the stairs or ladder that led to the tunnel. I saw none. At that moment he said, "Here comes the bucket." A crane, two hundred feet away placed a bucket hanging from a long wire on the ground in front of us. "Hop in," he said.

No sooner had he closed the little gate, than we were airborne. We swooped over the ground until a hole appeared below us. We hovered over it for a few seconds until we stopped swinging and then we dropped, at the speed of sound, four hundred feet into the ground. My heart was in my throat as we plunged into total darkness. Then we abruptly slowed and gently stopped on top of a wooden platform in a brightly lit area.

"How'd you like the ride?" he said with a grin. "Holy shit," is all I could manage.

We walked about a mile into the tunnel, through running water, me in my suit and tie; hardhat and boots. I looked like an idiot. Water was dripping on us from the ceiling and soon we were well away from the staging area with only the lights on our hats showing the way. It was eerie and unnerving. Eventually we rounded a bend and bright lights appeared ahead. "There's the leak," he said, "It's right behind the TBM (tunnel boring machine). Can you stop it?"

I couldn't believe my eyes. The "leak" was a stream of water a foot in diameter shooting straight out of the wall and splashing against the opposite wall, which was thirty feet away. The force was enormous!

"No problem," I said, parroting Terry.

"How?" he asked.

"I'll let you know after I consult with my partner," I said.

When I left the superintendent I called Terry on my new cell phone. (They'd just been invented. It was as big as my shoe.) I told Terry about the massive leak and he said, "No problem." As it turned out we didn't get that job but if we had, I learned from later jobs, it would have been no problem.

Past mistakes had taught me how to manage Green Mountain from the business side.

First and foremost, I needed to get on good terms with a banker. We were lucky. My banker asked *me* for a loan. He called me on his cell phone and said, "Jim, I've got troubles, can you give me a loan?" I said, "'Harold*, get off your cell phone. Those things are like radio transmitters. Anybody can listen in. Call me on a hard line." (It's against the law for bankers to borrow money from their customers.) A few minutes later he called. "You remember when I got you the bank credit card, bending a rule of two?" he said.

"Of course."

"Will you meet me at the bank's teller window and take $5,000 cash out on it?"

"Of course."

I never asked why he needed the money and didn't care. I was now on very good terms with a banker. (It took him three years to pay me back. He neglected to pay any interest. All the better.)

Next, I would keep fixed overhead to an absolute minimum, which meant the fewer employees the better. When possible, Green Mountain subcontracts deliveries, accounting, R & D, technical representation, testing, warehousing and whatever else we can. We use independent, commission only, sales reps whenever possible. We do not have a fancy office. Inventory is scrupulously controlled.

Lastly, I determined to keep suppliers happy and wanting to do business with us. I'd beat down their prices, of course, but not too much. They needed to make a decent profit on us so they'd jump, when necessary, to support us. We negotiated extended terms, 2% 15, and net

45, strictly adhering to them even if it meant borrowing from the bank. (No problem–see above.) Suppliers, I'd learned, are more important than customers, employees or stockholders.

After we'd been in business for five years and felt confident in the viability of the company, Barbara and I moved Green Mountain from Chicago to North Carolina. Although Chicago is a great city, and my heart will always be there, there were five good reasons to re-locate: November, December, January, February and March. And the traffic, of course.

In the rural mountains of North Carolina we found gold in the persons of Linda Jones, Office Manager, and Bill Phillips, Sales and Marketing. Smarter, more decent, more reliable people cannot be found, anywhere.

And we went international in our sales efforts. As I write this, our biggest customer is in the Middle East. Today we do business in thirty foreign countries and between Bill and I we've been to all of them. Greece is not my favorite. The people are grouchy, but their food is the best in the world, except for Singapore's. I've been to Singapore twice; it's my favorite, with caveats. You learn about their stringent laws before you get there. About an hour out the flight attendants issue Customs Declaration forms. At the top of the form, in red letters, it says: "If you bring illegal drugs into Singapore you will be executed." And they're not kidding. Takes about three days. Spit on the sidewalk: $300. Chew gum: $500. Litter: $500 and maybe a whack or two with a cane.

My customer, Mr. Eddie Tan, told me another Singapore law. "If you pinch a stewardess, and she reports you, they will arrest you when you land and give you three whacks with a cane. Happens to Japanese businessmen all the time." Until then the thought of pinching a stewardess never crossed my mind. Now I can't see one without thinking of it.

Bill's favorite country is Switzerland; he's been there often. For three years in a row our biggest customer was in Seoul, Korea. Next, a customer in Taipei, Taiwan took first place. Then along came Australia, mate. International business is fun and helps to even out the ups and downs of our domestic economy. We can be competitive anywhere in the world. Ocean freight is cheap.

Some of our prestigious projects include stopping water leaks in

The White House, stabilizing soils for NASA at Cape Kennedy, and stopping water leaks in the Athens, Greece subway tunnel extension built in preparation for the 2004 Olympics. Green Mountain was, and remains, a fun way to make a living.

Circa 1997 Jim, Jr. was working at Green Mountain and took a call from a golf course superintendent, Tim Johnson, who was consulting on the construction of a new Fazio designed course. It was a very private facility for the crème de la crème of Minneapolis society. The gorgeous property was purchased from the Cowles family of the media empire. (See chapter on Morley Ballantine later. Life is full of interconnectedness.) Tim said he'd heard about one of our soil stabilizers and wondered if it could be used in the base of sand traps in lieu of fabric liners. He told Jim he'd used fabrics before and knew they would eventually fail. Jim told him our product should work fine and after some experimenting and formula tweaking it did. We applied for a patent and we wound up in the golf course business. Terry and I formed Klingstone, Inc. for that purpose. A few years later I bought Terry's stock in Klingstone. (Terry is not interested in golf and is the better man for it.)

A year or so later Old Colonial Williamsburg in Virginia called and asked if we could bind their pea gravel trails together to make them ADA (Americans with Disabilities Act) compliant. Jim, Jr. went to Virginia and showed them that we could, using a juiced up formula from one used in the sand traps. Later my son, Zack (16) and his buddy Cassidy (15), and I did a large demo at Williamsburg. Klingstone Paths, LLC was born ushering us into the landscape business. We have done pathways at Thomas Jefferson's Monticello, James Madison's Montpelier, the Miami International Airport, Clemson University and on and on. We are fortunate. Our businesses are not boring.

CHAPTER 25

On Being A Fireman

By Carpenter Joyce

Ada has been on my case for years to write down the stories trapped in my mind and occasionally told to certain audiences at select times. It may seem that my stories are presented at scheduled times and places but that's not so. I never plan to relate my experiences; they just flow based on the audience and setting. I'm actually quite guarded.

I enjoy "storying" and I think I'm fairly good at it but I'm also really concerned about what a listener might think of the institution that I love so much, The Chicago Fire Department. My stories are much like those of other firefighters who worked in the same era under similar circumstances. The stories are best told by those who experience them. Even though we've heard each other's tales over and over, they get better and better as the years go by. In a neighborhood saloon with a few jars in us the stories flow, and they are great, but if a stranger attempts to sit in an unspoken warning goes up and the conversation takes a quick turn.

Many of our stories might seem to be pushing the envelope of legalities and civility, but that is only to the untrained ear. A veteran firefighter's face will light up with the mention of a few key terms or phrases. They seem to know where the story is going in the introduction long before the body is discussed and can often predict the denouement knowing which battalion, company or shift is being discussed.

There are a few of us who run into each other fairly often and it doesn't take much to trigger a story. I know what's coming when a friend might say, "Frank, tell us that one about the purchase of a new refrigerator for Engine Company 126." Frank will then go into a detailed setup outlining the characters involved, their quirks and habits and how each one contributed to the story. By the time he gets to the conclusion we are roaring. I could tell the story but it wouldn't be one tenth as good as Franks. Besides it's his story and it's for firemen only.

"Jerry, tell us about the three piece band riding on Squad 3 on New Years Eve." "How about the guy who lived in the firehouse and had a tuxedo hanging on a nail next to his bunk." He was a fireman and a "toastmaster" on his day off.

Rules and regulations are a big part of being on the fire department and there were those who studied them, some memorized them, and were ready to implement them during one of those rare circumstances that you may actually want to follow them. Most of us, however, were often pushing against the margins of the rulebook; that's what made many of the incidents so funny. But I don't want any reader to think less of the Chicago Fire Department based on a few very funny stories that went beyond the margins and fell off the page. That's why I'll not tell them here. Meet me in a bar some day and maybe you can pry some of them out of me. I enjoy Jack and ginger.

Some stories of our teen years in the guys in the gang went beyond the intent of the law and certainly caused me some concern about what family, friends and readers might think of my (our) moral compasses. Please give us the benefit of the doubt – stupid decisions made by unthinking teens and some "young adults" with no malice intended and consequences not yet firmly established in our lexicon. We've all evolved into law-abiding and contributing adults – essentially good people.

The same holds true with members of the Fire Department. I remember over-hearing a conversation between a frustrated Division Marshal and the salty old Chief of Personnel. The Division Marshal was venting on a particularly egregious violation of the Rules and Regulations by a couple of firemen. He asked "What could those guys be thinking of when they made that decision?!" The old chief said, "You mustn't forget that we don't hire a bunch of accountants to do this job. Most of the firemen are half nuts to start with, but tell those two guys that a kid is trapped behind that brick wall and they'll ram it with their heads 'til they find him." That pretty well sums it up. We're proud to be members of such a giving, self-sacrificing way of life.

I saw a lot of crazy things over thirty-nine years, some horrid things, happy things and sad things but overall I couldn't have made a better choice in my life's work. While on the Department I was fortunate to complete my college education, earn a Masters degree and attend Harvard for a month long program. Not bad for a fireman's kid and a fireman's grandson. (My Grandfather, Thomas Garry, died as a result of the Stockyard Fire of 1934. I wasn't lucky enough to meet him.) I loved my time on the job and look back on it with fond memories and hope to live long enough to tell my stories to my grandkids – in person.

CHAPTER 26
Foreign Travels

Carpenter Joyce and I traveled to foreign lands over a twenty-year period. It was mostly my businesses, Green Mountain and Klingstone, which prompted the trips, often aided by the United States Department of Commerce, International Trade Division. This agency effectively and efficiently promotes exports of U.S. manufactured products through special sections in our embassies. (Eddie Christie put me onto it.)

We have been to: Australia, Singapore, Bangkok and Phu Ket in Thailand, Hong Kong, Seoul, Costa Rica, Mexico, Ireland and Greece. Here's Carpenter on Greece.

"Selected Notes from Greek Trip in 1999"
by Carpenter Joyce
Hotel Herondion, Athens, at foot of the Acropolis

Friday, March 19
Dimitri Mantzakis (Ada's customer), Jim and me in one car, Stephanos and Helen in trail car to "starting point" for famous Greek coffee then off to Peleponese (southern region of Greece). Cold, rainy day. Mountainous area, peaks 6000 feet above sea level. Rockies have 50 peaks over 14,000 ft. but Colorado is at least 5,000 ft. above sea level to begin with. Some Peloponese peaks are 9,000 feet.

Town of Kastri. Stopped at Cave of the Lakes–huge cave with 13 ponds inside. Walked one mile into cave, which was discovered by a shepherd who was chasing a fox away from his flock or herd. Checked into Little Mount Helmos Hotel with 15 rooms, $10.00 U.S. per night. Homey but basic when compared to Courtyard by Marriott. Town of Kassri, pop. 500, quaint and much like pre-WWII town, a true village.

Traditional Greek lunch at 3:30 p.m. in nice ski town of Kalavrita–included mousaka, spinach pie, cheese pie, salad, pork, lamb and beef–fantastic! Went to ancient monastery of Agia Lavra and witnessed vespers. Bearded monks amongst ancient icons chanting in semi-darkness. Sent shivers down spine. One of the most historic monasteries, approx. 961 A.D. site of "Monument of 1821," year that Greeks finally drive out the Turks and remains a national holiday commemorating a major time in modern green history. Greece has suffered a long history of invasion and domination. Also the scene of mass murder of monks, pushed off the cliff, one at a time, by Nazi troops, on December 8, 1943. Peering over cliff will make you gasp.

Greek Orthodox Church is not an offshoot of Roman Catholic Church, Dimitri said. It always was Greek Orthodox since conversion to Christianity by St. Paul (we all recall that Paul came after Christ and was not an apostle–converted when knocked off his horse on the road to Damascus and set about conversion of Greece). Prior to this Greeks worshipped 12 mythical gods–Zeus, Athena, Aphrodities, etc., etc. Patriarch is leader of Greek Church which is headquartered in Istanbul, strangely, considering the enmity 'tween Turks and Greeks.

I digress. A most amazing witness to ancient Greek rite. Helen was not allowed in the monastery because she was wearing a pants suit and not a dress! A monk chased after her yelling in a panic, "Stop!"

This excursion in mountains with narrow turning roads was complete with occasional blocked roads from falling rocks and herds of sheep complete with shepherd and staff. Truly a trip back in time of hundreds, thousands, of years. It's called irony, although I personally prefer juxtaposition, to witness the ancient shepherd and dog as Dimitri negotiated hairpin, cliffhanging turns with a cigarette in hand (four packs a day) ever-ringing cell phone in ear and five-speed manual transmission. "Special tires and upgraded suspension system," he stated.

Walked into town for dinner; Dimitri ordered and we ate it all–delicious and without brown gravy like every Greek diner in Chicago. In fact, we saw plenty of olive trees but no brown gravy trees. Everybody went to bed early, too much climbing. Well, not everybody. J & J stopped at six stool hotel bar until 0200 hours, mountain time.

Sunday, March 21

Departed Kastri and visited the monastery in the rock, Mega Spelion. Incredible sight, monastery complex carved out of the side of a sheer cliff. Literally a whole complex of caves and carvings where monks lived in cells and prayed for hours in isolation. Circa 362 A.D. Now only 15 monks left after thousands were there since Hector was a pup. Monks wore long grey beards and black vestments. Caves full of icons and relics of saints in glass cases–bones, fingers, skeletons, etc. Some were for sale. Won't repeat what Jim said.

Stopped in middle of nowhere and observed a most unusual sight. Water coming out of the ground without explanation, trees in water are a thousand years old. Replete with open-air fish market, restaurants and vendors. No paved roads in this area. Contemplating the history of what we were observing was overwhelming, causing nighttime short circuits in the brain resulting in a cocktail hour discussion that only the ancients could appreciate. These mountain scenes are like settings from a Frederico Fellini movie!

Mountain goats observed negotiating steep cliffs as they changed quarters to lusher grazing areas. Amazing skill. Lesson learned–food chain–goats grow feta cheese.

Lunch in village of white water streams and falls. Boarded funicular train (also called gear train), narrow gauge, little cars going up and down 5,000 foot slope on cables and rails counter-balanced by the trains going the opposite way–genius. Beautiful journey ended in seaside town of Diakofto. Boarded train in Zahlorou.

Interstate highway–no speed limits in Greece only "suggested" speed. No shit. Dimitri, chain smoking, managed 102 mph (not kph) while on phone. Parked on shoulder. We flipped fence and entered underground ancient caves carved out of rocks. This is known as site of first civilization, 10,500 years ago, according to Dimitri.

Saint Paul visited Corinth in 50 A.D. Ancient City of Corinth has an Acropolis. Every major settlement in ancient times built a fortress on its highest peak called Acropolis. It served as place of worship as well as a place of refuge during invasions. Climbed to Corinth Acropolis and visited ancient city ruins. We could make out homes, shops and a building with baths. "World's first cathouse," according to Dimitri.

Corinthian canal–incredible sight–two miles long, 220 feet high. Picture a tee cut into a rock of the above mentioned dimensions! Carved through this part of Greece to allow ships to cut travel time by days or weeks when going to the Aegean Sea from the Ionian Sea. Begun by Emperor Nero in 67 B.C. but he took a leave of absence and not completed until 1891. Ships towed through by tugs and cross *over* one bridge. Narrow automobile bridge is lowered to the bottom of the canal as ship passes through. Rode through the canal on pilot boat to observe damaged rock in anticipation of Green Mountain getting the contract for repair.

Day Five (Maybe)

Three days of intensive business calls with major players in engineering circles of Greek infrastructure. These visits began as International Business 202 and ended up in American Embassy on Wednesday afternoon, ancient time, with the awarding of a Masters Degree in "How it's done" east of the Bay of Fundy.

Monday, March 22

Met "The Frenchman," Mr. Y. Mille, now in charge of Athens subway extension. He is an imposing figure; five years in Hong Kong tunnel, five in Cairo, couldn't join us for dinner because he was going to the theater that night to see the animated "Mickey Mouse" that all of France is apparently infatuated with. The movie is the only thing Mickey about "The Frenchman." He is a man who gets things done and answered our question of why foreigners come to Greece to run the major projects. "Greeks, too much time spent on coffee, cigarettes, lunch and holidays." Likeable guy our age.

Tuesday, March 23

National telecommunications company–public monopoly phone company. Met Eva and her boss to discuss future project of sealing leaks in 150,000 phone junction vaults. Dimitri worked hard on securing this business relationship. Jim excited. Very interesting. Met for dinner that night with Eva and her boss who, we found out later, doubles as her husband—timid fellow—Johnis (my spelling) (in Greek means Paddy Boy).

Dinner that night was in Homeric restaurant in downtown Athens. This restaurant serves food eaten by ancient Greeks. Delicious pork tenderloins stuffed with plums, humus, pureed peas, leeks—outstanding.

Wednesday March 24

Climbed Athens Acropolis and St. Paul's rock next door. Slippery. Parthenon on same mountain top. Incredible sight, wonder how ancient Greeks designed and built without cranes, circular saws and laser beams.

Back to Embassy. Warned us to stay off the streets tonight because bombings and demonstrations about to begin over Kosovo. We weren't scared but we did avoid the demonstrations, and got bombed at the hotel bar. Next day home.

"More Foreign Travels"
by Ada Joyce

A few brief observations of other countries using Carpenter's pithy style.

Australia: Beautiful, fascinating country but a long way to go (24 hours in *air* from Asheville to Cairns) to experience culture so close to ours. People friendly "We love Yanks." England spawned Australia—food just okay. Australia is as big as the continental U.S. Tried kangaroo. Tastes like old chickens. Great Barrier Reef can be seen from outer space. Driving on left is unnatural/terrifying. I damned near killed us twice. TV weather reports were very brief: Tomorrow will be "fine." No details.

Best thing: Seeing my son, Walter, who joined us from Solomon Islands where he's in the Peace Corp. (Talk about proud of a son!)

Singapore: Repeat! Don't pinch the stewardess! Super clean and safe. Fabulous food. Fabulous weather. People not unfriendly.

Bangkok, Thailand: Buddha statues *everywhere*. When you meet someone, whether you know them or not, put hands together in front of chest, as in prayer. Bow. Great custom. Tom Doughton (you'll meet him later) with us. He bought clothes from Indian tailor who came to hotel room. Tom stripped to underpants. Measured top to bottom. Ordered suits, overcoat, shirts from sample fabrics. Tailor delivers next evening on his moped. Clothes fit perfectly. Tom happy. Tailor's name was Nit.

Phu Ket, Thailand: Seaside town. Beautiful beaches. Many Europeans topless, we noticed. Went sailing with Barbara's sister, Cheryl Beck and husband, Jim, who were circumnavigating globe in their 41-foot sailboat, "Ptarmigan." When we left the harbor, porpoises followed on both sides of boat. At nightfall dropped anchor, took dinghy to shore to Beck's favorite "restaurant." No doors, no walls, thatched roof, one long table, no menu. Food kept coming. All agree best meal we ever ate. Period.

Hong Kong: From hotel room on harbor, 19th floor, saw boats of every description: "water bugs" to carry workers from ships to shore and back, luxury ocean liners, harbor ferries, house boats, Naval war ships from many countries, container ships the size of small mountains, pleasure craft both sail and power. People not friendly. Chinese food. Took walk by harbor. Heard sound of thousand birds. Did not see birds. Sound got louder and louder as we walked. World's biggest aviary? No! Rounded corner of big building. A thousand women on benches, walls, steps, and grass chirping at each other. Philippine domestics of Hong Kong millionaires. They all get same day off.

Customer Alex Cheung and wife took us to dinner. Two men from kitchen carried big glob of dough between them. Started twisting—round and round while backing away from each other. Then twirled like jump rope. The great glob was now twenty feet of individual strands. Chinese noodles. Very clever.

Seoul: Poster city for traffic jams. No downtown. Thirty story apartments to infinity. Food was interesting, I say. Carpenter hated it. People border on surly.

Costa Rica: Beautiful country, mountainous jungles but an armed camp. San Jose capital with iron bars on windows and doors, concertina wire on walls. Same in rural including churches. Uzi armed guards all over—even grocery stores. Drove rental car 3 hours to grand golf resort. From balcony watched Japanese golfers drive carts onto greens. Left ruts. Sign on beach: "Do not be here at night. You might be killed."

Rented taxi to see active volcano. Driver Francisco spoke *poquito Ingles.* Stop for lunch. We invite him to join us. Not the usual. Very grateful. Order ice-cold beers. He took swig, said, "This dee LEE ceeous!" I've been saying it ever since.

Mexico City: Fresh, outstanding food. Never saw taco or burrito. Friendly, happy people. Surprise. Few spoke English by comparison to other countries. Felt safe walking streets. Biggest city in world. Smog free on weekends. Traffic okay. Center of city sinking, including cathedral. I explain "Mountain Grout" can stop. Still waiting for order.

Cancun: Miami Beach.

Ireland: 79th Street in 1950s. We recognize faces from old neighborhood. Deals Griffin tends bar, Pat Carroll is a torch singer. Father Mollahan is a waiter. Jim Brennan's a golf pro. Picture taken with James Joyce statue in Dublin. (Wouldn't he say "shite and onions!" Us calling ourselves writers next to him?) In James Joyce museum there's a photo of him age 20. He looks exactly like Carpenter's brother, Tom. As he aged, James, that is, was the spitten' image of my dad. Eerie–our genes.

Checking into hotel, Dublin, clerk saw names. "You don't mean it! Thars two of ye?" Irish culture inclusive. On the ten spot was Joyce, the atheist. On the fiver was Mother McAuley, the saint.

Visited "Joyce Country" near Galway. Bleak landscape. Joyce name everywhere on stores and buildings. Saw Galway Bay where ancestors fished for a living. More left side driving. Carpenter about killed us, twice. Plus he's a speeder. He claims he didn't know speed limits were posted in kph not mph. Idiot. Thank God he doesn't smoke or own a cell phone.

Charming country. People welcoming. Green, green fields, friendly pubs, soft rain, torrential rain, soft breezes, wild winds, bland food, beautiful brogues. Home, we were.

Business meeting at big corporate guy's office. We barely sat when Carpenter Jimmy tells joke. "Mike," he says, like they're old pals, "When an Irishman gets the Alzheimer's what's the last thing he forgets?" Mike doesn't know. "The grudge," says Jim. Mike roars.

Taxi in Dublin. Driver says, "Yer from Chicago? Sure 'n me dotter lives in Chicago! Married a fireman." They lived two blocks from Jim.

People Along the Way

———————— ⚭ ————————

CHAPTER 27

Palmer

Palmer Haines was an enthusiastic liver of life. He had a degree in engineering but was unlike any engineer I ever met. His personality was engaging and his curiosity about all things made him a joy to be with. His favorite expression was, "That's hot shit!" He was also unlike any of my friends from the south side of Chicago. He liked fast cars, fast women, Broadway shows and scuba diving.

Palmer was honest to a fault, generous and kind. His incredible smile and blue eyes embraced you. His laugh made you laugh. No one who ever met Palmer Haines forgot him. We became buddies at Ft. Rucker, Alabama in 1965 where we were classmates in the U.S. Army Aviation School. We lived in the same BOQ (Bachelor Officers Quarters), a cluster of two-story, motel-like buildings with large grassy areas between them. It was a nice setup, not something you'd expect from the Army. In the BOQ across the grass from us lived another student pilot who had a Doberman Pinscher. When he returned from the flight line in the late afternoon he'd let the dog out to roam freely around the area.

One afternoon Palmer and I were walking to our BOQ and Palmer saw the dog trotting next to a row of hedges about one hundred yards away. Palmer loved dogs and this was the first time he'd seen the Doberman. He handed me his helmet which we carried in clothe bags, "Hold this," he said, "I'm gonna go play with the Dobie."

He walked to the middle of the grassy area and called out, "Here puppy! Com'ere, puppy!" The dog's ears shot forward, he saw Palmer and came running. "Good boy!" said Palmer. "You want to play? Come on!"

When the dog got close, Palmer put his arms out to give it a roughhouse hug. When the dog saw this, his running became a charge.

He growled, bared his teeth and lunged at Palmer's head. Palmer ducked and side stepped as the dog went over his shoulder snapping at his ear. The Doberman landed, whirled around and got ready to lunge again.

Palmer had good reflexes and was powerfully built with broad shoulders, muscular arms and no fat. He'd wrestled in college. As the dog left the ground Palmer said, "You son of a bitch!" and punched it, hard, on the nose. It came to a stop in mid-air and let out a, "Yelp!"

The dog lay on the grass for a few seconds, staggered to its feet, shook its head and weaved its way back to the BOQ.

Palmer was full of remorse for punching the dog. "That's the only time in my life I ever hurt an animal," he said, "All I wanted to do was play with him." When we told the story at the mess hall that night we learned that the Dobbie had snapped at other guys and two days later he bit one. Palmer felt better and the dog was escorted from the fort.

Palmer was a graduate of The United States Military Academy at West Point. Most graduates of The Point were proud as the dickens of their accomplishment, but Palmer hated the place. When we'd meet girls on our travels one of the first questions asked was "Where did you go to school?" Palmer always replied, "I didn't go to college, I went to prison."

But he did make a name for himself at The Academy. At the beginning of his fourth year the popular folk singing group, "Peter, Paul and Mary," performed at the school. When Palmer and two of his friends arrived, all seats were taken so they waited at the back of the auditorium until just before the concert began. They were wearing Russian Cossack hats. They'd been drinking. As Peter, Paul and Mary began to sing, Palmer and his buddies goose stepped up to the stage and sat on the floor in front of the dignitaries, which included the school's Commandant, General William Westmorland. For that stunt Palmer spent his entire last year at West Point "in confinement;" all privileges revoked. The performance, for many years after, came to be known as the "Peter, Paul and Palmer" concert.

A few days after Palmer was born in Texas, his dad, an Army officer, was shipped out. World War II had begun. Palmer's mom had always regretted that Palmer had not been baptized. While we were in flight school, she asked her son to please have it done for her. She knew he was headed for Vietnam.

Palmer knew nothing about religion. "I thought it was for simple-minded people," he said. But he loved his mother, so he found a chaplain and took a few lessons in the Christian faith. He could now be baptized, but the chaplain said he needed two witnesses. Palmer asked our classmate Ray Alexander, a Catholic, to be one of them and me to be the other. Ray and I had to stifle smiles when the water was poured on Palmer's head but we got through it and are proud to say, to this day, that we are Palmer Haines's godparents.

After flight school Palmer was sent to Vietnam. He was a Birddog pilot assigned to a Marine Corp unit. Birddogs are small, single engine propeller driven airplanes used as aerial observers. He spent his days flying high above battlefields directing artillery and attack aircraft. At night he hung around with the Marines.

One evening he learned that a Marine squad was going on a reconnaissance patrol. This meant that after nightfall they would leave the safety of their compound and wander around in the dark attempting to locate, surprise and kill the enemy. This sounded like fun to Palmer so he went to the Marine commander and asked if he could join the squad.

"Let me get this straight, Haines," the commander said, "You want to spend the night in Injun Country?'

"Yes, sir."

"When you die, Haines, I want it to be with your ass in one of my airplanes. Permission denied." He then said something about pilots being too valuable to be wandering around in the dark.

Flying aerial observation was boring for Palmer because he couldn't get into the fight; he directed others. When his tour was over, he returned to the States and requested to be sent to helicopter transition school. He wanted to return to Vietnam flying a gunship. For whatever reason, the Army denied his request so he quit the Army and joined the Marines. The Marines happily sent him to jet fighter school and he returned to Vietnam in the attack craft, the A-10. He loved it. "I'm in the thick of it now, Jim," he wrote "I feel like I'm finally serving my country."

While Palmer and I were in Vietnam, his dad, now a four star general, was made the Army's Vice Chief of Staff. He and Mrs. Haines lived in a grand house on General's Row at Fort Belvoir, VA, not far from the Pentagon. After Palmer and I returned from Vietnam, he invited me and two girls from Chicago that I knew to stay at his parent's house over New Years Eve. One of the girls was Pat Carroll, Tommy's sister.

Army living is formal and sophisticated at the general officers' level. Housekeepers, butlers, waiters, drivers and cooks are provided in the form of Army personnel. Our first night we had dinner with General and Mrs. Haines. Mrs. Haines sat one end of the table, closest to the kitchen, and the General at the other. When we were seated Mrs. Haines rang a little bell and the first course appeared, served by two sergeants in dress blues. When we were done with that course, she rang the bell again and these dishes were cleared and the next course appeared. This procedure was repeated through the dessert. The dinner conversation, steered by General Haines, with four stars on his epaulets, was subdued, polite and informative. The general, it seemed to us, knew everything about world affairs. The two girls and I were blown away by the grandness of it all.

The next night the Haines's had another engagement, leaving the four of us for dinner. Palmer was the senior member of the group so he was assigned the bell. When we got to our places, a sergeant formally pulled Palmer's chair out for him. Palmer missed the chair on purpose and fell to the floor. He got up howling with laughter and proposed an off-color toast. Decorum further deteriorated from there.

The sergeants were at first uncomfortable with this destruction of protocol but Palmer put them at ease. "Join us for dinner and drinks at the table, men," he said, "And that's an order." Palmer was a captain, outranking them, so they had no choice. To further put them at ease he said, "And don't worry. I won't tell my dad; he'd kill me." We had a ball.

After my three years commitment was up I left the Army and was working for GDC. One night Palmer called just to chat. He was stationed at Cherry Point, NC. I happened to mention that we were having a large gathering of salespeople at Lou Herring's resort near Melbourne the following weekend. "How would you like a private air show?" he asked.

"What do you mean?"

"I can borrow a fighter and come down and do some aerobatics for you," he said. I thought it was the coolest idea I'd ever heard and we made arrangements.

We all gathered on the beach at the appointed time and looked north to see a dot on the horizon with smoke coming out behind it. It was Palmer flying low level over the ocean. Within moments he was upon us and way too close to shore. Right in front of us he pulled back on the stick and the plane went straight up. The noise was phenomenal. The earth shook. He did barrel rolls, inside loops, outside loops and other fancy maneuvers that only a jet can do. This was better than hot shit. When he finished the show he landed at Patrick AFB just up the beach next to Cape Kennedy. He joined us for the party that night.

When Palmer left the armed services he got a job as a pilot with Delta Air Lines. By this time he was married to Robin, an admiral's daughter and former Miss Hawaii. They had three children, Lark, Lance, and April Lee. One summer the family went camping in the mountains near Ouray, Colorado. As they were setting up camp Palmer thought April Lee, they called her Lee Lee, was with Robin. Robin thought she was with Palmer. Two-year-old Lee Lee was nowhere in sight.

There was a rushing mountain stream near the campsite. Palmer ran to it yelling his daughter's name. Still no sign of her. He jumped in the water and ran downstream stumbling and falling. He went about a mile until he found her. As he made his way back up the stream carrying his dead daughter, Palmer Haines began to lose his mind. As the years went by, his marriage crumbled; he was placed on medical leave by Delta. Depression and anxiety overwhelmed him. He was hospitalized. They called it a nervous breakdown.

These horrors would have destroyed many people, but they did not destroy Palmer. When he was emotionally stabilized, he got his Texas real estate license and started selling ranches. He was very successful and bought one himself. He wrote a sports column for the Denton, Texas newspaper. He got exclusive interviews with the famous pitcher, Nolan Ryan of the Texas Rangers, and with the little known part owner of the team, George Bush.

All the while Palmer's brain was healing. He was smart enough to stay close to his doctors, scrupulously following their orders. When he, and they, felt he was ready, Delta reinstated him. Many years later he retired; his last position as a captain on the L-1011 jumbo jet flying the plumb route from Los Angeles to Honolulu.

He also got his wonderful sense of humor back. When he was flying the 727, he had a layover at O'Hare and decided to stay at our house. Barbara and I hadn't seen him in a couple of years and we had a great night catching up. The next morning I took him to the airport. On the way we stopped at a 7-11 for coffee. When we walked in the door all eyes were upon him. No one had seen an airline captain, in uniform, in the 7-11 before and Palmer was movie star handsome. He, of course, noticed this and came to attention with full military bearing. With eyes straightforward, he marched down the main aisle of the 7-11 like a one man parade. At the end of the aisle he halted. Heels together. Feet at a forty-five degree angle. He did a smart left face and marched to the coffee machine. He prepared his coffee, did a perfect about face, marched to the check out-counter, paid, and marched out the door. I was watching the people; their mouths agape. When we got back in the car we cracked up. "Did you see the look on their faces!" he howled.

Palmer was always funny, much of his humor directed at haughty people, be they military or civilian. During flight school we ate three meals a day at the mess hall. The food was just fine. Breakfast and lunches were often rushed but suppers were relaxed. One night the place was crowded and Palmer and I had to sit next to two fellow students we normally avoided. They were from extraordinarily wealthy families and let that be known whether anybody wanted to hear it or not.

As Palmer and I sat down, they began asking each other about their favorite foods. This was a competition to out-snob each other, with a dual purpose of letting Palmer and I know that we were, by comparison to them, culinary cretins.

Student One said, "I really enjoy escargot as an appetizer."

Two said, "That's ok but I think vichyssoise is the best way to start a fine meal."

One said, "Crème bruile is a good way to end it along with espresso."

Two said, "At our house the cook prepares cherries jubilee."

That did it for Palmer.

"Jim," he said, "Do you know what I really like?"

"What, Palmer?"

"Mashed potatoes and gravy."

"Me, too," I said, "but a nice green bean casserole is my favorite."

"Do you like milk?" he asked.

"I love it, especially with cookies."

"How about toast? Do you like toast?"

One and Two got up to leave, in a huff, and Palmer asked them if they liked hot dogs and beans. As they rapidly walked away he yelled across the crowd, "How about peanut butter and jelly!"

The day after his wedding in Texas to Pam, his second wife and soul mate, I drove him to DFW. As we came into the airport the road paralleled a runway where a giant jet, like the kind he was then flying, was taking off. "Palmer," I said, "How the hell do those things get off the ground?!" Without hesitation he said, "I have no idea."

When Palmer retired from Delta he and Pam moved to their ranch in the magnificent Texas Hill Country, but total retirement was not for him. He continued selling ranches, flying his prospects around the state in his own plane. He and Pam traveled regularly to Honduras with their Episcopal Church to dig deep-water wells in rural areas. By now Palmer was taking his religion very seriously.

One morning Palmer took off from Angel Fire, NM, headed for Austin in a prospect's airplane, a twin engine Cessna 421Q, with the prospects aboard. Well into the flight he had engine trouble and declared an emergency. He could not reach an alternate airport and the plane went into trees. Palmer and one of the two passengers perished.

Palmer was buried on his ranch. Friends from all over the country were there. One of the speakers accurately described Palmer by saying it was wonderful when Palmer started having grandchildren, "He finally had people his own age to play with." He had seven pallbearers, one each from: the Marines; Delta Airlines; West Point; a fellow Christian Missionary; a fellow member of a Texas horse club, a high school friend and me, from the Army. At Pam's request we wore cowboy boots, new blue jeans and crisply starched long sleeve shirts. Cowboy dress up. From the small Episcopal Church, which sat alone on a mesa, we put Palmer's casket into the back of an SUV. On the way to the ranch through rugged countryside the long funeral procession forded three streams – water halfway up the hubcaps. We were in Texas.

A Marine honor guard was there. One of them slowly walked up the hill above the grave. He turned around, raised a bugle to his lips and began *Taps*, the plaintive, heart wrenchingly beautiful melody reserved for the special among us. In the gathering below were some of Palmer's old war buddies, standing at attention and weeping without shame. *Requiescat in pace*, dear Palmer.

Because Palmer's personality was so bubbly and his laughter so infectious I did not realize, until I wrote this, that he was probably the most courageous man I've ever known.

CHAPTER 28

TOM

"Thanks for taking me to the emergency room last night, Jim," Tom said, stopping the conversation. I didn't know where he was going with this so I said he was welcome and was glad he was okay. This was at the Breakfast Club, which met at Clyde's Restaurant in Waynesville, NC (pop.9200). It was an unofficial club but everybody knew you could not sit at the table unless invited by members who were some of the town's important people. There was a banker, a stock trader, a concrete executive, assorted business owners and the district attorney. All were Republicans except the district attorney.

The banker died of old age; the district attorney of a sudden heart attack. My buddy, Tom Doughton, a retired banker himself, and I were invited to join. We did so with reservations.

Republicans, Tom and I believed, are, as a group, up tight, tight fisted, holier-than-thou, humorless, sanctimonious and self-righteous. We'd heard they often suffer from constipation, which we believed was a symptomatic condition mirroring their view of life. In case you are wondering, Tom and I are Democrats.

As individuals we liked most of the members of the Breakfast Club, but when they got together they could be difficult to be around. Inevitably, someone would mention the federal government and that would get them started on a litany of its sins: Social programs, foreign aid, the control of automatic weapons, protecting the environment, labor unions, all things minority and, of course, taxes of any kind. Plus that bullshit about global warming. They would soon be frothing at the mouth. Tom and I would eat our breakfast in silence.

It was during a particularly heated tirade about border security that Tom mentioned the hospital visit. The Republicans quit talking and all eyes turned to him. "What happened?" they asked with genuine concern. With a straight face he said, "I took a Viagra last night, and my erection lasted more than four hours. I called Jim to take me to the emergency room."

Tom was my best buddy in Waynesville. (Ironically, Tom and Palmer were classmates at West Point, although they never met. Tom dropped out after the first year.) Tom's and my relationship started as banker to client, but soon became less formal, occasionally socializing with our wives and other couples. When Tom retired from the bank I invited him to go on a business trip with me and Carpenter to Singapore and Thailand. When I got to Singapore work would begin (a trade show) so Tom decided to go two days before me to sightsee and have breakfast with the orangutans at the Singapore zoo. Somebody told him about it. "That's sounds neat," he said.

"How was breakfast?" I asked when I got to the hotel.

"A rip-off," he said. "I thought we'd be sitting at the same table but a glass wall separated the people from the gorillas. And god are they disgusting!"

"Did they crap all over their cage?"

"Naw, they were wearing diapers. It was a rip-off."

It was on that trip that we bonded as friends and over the years took many other trips together.

Tom was 6'3", 220 pounds of sinew and muscle with big, strong hands and a face like a Great Dane, strong, alert, don't-even-think-about-messing-with-me. His voice was unforgettable – deep bass, sonorous, seductive.

Other than our Democratic upbringing, our backgrounds were dissimilar. He was raised Methodist in the tiny town of Sparta, NC (pop.1700). Growing up he milked cows to earn spending money. In high school he was a superior athlete in all sports including boxing. I was mediocre. He was a math whiz; I was an English major. His accent said, "Southern." Mine said "Yankee." But we grew to love each other - hell, we could read each other's minds.

One of the interesting parts of our friendship is that we always agreed on our assessment of other people. We both knew hundreds of people in Waynesville, men, women and children, and our opinions of them never varied. Thumbs up or thumbs down, we either liked them or we didn't.

Our houses were near the Waynesville Country Club golf course and in the mornings we would walk our dogs across it. We both had two. His were purebred boxers, Sadie and Molly, and mine were mutts, Chelli and Darby. During our walks Tom and I talked freely and intimately about our fears, guilt's, past mistakes, yearnings, frustrations, finances and families. One morning we discussed each other's children; which ones we liked the best and which ones the least, and why. He had three girls; I had four boys. And we talked about death and dying: "I want to be buried next to my mama," he said more than once. I had decided on cremation.

An important part of our friendship was betting. We had a bet on every football game played by NC State and the Carolina Panthers (his teams) and on every Notre Dame and Chicago Bears games (mine). One year when Michael Jordan was still playing we bet on every single Chicago Bulls game. We always used the Vegas point spread so the bets were not lopsided. We bet on every PGA tournament. With all those hundreds of bets over many years, we could have lost thousands of dollars but essentially we broke even, a testament to the brilliance of the odds makers.

The most bizarre bet we ever made was on our mothers. One day as we were strolling along the golf course watching our dogs run through the sand traps (the grounds superintendent hated us) Tom told me how wonderful his mother was when he was growing up. I said, "I'll bet my mom was nicer." He said, "That's a bet. $5. But how can we prove it?"

I said when I was little, during Chicago's cold winters, my mom would get up a half hour early to put my socks and underwear on the radiator. When they were nice and warm she'd wake me up and put them on me while I was still in bed. He thought about that for a minute and said, "I owe you five bucks."

Tom was afflicted with malapropism. Although a genius with numbers he was forever screwing up words. Over lunch at Clyde's he mentioned his sisters were coming to town for a visit. I asked if they'd be staying at the house. He said, "No. They want to stay at the new bread and breakfast."

Tom and his wife, Gayle, took many trips to faraway lands. Gayle was a top producing insurance sales agent. The trips were awards she'd earned. Once they went to Turkey. When they returned I asked

Tom how the trip went. "Oh, it was okay," he said, "but I didn't like Instantbul."

Tom and I had a mutual friend in Waynesville, Danny Wingate, who had grown up without much money but became, through hard work, a very successful businessman. Tom had been his banker and was proud of Danny. He even graciously overlooked the fact that Danny was a Republican. "As important as he's become around town," Tom said, "he hasn't let it go to his head. He's still just a good old local jokel."

One night we attended a fundraiser at a rich lady's house. She had on display numerous and expensive figurines and artifacts that she'd collected from around the world. We were admiring them and Tom said, "she's got some pretty nice snick snacks."

Food was a big deal with Tom and me. We never walked without asking each other "What's for supper?" We were the main cooks in our houses so we also wanted to know how the entrée would be prepared and what would accompany it. One time Tom and Gayle invited Barbara and me, along with some other couples, to a dinner party at their house. On the morning of the party Tom and I were walking the golf course and I asked what he'd be feeding us.

"Steaks on the grill," he said.

"What kind of steaks?" I asked.

"Tenderloin."

"Where'd you get them?"

"Ingles," he said. (Ingles was our local supermarket.)

He continued, "I think Ingle's steaks are just as good as the ones you get from Mutual of Omaha."

The diagnosis was pancreatic cancer. Our walks across the golf course ended and were soon limited to the end of his driveway and back; then halfway; then to lawn chairs by the back door. The last walk we took was from his bed to his desk – about 20 feet. Tom had quit smoking, but one evening in the lawn chairs he asked to take a drag off mine.

"Tom you're on oxygen. You'll blow yourself up," I said.

"I just turned it off. Gimme that smoke."

As we shared the cigarette he said, "Jim, I know I'm not going to make it. I haven't given up and I don't want to die, but I'm not stupid. I

212

don't have much time left so I've made my arrangements and I'm asking you to speak."

"Only for you, Tom," I said.

"Make it short and funny," he said, "not maudlin." This was a word he would normally mangle but he pronounced it perfectly. He even defined it, "overly sentimental," in case I didn't know.

In the terrible days that followed I was riddled with anxiety. Not only was I losing my friend, but now I had to "speak" at his funeral, in the tiny southern town of Sparta, with my Yankee accent and where I knew no one. I don't know what was more upsetting, but, honestly, it was probably the speaking. How do you get in front of a crowd and speak about your just dead friend and, on top of that, make it funny? That's not possible. I wanted to say to Tom, "You prick! I can't do what you ask!" But, of course, I couldn't. The prick was dying.

Fortunately, Tom asked three other friends to speak: His cousin, Richard Doughton, a judge; his life-long best friend, Johnny Sanders, an electrical contractor from Mt. Airy and Jim Swofford, another friend who owned dozens of fast food restaurants, and who also had preacher experience.

As the hundreds of people were flocking into the chapel Johnny, Richard and I gathered together and unanimously decided, "We can't do this. It's too hard!" But then Swofford joined us and calmed us down. He said one way or the other we'd get through it together and we'd be doing it for Tom.

Because I was Tom's newest friend I volunteered to talk first. I started with the words *de mortium nil nisi bonum est,* my voice shaky. "This means, concerning the dead say nothing but good. That may work for some people, but not Tom." I said, "The man had many faults - for one thing he was a slacker." The congregation laughed. I relaxed.

I told them about walking the golf course and how he constantly complained about the highest hill, a tee box for a par three. He always wanted to stop short of it but, with much cajoling and badgering from me, he usually consented to go to the top. But one day he balked.

"I'm not going to the top today," he declared.

"Why not?" I asked.

"I don't feel like it," he said.

"C'mon, Tom, we'll take it slow and, besides, you have nothing better to do," I said.

"No!"

He saw that I was disappointed so he said, "But I promise I'll go to the top tomorrow."

"Your promises to me mean nothing, Tom," I said, "I want you to promise God."

"Okay," he said, "I promise."

"Not good enough. I want to hear it out loud."

He stopped walking, bowed his head and said, "Dear God, I promise to walk to the top of the hill tomorrow with Jim." Then he paused and with his head still bowed he added, "If you give me the strength."

The chapel burst out laughing. This was the Tom they knew. I then added some of his malaprops, which they loved, especially about buying steaks from Mutual of Omaha. My speech, mercifully, was over and Johnny, Richard and Jim Swofford did great ending the service.

I was standing with Danny Wingate outside the chapel as Tom's casket was carried to the hearse. "Look at all these people!" he said. "They're gonna have to hire people to come to my service." A few weeks before he died I asked Tom what was one of his regrets. "I should have been closer to my girls," he said. "And what are you most proud of?" I asked. "I have many great friends."

Most funerals are well-planned productions and Tom's was no exception. Because I was part of the cast I could not participate in the purpose of the funeral, the mourning of my friend. As soon as the graveside service ended I split for home, driving in a daze.

A few weeks later I drove the three hours from Waynesville to Sparta and back to the little cemetery. It was out in the country and it took a while to find it. When I finally got to his grave I reflexively got on my knees, a Catholic thing. But after a few moments and a few rote prayers, I stood up and started talking to him. I told him how much I missed him and how much his friendship meant to me; then added out loud, "Hell, you know all that, this is stupid. You could read my mind when you were alive."

So I wandered around his new neighborhood checking out the markers. His grandfather, U.S. Congressman Robert Doughton, (the former chairman of the House Ways and Means Committee) was nearby as were a bunch of other Doughtons. Tom, I was glad to see, was next to his mama.

"See you in my mind, Buddy." I said as I walked down the hill. "What's for supper?"

CHAPTER 29
Uncle Bob

Thoreau said, "The mass of men lead lives of quiet desperation." He had a point but I know men who are completely comfortable living life as it comes. They don't hanker to get rich, be famous or get their names in the paper. Their goals are simple and easily attainable: a secure job with benefits, a wife, some kids, three bedrooms, two baths and a nice car. Their plan for life is to work until they retire and then kick back until they die.

They are not needy. They are not trying to maximize their potential; they aren't even looking for it. They are happy with their lot in life and enjoy being in their own skin. Their pressures only come from day-to-day life, not from deep, inner yearnings. They are devoid of insight. They shrug at introspection. They are not envious.

How could you not want to learn more about yourself, find your latent strengths, explore and question your beliefs, thoughts, feelings? How could you not want to continue to rise in society, be noticed, be talked about and quoted? How could you not strive to be rich? How could you decide that you were a Catholic, a Methodist, a Jew, a Republican or a Democrat and never look back (or within or around) but simply declare, "That's who I am. Period." I admire (envy) people like that and have just described my dad and my Uncle Bob, two very different personalities with the same philosophy of life: Deal with it. Die. Go to Heaven.

Uncle Bob Anderson was a fair haired man of Swedish descent, six feet tall, over two hundred pounds. He had one of those large stomachs that are hard as rocks. He and his six siblings were raised Lutheran in Joliet, Illinois where their dad owned The Anderson Dairy Company. Uncle Bob and two of his brothers married Catholic girls and the boys converted. Uncle Bob took his new religion seriously, never missed a

Sunday mass and even joined the choir. He became convinced that the Catholic Church was the one true church. Period. When Uncle Bob returned from World War II, he joined the Joliet Police Force. He served for decades, never thinking of doing anything else.

Uncle Bob was married to my favorite aunt, Margie, Mom's sister, and he was an inspiration to me. He was a loud, happy, opinionated man who was genuinely interested in everything I'd been doing and everything I had to say. We loved each other. His favorite saying was, "It's a great life, Jimmy!"

As a teenager, I developed a case of hero worship on Uncle Bob. From him I learned to drive a car at high speed (look way out in front of you), smoke cigarettes, shoot a rifle, operate a boat and cook spaghetti. He was the only man I knew who cooked but there was nothing sissy about him. As a police officer he liked nothing better than to rough it up with bad guys on the streets of Joliet.

I suppose my fascination with Uncle Bob was that he was so unlike my dad. My dad's favorite expression was, "This, too, shall pass away." Unlike Uncle Bob, Dad preferred the company of "things" to people. Dad reveled in all things electrical, mechanical and electronic. Uncle Bob liked to socialize. He was active in the American Legion, becoming the commander of his Post. Dad didn't like socializing. Although I respected my dad and his inclinations, Uncle Bob was a lot more fun. The strongest word I ever heard my father say was "shucks." Uncle Bob used all the four letter words and didn't care if I did, either.

Whether in a squad car or his own car Uncle Bob drove like a maniac. After retiring from the Joliet police force he got a job as a car hike for auto dealers delivering cars back and forth among dealerships in the Midwest. He was forever getting stopped for speeding, one day three times, by three different cops, in two different states, but only once got a ticket. All the other times (dozens) when the cops asked to see his driver's license, he opened his wallet where his policeman's badge was prominently displayed. They let him go. There's honor among cops.

When Uncle Bob was in his late 70s he and two grandchildren visited us in North Carolina. Uncle Bob was slipping and the boys, at their insistence, did most of the driving. On that trip I inquired about his health. "Jimmy, as far as I know everything's fine. A little blood in the stool, but that's about it." Shortly after that Uncle Bob lost his license. He ran into a lady's parked car at the Joliet Mall. A cop showed up and told him to move his car. Uncle Bob hit her again. It was later discovered he'd had a stroke.

Uncle Bob didn't always play by the book, but his character was solid, his heart was big, and his priorities were right on. When Uncle Bob and Margie's daughter, Patti Bersin, got divorced she moved back in with them bringing her two toddlers. Well into their 50s at the time Uncle Bob and Margie willingly and lovingly helped raise the kids as their own. Uncle Bob was also especially kind to my grandparents as they aged, "You're always welcome in my home," he'd tell them with gusto. They'd stay for weeks. He was the same when my mom aged. She stayed for months. Many smarter, wiser, more introspective people wouldn't dream of putting up with such an intrusion.

When I was thirteen Uncle Bob, Margie and their kids took a family vacation to Colorado. They invited me to go along to help baby-sit. I was thrilled; it was my first time out of Illinois. Uncle Bob drove with Margie up front and me and their three little kids in the back. I had a wonderful time. Many years later Uncle Bob told me that on the way home from Colorado I whistled all the way across Kansas. "You were right behind my head and almost drove me crazy," he said.

"Why didn't you tell me to stop?" I said.

"Nah. You were enjoying yourself."

Only once did I hear Uncle Bob speak of his time in WWII. We were having dinner the last time he visited North Carolina. "Jesus, Jimmy, you never saw so many boats. They were in the English Channel out as far as you could see. And the airplanes! They darkened the sky."

"Is that when you went over, Bob?"

"No, it was about two weeks later. I was bomb disposal."

"What was it like?"

"Mostly I remember the smell. God almighty it was awful."

"The smell?"

"The bodies," he said, looking off.

Two years passed before I saw Uncle Bob again. I had business in Chicago and he was now in a nursing home, too big and too feeble for Patti to continue to care for. Aunt Margie was deceased. When my meetings were over I called Patti to get directions to the nursing home, thinking it was in Joliet, but learned he'd recently gone to the Illinois

Veterans Home in Quincy, Illinois, six hours away. No problem. I wanted to see him.

The Illinois Veterans Home is a sprawling complex of brick buildings with lots of grassy areas and a vintage cannon at the entrance. The place was very old but well kept. The staff was helpful and cheerful. I found Uncle Bob's building and got on the elevator to the second floor. The door opened into the dayroom where fifteen or so veterans, mostly in stupors, were seated in wheelchairs watching a *Rambo* movie on TV. I asked a nurse where I could find Robert Anderson and she said, "Bob is right there." I would have walked right past him.

"Bob," I said with a big smile, "It's Jimmy. How you doing?"

Nothing.

Louder, my mouth next to his ear I said, "Bob, it's your nephew Jimmy Joyce. I came to visit!"

Nothing. What I did not know was that his Alzheimer's was in its advanced stages. I helplessly kissed his head, told him I loved him, thanked him for everything and left.

At his funeral two months later his sons, Bobby and Mark, and I reminisced. They told me how they liked to visit our house in Chicago when they were kids so they could go down in the basement to hang out with my dad. They called him, "Uncle Petes." They said they got their first interest in electricity, mechanics and electronics from him. Both had successful careers in those fields.

On my way home I thought about that conversation. From my dad, Mark and Bobby learned about the fascinating world of science. From their dad I learned to drive fast, smoke cigarettes, cook spaghetti and shoot turtles off a rock. It made me smile.

"It's a great life, Jimmy!" said Uncle Bob. "This, too, shall pass away," said my dad.

They were both right.

CHAPTER 30

Mr. B. C. Cho

In July of 1996 Mr. and Mrs. B. C. Cho and their two children came to stay with us for a few days. Mr. Cho was our good customer from Seoul, Korea. In the lower level of our home in North Carolina's mountains we have an apartment. On the first night I got them settled in explaining, in broken English, that we did not have air conditioning but, "no need. Leave windows open. Nice breezes," I said and mimed pulling air through the screens with my hands. "Do you understand, Mr. Cho?"

"Yes, yes, Mr. Joyce. Open window all night. Good weather come in."

But when I went down in the morning to get them for breakfast the apartment was very warm and the windows were closed and locked. "Mr. Cho," I said, "you should leave windows open. Otherwise too hot." I opened the windows. "Yes, yes, Mr. Joyce. I understand."

That night I again explained about the windows and wished them a good night. The next morning when I went to get them it was the same thing. Windows closed and locked. Mr. Cho understands English much better than he speaks it. I again opened the windows and asked, "How come shut?" He blushed and took me off to the side. In a low voice he told me, "Mrs. Cho say, 'Mountains? Tigers'!"

The next night I put fans around the apartment. "Thank you, Mr. Joyce."

Entertaining people who don't speak English is challenging so I was delighted to hear the Chos played golf. Before they arrived Mr. Cho told me that he and Regina (Mrs. Cho) had been "much practicing." I got a tee time.

I'm not much of a golfer, my lowest handicap was 18, and I have played with some terrible golfers but the Chos were something special.

On the first tee Mr. Cho whiffed his drive three times before dribbling it onto the fairway. Mrs. Cho knocked her ball about ten feet and then grabbed her camera to take photos of the flowers next to the tee box. By the time we finished the first hole, three foursomes were lined up behind us. My stress level was rising by the minute, but then I caught a break.

On the interminable ride to the first green Mr. Cho said that he and Mrs. Cho had never been on a golf course before. All their much practicing had taken place on the roof of their hi-rise in Seoul, hitting balls into a net.

When we finished the first hole, I bypassed the next three tee boxes and we teed off on number five. When the foursome behind us caught up, I skipped a few more holes. That day the Cho's and I played six of the eighteen. They didn't have a clue. They had a marvelous time, and I wasn't asked to give up my membership to the Waynesville Country Club.

Mr. Cho spoke pidgin English, Mrs. Cho spoke no English and neither did the kids. We Joyce's didn't know one word of Korean. So there were lots of yes, yesses, head bobbing and smiling. The only word we all understood was "okay." Everybody on earth knows "okay."

We were sitting around the den after dinner trying to make conversation with Mr. Cho as interpreter. He asked if we knew karls. "What's a karl?" I asked. "You know, Christmas Karl. Sing," he said and started in with *God Bless You Merry Gentlemen*. His family joined him; they knew every single word in English. Then we joined in. They knew all the words to about a dozen karls. They knew them better than we did. It was Christmas in July with the Joyces of North Carolina and the Chos of Seoul. We had a ball, repeating the songs over and over. When we were done, Mr. Cho, who had been drinking heavily, fixed another Scotchie and Mrs. Cho gave him the glare known to all husbands. He pretended not to notice. Mrs. Cho took the kids to bed. Mr. Cho then had more Scotchies.

Like all of us, the more he drank the more he talked. That night we learned he had been raised in a Catric orphanage in Seoul. "I know Ratin," he said proudly. "Dominus vobiscum," he said "Et cum spiritu tuo." I replied. "Oh, you catrik too, Mr. Joyce? That Good!" He told us he made much money and each month had to decide, "How much for me? How much for Jesus?"

It was now late and when he got to his feet, he was weaving. He told our kids, "Get me rock. I break with hand!" I told him we didn't have any rocks. He took the hint and went to bed.

Next day we went rafting down the French Broad River near Asheville. We were having a wonderful time except for Mrs. Cho who kept staring at the mountains looking for tigers. Halfway through the trip we stopped for lunch. There were numerous other rafters spread out along the bank. I lost track of Mr. Cho and the kids.

As I put a hot dog in my mouth, I heard, "Crack!" Followed by a chorus of "Wow!" I looked toward the sounds and there was Mr. Cho, surrounded by the kids and other rafters. He was smiling and holding half of a flat rock in his hand. The other half was on the ground. It was at least two inches thick.

"You think you can break rock?" he told the crowd. "You can!" A few years later I was in Korea. One of Mr. Cho's employees told me "Mr. Cho can break rock with hand." "I know," I said.

During our trip to Seoul, the North Korean leader, Kim Somebody, was being particularly obnoxious threatening to attack the South. On the way from the airport I asked Mr. Cho how far away North Korea was. "Not too far. Over those hills."

"Are you worried about the latest threats," I asked.

"No," he laughed, "North Korea not make war. They have no money!"

Carpenter Joyce accompanied me on that trip to Seoul. Mr. Cho took us to an elegant restaurant on the top floor of a downtown hotel. From our "special table," reserved for Mr. Cho, we had a spectacular view of the city with the Han River below. The buffet tables were extensive, laden with hundreds of things to eat. Unfortunately for Jimmy and me, they were not labeled in English and most items were unrecognizable to our Western eyes. As we moved along, tentatively picking small portions of stuff we thought we recognized, we came to a large platter of what looked like octopus tentacles in green slime sauce.

"I wonder what that is?" Jim said. In front of us a middle aged, dowdily dressed, Korean woman heard his question. She looked like a librarian. She turned to face us, raised her arms as though flexing her biceps and said, "You should eat. Make man strong all night long."

Some years later the Asian economy was in shambles. I hadn't seen Mr. Cho in a year or so, but met up with him at a trade show in Las Vegas. We shared a cab from the Convention Center back to the strip. I asked how his business was doing. "Oh. Mr. Joyce. Last year. Everyday rain." Shortly after that he lost his business and moved to England.

CHAPTER 31
My Most Unforgettable Person

Without question it was Jean-Luc*, a reclusive artist who lived near Telluride. He would not have wanted to have been identified. Nor would he have wanted his art works tied to his disabilities – because they weren't.

Jean-Luc was born in France where his dad was a skilled craftsman. When Hitler conquered his area, he forced the dad to move to Germany to help with the war effort. Jean-Luc and his mother accompanied him. The family resented the move and hated the Nazis.

When Jean-Luc was ten years old, Allied planes started nightly bombing runs on his village. He and his friends, the children of other displaced workers, thought of the bombers as their saviors from the Nazis. "Angels of the Lord," they called them. When the Nazis temporarily retreated from the village, Jean-Luc and his buddies broke into their ammunition warehouse to defuse their anti-aircraft ordinance. Jean-Luc began banging a metal pipe on a 50mm shell to remove its head. It exploded, tearing off Jean-Luc's left arm above the elbow and half of his right hand. Only the little finger and the one next to it remained. He lost an eye. His legs were shattered. Ironically it was a Nazi surgeon, a woman, who saved his life with numerous, unauthorized operations.

After the war, Jean-Luc and his dad came to the United States. His mother had split. Jean-Luc attended one of our best art schools. With two fingers, he painted in oils and sculpted in bronze. Famous people bought his works from galleries in San Francisco, Denver and New York, none knowing of his handicap. As a hobby he restored old motorcycles. He built his beautiful house out of rocks doing almost all the work himself.

After we became friends, I'd drive the three hours to Telluride (To-hell-you-ride) for the weekend. I enjoyed his perspectives: "The Swiss are the squirrels of Europe, they gather nuts and hide them; don't rush through life, let life rush through you; let's go up the mountain tonight, lie on our backs and be in the universe. I like to listen to it; I build my house with rocks because I live in the Rockies. Others here don't live in the Rockies; they live in Telluride. They use glass. They want to be seen." Some of Jean-Luc's best friends were Ute Mountain Ute's. He was the only Anglo invited to their secret rituals. Jean-Luc had two artificial left arms, one with a hook, "for working" and one with wooden fingers "for going out to dinner."

Usually I went alone to visit, but occasionally I'd bring a friend. Jean-Luc never held back his opinion of my friends, and he was a very opinionated man: She is cold. He is dumb. He doesn't get it, and never will. She's not an artist; she's a mechanic, and so on. One friend, who was born and raised in Phoenix, he called "shallow." He believed you could not have depth of character when raised in a place where the sun always shines.

When I started dating Barbara, I got a lot of heat from my friends and colleagues in Durango. My most vocal critic was my psychoanalytic mentor, Jean Rosenbaun. We didn't speak for weeks. By then I was certified and in my own private practice, and frankly, didn't need him. His problem was that Barbara was twenty-two and I was thirty-six. "It can't work, Jimmy," he said. "Don't come back to my house until you stop seeing her." I told him to butt out. Barbara and I were in love and determined to see each other no matter what anyone said. One weekend we took off for Telluride. When the weekend was over Jean-Luc whispered to me, "Marry her, Jimmy." "I intend to if she'll have me," I whispered back. Barbara got Jean-Luc's rare imprimatur. Seeing essence was his business. Nice. Some weeks later Barbara, unannounced, knocked on Rosenbaum's door. He let her in. They talked. He melted.

One of the memorable things about visiting Jean-Luc was his father's grave. It was a mound outside the kitchen window. After Barbara and I left Durango, many years went by before I made contact again. One night on an impulse I picked up the phone. "Jean-Luc, it's Jim Joyce. I'm calling to see if you are still alive."

"So far, so good," he said, "Where are you? Are you coming to see me?"

"I'm in Chicago," I said, "I moved here five years ago."

"Are you crazy?" he said.

We chatted for a while and he sounded good. He said he had given up art and was engaged in "self-analysis." I said nobody could analyze himself. "I can," he said. Before we hung up I asked if his father's grave was still outside the window. "One hundred paces. He has not moved yet," he said. Then added, "His grave is my preview of coming attractions."

Jean-Luc's paintings are at once stunning, thought provoking, strong yet delicate. I own three. One, a reclining angel grinning ear to ear, is tiny, 1.5" x 3". The other is a self-portrait he gave me after a visit, signing it, "To Jimmy." It is on a large canvas, mostly blank except for his face in the upper right hand corner. I treasure it but can only look at for short periods. It was painted after a personal loss. His grief is undisguised. The third is entitled, "Jesus." It is 2' high and 1.5' wide. It is Jesus walking, carrying an orange backpack. His oversized hands clasp the straps at his chest. He is wearing a white robe and oversized beige waffle stompers with silver clasps and red laces. His body is half-sized. Jesus' gait is jaunty but his face is sad with down turned mouth and hooded eyes. His shoulder length hair is straight, neatly combed, and stylishly cut. A bright golden halo surrounds his head. The background is black.

CHAPTER THIRTY TWO
It Could Happen to Anyone

I have always had great friends. In that I have been fortunate but, then, so have they. Friendship has always been precious to me and I think I gave as good as I got. At least I hope so. Most of my friends were natural choices in that we shared much in common – the block, the parish, the schools, the Army, the job, the book club, business etc, but one friend did not make sense. Her name was Morley Cowles Ballantine and we had nothing in common. We were not even in the same generation. One of her sons was, like me, a Vietnam vet.

For instance, if you are sailing your yacht around the island of Antigua and see a sprawling complex with a lighthouse attached, that's Morley's place. It is in the Mill Reef Club, one of the most exclusive properties on earth. The Mill Reef club is not a resort. It's a private haven for the very wealthy founded after World War II. Don't try to get in. You'll embarrass yourself unless you have the right name and a ton of old money.

I first met Morley in the mid 70s. She was a stunned widow reeling from the loss of her husband, Arthur, who'd died of a heart attack. About the same time I'd become a divorced man, also reeling. We found each other in our wounded states and, thanks to God and tennis, we bonded.

At this time, I was a psychoanalyst at The Institute for Child Development and Family Guidance in Durango. The Institute was a new venture. The founder, Jean Rosenbaum, MD, asked me to take on the extra role of executive director. In that capacity I was to contact Durango's prominent citizens and tell them what the Institute was all about. He handed me a list. On the top of it was the name of The Durango Herald's publisher, Mrs. Ballantine.

I was a bit intimidated; I'd heard she was really rich, but I worked up the courage to call her and, brazenly, now that I think about it, invite her to lunch. She graciously, although I sensed reluctantly, agreed.

At the time I drove a Chevy pickup with a friend's camper top on the back. He needed a place to put it until he closed on his new house. Mrs. Ballantine and I walked out of the Herald and I escorted her to my truck. She looked at it and said, "Do you live in your truck?" I figured this would be a short lunch.

I took her to a nice restaurant and we ordered drinks. They tasted good, so we had two more. After lunch we had another round and were now talking freely. I asked her if she believed in God. She looked at me like I was nuts, "Nobody ever asked me that before."

"Well, do you?"

"Yes."

"Me, too."

A few years before I had seen the Ballantine family playing tennis.at Tamaron. I asked if she still played. She did, and so did I. We arranged a doubles match for the coming weekend. Our friendship began.

We knew people gossiped about us but neither of us cared. Many nights I'd leave her house in the wee hours after having numerous "just one more." Talking and drinking was our favorite thing to do. Once as I was leaving I asked what her neighbors must be saying about the man who leaves her house in the middle of the night. "Oh," she said with a dismissive wave of the hand, "what are neighbors for?"

I'd never met her Arthur but had heard he, too, enjoyed a drink. Morley told me he always kept a bottle close. "What are briefcases for?" he used to ask.

I was attracted to Morley almost from the start. She was bright, interesting and interested in all things. She was ridiculously well traveled. (How many times have you been to Europe, Morley? I have no idea.) She also traveled in circles way beyond my experience. Presidents, governors, senators and titans of industry were in her life on a personal level. David Rockefeller was Arthur's roommate at Harvard. Arthur's father was the Ballantine of Dewey/Ballantine, the famous New York City law firm. I was fascinated (not too strong a word) by her access to, and being a part of, all that power.

Morley's wealth came from Cowles Media, Inc. which owned the Minneapolis Star Tribune, The Des Moines Register and who knows what else. She grew up in an estate in downtown Minneapolis. On the walls of the many rooms hung the works of grand masters; on tables were their sculptures; in the garage was a limousine and, in uniform, was Randolph the chauffer. There was a ballroom in the house.

I visited there for the wedding of Morley's brother, Russell. Morley and I had lunch in the house with her dad, a widower, and former CEO of Cowles Media who discretely pushed a button under the table to order each course from the kitchen. A bell would have been too effeminate, I guess.

During lunch we discussed world affairs. I said something like, "How can we criticize the president's decisions when he has so much more information than we do?" Mr. Cowles said, "If someone reads the *Wall Street Journal*, the *Washington Post* and the *New York Times* every day he knows *more* than the president. The president's information is filtered by his aides."

At the wedding reception I met some of Morley's childhood friends, the Pillsburys. I danced with one of them who told me her son had been a college roommate (Yale, I believe) of Gary Trudeau, the creator of the Doonesbury comic strip. "He started it while in school," she said, "and the 'bury' in Doonesbury is named after my son."

Cowles Media owned a retreat called Glendalough in the Minnesota north woods. There were lakes, a game preserve, swimming pool, a tennis court, a dozen cabins or so and a main lodge. Pictures of powerful Americans, holding up fish, hung on the walls. A movie setting. I spent time there with Morley and her family and two memories stand out: The wild turkey raising pens (I'd never seen a wild turkey) and the fact that every morning at the long breakfast table we each had our own *Minneapolis Star Tribune*. No need to share the sports section.

Antigua (pronounced An TEE Gah, the "u" is silent, I was told) is way out in the Atlantic, a three-hour flight from Miami. Morley's storybook vacation home sits on a bluff overlooking the sea. The neatest room is the dining room. Side walls come up about four feet and stop. There are no screens or windows. Through this open air room fly gorgeous, tiny birds. They momentarily land on the walls, or on the table, then flit away. Not once did I see bird poop. They don't dare.

One morning I got up early and went looking for coffee. I opened the kitchen door and saw Morley's cook and a local fisherman watching lobsters crawl across the floor. I learned he came every morning when Morley was in residence with his catch of the day and today was lobster day. The maid explained that the lobsters were on the floor because she wanted the liveliest. They tasted better.

Antigua (remember, the u is silent) provided some great memories - golfing through the lush flora; listening to the exotic birds in the jungle bordering the fairways. Unfortunately, I missed seeing Jackie O, a frequent visitor who'd been there three days before.

Morley had another couple to the house for supper one evening. Afterwards we sat outside on the veranda. Far below us waves crashed against rocks, far above us the sky was filled with stars. Filled! Morley told a maid to turn off the house lights. There was no moon. The show was unbelievable. A blanket of celestial bodies engulfed us with shooting stars everywhere we looked. For the first, and only, time in my life I saw that the earth was *in* the cosmos, not below it. For many moments we stared in awe.

"Isn't this marvelous?" said Morley.

"God's cathedral," said the man.

"Amen" I said.

"Fuck God," said the woman.

Given all the wondrous action above, my first inclination was to dive under the table but I was too stunned to move. We turned to look at her, mouths agape.

"I mean it," she said, "Fuck him. He has taken from me everyone I've ever loved. And now I have cancer." Morley turned a light on and we freshened our drinks. The lady told her story. It was a stunning paradox: heavenly beauty and majesty in the sky; hellish grief and rage on the porch.

Over the years Morley and I often mentioned that evening, a life moment never forgotten. A police car that went out of control in a high-speed chase killed the lady's husband. He was sitting at a red light on his way to work. Her daughter died of a rare disease. It's no wonder she was pissed off at God, we agreed. (Then quickly went on to other topics.)

A mutual acquaintance of ours in Durango was Cecil Cooper. He was a CPA by vocation and a staunch John Birch Society member by avocation. Cecil was a controversial figure in town who, back in the late 70s, decided to run for the U.S. House of Representatives. I submitted an article to The Herald, my first writing for publication, about Cecil's candidacy. Morley published it and it was well received. With Morley's encouragement I wrote more articles and eventually wound up with a column.

Morley was nuts on the topic of writing. If anyone had even the smallest hint of talent she encouraged him or her, to "keep writing." Whenever we'd meet after a time lapse she'd ask, "What are you writing?" Most people ask what are you reading? She was relentless and I thank her for that. Writing has added much joy to my life.

But it was not my meager writing skills that attracted Morley to me. It was because I was a psychoanalyst. She knew essentially nothing about the works of Freud and Jung and the concept of the unconscious mind. She felt that was a gap in her education. Morley was the learningist person I'd ever met. Everything was of interest to her.

Like most who are first introduced to psychoanalytic principals (which sound whacky), she, I'm sure, was also skeptical but was too polite to say so. But early on in our friendship I mentioned in passing that the main tool we analysts have to unravel emotional problems is by analyzing dreams.

"You analyze dreams?" she asked.

"Yes, but I have to know the patient's history to do so," I said.

"I have a recurring dream that bothers me. Would you listen to it?"

"Sure, but no guarantee I can figure it out."

She told me the dream and I knew just enough about her past to accurately interpret it.

"Whoa," she exclaimed. "That's amazing! So Freud was not a fraud," she laughed.

"How did you put that together?"

"Nothing in the mind stands alone," I said. Morley liked that concept.

At 5:00 one evening the phone rang at my office. I had a patient in extreme distress (suicidal) so couldn't answer it. Hours later I retrieved the message from my answering service. "Call Mrs. Ballantine. Important." By then it was too late to call Morley so I waited until morning.

"What did I miss?" I said. "I was tied up with a patient."

"Oh, Jim, you would have enjoyed it. Dick Lamm (Colorado's

governor) and I had dinner and drinks at the pool. Just the two of us."

Lamm was very popular and thinking of running for president. He was at Morley's house to pay homage and get her opinion…and I missed it. But no regrets, not many, anyway. That patient is alive to this day. (And would she have killed herself? I mean, really? I think so.)

Morley was also attracted to me because of my relative youth. I was 34 when we met; she was 52. Most of her friends were married with commitments, whereas I was ready to go. One of our favorite weekend trips was to Telluride to see Jean-Luc and Morley's Aunt Sal.

Aunt Sal, a tall, stunning woman had been an actress on Broadway and in Hollywood. She had a hundred interesting stories, one of them set in 1920s Paris: "At that time the bar in the Ritz Hotel was off limits to women, but my escort defiantly took me there anyway, and nobody objected. Guess who my date was?" We didn't have a clue. "Ernest Hemmingway," she beamed.

Jean-Luc, Aunt Sal, Morley and I had grand times drinking, dining and solving the world's problems. Once Aunt Sal said, "being old is wonderful!" Jean-Luc said, "I can hardly wait." He meant it.

One of Morley's and my favorite things to do in Durango was have lunch at Lemon Dam. I'd pick her up at the Herald and on the twenty minute ride up the mountain we'd have a couple of beers. Then I'd park on the dam and we'd eat a sandwich while taking in the beautiful mountain lake. Sometimes eagles would be fishing. Our Lemon Dam lunches were the best.

After I got divorced my sons, Jim and Walter, moved to Alabama with their mother. When the boys came back to Durango to visit, Morley often joined us. We took them on their first cross-country skiing excursion. There was a steep hill that Jim, nine, was determined to climb. It is difficult in cross-country skis to climb a hill and he kept falling. He'd lose the skis, retrieve them, take forever to get them back on and try it again. It was exasperating to watch.

After his fifth unsuccessful attempt, I said, "That's enough, we've got to go." Morley said, "You stay right here. He wants to keep trying, let him." Two tries later he made it to the top.

North of Durango in the Animas Valley is the Cowboy Barbecue. It features excellent BBQ beef and a stage show of singing cowboys. It was a fun place enjoyed by both tourists and locals. The show was in a big tent, the food was prepared next to it.

Morley, Jim, Walter and I sat down in folding chairs and the cowboys started singing. Soon Walter, seven, got bored. He wandered to the side of the tent, picked up the canvas flap, and peeked under it. I started to get up to bring him back to his seat and Morley stopped me. "Leave him alone," she said, "he wants to see if the cook has hair on his legs."

For all her wealth and its accompanying power, Morley was unpretentious, gracious, polite and interested in you, no matter who you were. Her home in Durango was nice enough, but nothing like the one she grew up in. Her Durango house sat in the middle of a block. She drove a small Ford. After Barbara and I married they became friends. When we moved to Chicago, and later North Carolina, Morley would visit, spending a night or two. Yes, we cleaned up the house, because a guest was coming, but not that much. Morley was as easy to be with as anyone we'd ever known.

When she called to tell me she had throat cancer the first thing that popped out of my mouth was "Are you scared?"

After a short pause, she said, "Not really."

"I'll be on the next plane."

"Don't come now. Wait until the medical procedures are over."

Six months later I flew out. She was frail and on oxygen, but was game to go to Lemon Dam for lunch. There were no beers on this trip. I parked on the dam and we ate egg salad sandwiches, easy to swallow. When we finished, she unhooked her oxygen and said, "Let's have a cigarette." I gave her a Marlboro. She pinched the filter off and lit up. "Ah, dear boy," she said. "This is wonderful." On the way home we held hands. "I've never had a better friend," she said. "If you ever need anything, just ask." Same here, Morley.

Two years later the call came from her daughter, Elizabeth, "Mother is dying. She wants you to know." I was on the next plane. When I landed in Durango I bought a *Herald*. I scanned the paper to see if I would recognize anyone from thirty years ago. Toward the back of the paper I did see a name I recognized under the picture of a very old man.

Let's call him "Ted." He and his wife had been part of Morley and Arthur's crowd of movers and shakers in Durango. When I got to

Morley's house she was in a special bed in her living room. She was, indeed, dying; her body a wisp. I think she was blind, but she could hear just fine and was perfectly lucid. She recognized my voice, and asked about Barbara and the four children, by name. She listened with interest as I described their doings.

I told her I was surprised to see a picture of Ted in the *Durango Herald*. "Yes," she said, "He's in his nineties." I asked her if she remembered the great story she told me about Ted, over thirty years before, when he took a business trip to Denver. "What was it?" she asked. I repeated it.

Ted had flown from Durango to Denver for a meeting. When the meeting was over he returned to the airport to fly home, but his flight was delayed due to weather. Ted spent the next hours having far too many drinks in the bar. He finally boarded a plane and woke up in Kansas City.

"Do you remember that, Morley?" I said.

She nodded and said, "Yes." Then smiled, thought about it for a moment, and said, "It could happen to anyone."

Like Palmer, Tom and other friends who are physically gone, Morley remains alive in my mind. I talk to her, she listens, and, sometimes, she talks back.

Hop in the truck, dear Morley. Let's go to lunch. The eagles are fishing.

Note: Elizabeth Ballantine recently had published *Mill Reef Style*, a book of facts and gorgeous photos of the Mill Reef Club, available on Amazon.com. (Here's your chance to see how the other half live.)

SECTION VII

Snippets From Life

CHAPTER 33
The Wager

At mass this morning the priest interrupted his sermon about the loaves and fishes (and man not living by bread alone) to complain about the people who come to the rectory looking for money. He said almost every day he's asked to pay an electric bill, a phone bill or a grocery tab. He said he explains to these people that the church is not here to help with their finances; it is here to save their souls.

This reminded me of the time I went to a rectory with a money problem. It was in the late 70s in Durango. I was in between marriages and spending too much time in taverns. One night a guy walked into my favorite tavern, The Solid Muldoon, and saw me at the bar. "Hey Joyce, Notre Dame is playing Texas for the National Championship next weekend. You want Notre Dame? The spread is Texas by 7." I told him I would take Notre Dame for $300.00. This was a big bet for me. I didn't have $300.00.

A few nights later the game was played. By now I was full of remorse for making the bet. Texas had Earl Campbell in the backfield, the Heisman Trophy winner that year. Just before the kick-off I made a deal with God. I told Him that if, by some miracle, Notre Dame beat the spread, I would split the winnings with Him fifty/fifty.

Notre Dame kicked off, Texas fumbled, Notre Dame recovered and scored. The rout began. Notre Dame won big so when it was over God and I were each $150 richer. Now then, how to pay Him?

The next day I rang the bell at St. Columba's rectory. The old priest and I were not acquainted. I was an "in and out" church attendee never hanging around after mass or joining the various organizations. I introduced myself and asked if we could speak privately. He escorted me to the parlor and we sat. "What can I do for you?" he asked.

I told him that I had placed a bet on the Notre Dame–Texas game.

I noticed he stiffened up a bit. "As you know, Father, Notre Dame won," I said. (He didn't know.) "So now I have a problem and I hope you can help me," I said.

By this time he was really stiff, sitting all the way back in his chair. "We don't have money to lend," he said firmly, "especially on gambling losses." I laughed and told him that I hadn't lost, I'd won. I explained the details. "So I want to give you God's $150 and let you pass it on to somebody who needs it."

When he composed himself he said, "In all my years as a priest I've never heard anything like this." I handed over the money. He took it but couldn't help giving me a lecture about how it is wrong to make bargains with God. I didn't argue with him, he was just doing his job, but I know, for sure, that without that bargain Notre Dame would have been creamed.

A couple years later I rented golf clubs at the Durango Municipal Course. When I got on the course I discovered two $100 bills had been left in the bag. After the round I turned them in to the pro shop. A month went by and nobody claimed the money so the pro returned it to me.

So back to the rectory I went with another hundred bucks for God. "Did you win another bet, Mr. Joyce?" I told him what happened and he was delighted. "I know exactly who needs this money," he said adding, "you are a strange man, Mr. Joyce, but God bless you."

"Same to you, Father."

CHAPTER 34

Tastes Like Chicken

When Jim (7) and Walter (5) were living with me in Colorado, my buddy, and their pediatrician, Dick Geer, invited us to a goat roast. It was at a ranch way out in the country. At this time we were raising a goat that had become sort of a pet. So I decided to tell the kids that we were going to a friend of Dr. Geer's for a chicken cookout.

There was a big crowd and lots of other kids including Dick's young sons, Garth and Stewart. The food was fabulous, especially the goat which was cooked in the ground. Jim and Walter, who were very polite, kept asking me if they could go back for more chicken, saying it was the best they ever had. I said, "Sure."

On the way home in the truck – country roads, full moon above the mountains, peaceful – the boys were almost asleep when Walter said, "Dad, that wasn't chicken, was it?"

Sometimes honesty is the best policy with kids so I said, "No."

"It was goat, wasn't it, Dad?"

"Yes," I said, "How did you know?"

"Garth and Stewart told us."

Many more minutes went by.

Jim spoke up, "Dad, when do we get to eat our goat?"

CHAPTER 35
The Gang's Still Going

By Carpenter Joyce

Today there is a sub-gang within the original guys in the gang that still gathers on a regular basis. Wes Nelligan cleverly refers to us as "The Eighth Graders," a time we were the most cohesive. All others in the neighborhood were forever fixed in time by their grade in school. For instance, Wes recently told me that Mike Lyman died. "I didn't know him," I said. "Sure you did," said Wes, "He's a fifth grader." (Mike was 65.)

The sub-group is now Wes, Cy Watson, Tommy Carroll (TC), Jerry Joyce and me. We are all retired and need entertainment to fill our days so we take field trips together. We've been to Canton, Ohio for the Pro-Football Hall of Fame; Springfield, Illinois to see Lincoln's tomb and Milwaukee, Wisconsin to see Milwaukee, Wisconsin. In Chicago we go to Sox games, museums, city parks and boulevard tours and the like. We often end our Chicago field trips at Cullinan's Stadium Club at 116th and Western Avenue to take advantage of the "Buy one, get one free" hamburger deal that they have on Tuesday, Thursdays and Saturdays.

The beer at Cullinan's is especially cold and one day as we were enjoying same I mentioned that my friend Bernie Kelly, a retired police commander, owned a condo on Bourbon Street and it was vacant at this time. Immediately the wheels turned: "Let's go! Why not? Nothin' better to do! Hey! I got a great idea! Let's take the train!" Even Jerry agreed to go which surprised us. He's more of a jet plane man than a train man.

Cy, an ex-Army officer, pilot and retired judge, is a born organizer so he grabbed the lead in arranging the trip. He got us reservations on The City of New Orleans – first class sleeper births, of course. I went over to Bernie's house and got the key and a few nights later we got on the train at the Union Station in downtown Chicago. All aboard!

A young railroad man got us oriented, showing us where to store our luggage at one end of the car, the bathrooms at the other end of the car, and then to our "quarters." Most dining room tables are bigger than these quarters. We stood in the aisle laughing hysterically and berating Cy for those travel arrangements. I felt sorry for the Amtrak guy, who thought we were nuts. He did not understand what was so funny. He thought the accommodations were plush.

As soon as the train left the station, at 8:30pm, we were summoned to the dining car for our all inclusive dinner package. To accompany our flatiron steaks we all ordered five beers apiece. As we were enjoying our very good salads the conductor came through announcing that our first stop would be Homewood, Illinois, a far southern suburb. By now Jerry, we noticed, was no longer laughing. He is particular about many things including sleeping accommodations and food. He seemed to be deep in thought, no doubt contemplating what the next eighteen hours would be like on The City of New Orleans. When the train stopped at Homewood he jumped up, grabbed his bag, told us we were "out of our minds" ran down the aisle and bolted the train. TC yelled after him, "Can I have your dessert?" After more hysterical laughter, the four of us remaining travelers finished our fine meal and ordered more beers, settling in nicely to the sound of clickety clacks.

Wes excused himself to go to the bathroom and when he returned he was limping. After a number of sincere questions pertaining to his health, he said he injured his foot but didn't know how. We told him to take his shoe off and when he did his reading glasses fell out. A bit later the very nice lady who served us dinner said that we had drunk all the beer on the train. Must be time to go to bed.

Wes and I shared quarters. I volunteered to take the top bunk because Wes, although he'd lost weight recently and was down to about 315 pounds, still wasn't climbing so well with his injured foot. He got settled into his space and I was sizing up my options. Our compartment was about thirty feet from the bathroom so I couldn't change clothes there. The only way I could get undressed was to stand in the hallway outside the bunks. I did that, much to the amusement of fellow travelers.

For those of you over the age of sixty with prostate issues, you can imagine how many times you may need to use the lavatory after an evening of storying and cocktailing on The City of New Orleans. Climbing up and down from the top bunk reminded me of some of the training exercises in the Fire Academy forty-five years ago. I enjoyed those tricks in 1965 but if the "eighth graders" talk me into another train trip, you'll find me in the club car – even if they run out of beer. (Or they can just hang me from a hook in the mail car.)

Overall, we eighth graders had a grand trip and will be laughing about it for years to come. Long live The Guys in the Gang!

CHAPTER 36

Finding Tula

By Carpenter Joyce

With the exception of our parents and a few interested aunts and uncles many of the guys in the gang trusted the opinions and advice given by Gus and Tula more than any other adults. Gus and Tula owned DeLites at the corner of 79th and Racine. Through our high school years we could be found at DeLites. When we went away to college or to the military upon our return we reported directly to the corner to catch up on current events.

Gus to me was a hip father figure when my own father didn't seem too hip. Gus had a man of the world way about him. Tula listened to what we were talking about even if we didn't want her to. She had great ears. From twenty paces she knew who was flipping the lid on the sugar shaker in the rear booth! She had an informal opinion on many things and didn't mind sharing them with us. Both Gus and Tula looked to me like distinguished Greek figures from history. Tula wore dresses that were "dress up" and high heels as she worked the crowd and kept control of a restaurant full of young people.

As Jim Ada and I tossed around ideas for the book we both wished we could sit down with Gus and Tula to listen to their version of our teen years. We valued their opinions then and would love to hear them now to see how they stood the test of time. The subject of Gus and Tula was raised from time to time when the "eighth graders" got together for a field trip or just lunch and beers. The consensus was that both Gus and Tula had passed away some years earlier. That was accepted as fact until one day a couple of years ago Spooks Cavanaugh said that he recently had seen Tula shopping for groceries on 95th Street. That declaration was met with more than a few ha-ha's. "Remember, it was Spooks who saw Tula," was the comment. Spooks was known to fabricate sometimes. I followed up with Spooks and he convinced me that he was correct and he even had a vague idea of where she lived. That was in 2009. I put that on the back burner until last week, October 2011, and thought more about how important it would be to find her if possible. While searching through old boxes of photos in my basement I came across a scrap of paper with an address that was close to where Spooks figured Tula lived. I'll give it a try.

On Wednesday October 26th, 2011, I found the address and had notepaper ready to leave a note on the mailbox if I found her. I wasn't so sure that it would be wise to ring the doorbell; I hadn't seen her since 1966.

I couldn't believe my eyes, there was Tula's name on one of six mailboxes in the entrance hallway. I didn't leave a note; I was so excited that I rang the doorbell. A voice yelled down from an upper floor, "Who's there?" I answered, "Jim Joyce from DeLites." "Who?" was the response. Down she came and asked again through the door who I was and I again mentioned DeLites and she smiled and opened the door.

I explained that there are two Jim Joyces and that we're writing a book on growing up on 79th Street and that DeLites was central to our story and that Gus and Tula were also important figures in our narrative. Tula was full of questions about us and it was clear to me that she remembered most of us. She still had the classic Greek features but without the high heals. She was a little shorter than I remembered but I guess that I'm also a little shorter than I remembered. At age 87 she is well-read and current with local events. I couldn't wait to tell Ada that I found Tula and that she asked about him as well as others.

Tula asked if I was the fire commander. The other Jim went to college in Ohio, what ever happened to him? I explained that, yes, that was John Carroll University and he came home for a few months after graduation and drove a Highland Cab prior to the Middle Eastern cab driver take-over. He was a regular at DeLites while the U.S. Army was attempting to find a position for him so that he could join their staff. After that Jim was gone and, while gone, DeLites became gone.

What about Jeremiah Joyce? What came after politics?

How about the two brothers, one became a judge? (Mike and Cy Watson.)

My sister, Noonie, worked for Gus and Tula during her high school years and has vivid memories of them. Tula asked about Noonie Conlon and when I called her to tell her about Tula she came up with some of her own stories of her days as a waitress. She remembers Tula for her classy black dresses, high heels, beautiful skin and dark eyes. Tula took public transportation to a hair salon in downtown Chicago for nails and hair. When Noonie was preparing for the Saint Sabina Cotillion, the dance of the year, Tula took Noonie to her downtown hair salon and had her hair done professionally. As Noonie became more experienced in the restaurant, Gus let her put the burgers on the grill and drop the fries into the grease. He, on occasion, would go to his car and nap. Noonie remembers two of the nicest customers as Dan Curley and Jim Brennan who would have morning coffee together and then return for lunch. She was a little afraid of Jerry Joyce because he had very definite ideas on the proper consistency of his chocolate shake. If it wasn't perfect he wouldn't drink it. Noonie then showed me a big silver candelabra that Tula gave her as a gift, for no apparent reason other than her generosity.

Tula asked about Tommy Carroll saying that she had occasionally met him on the train going to work in the morning. She said how tragic it was when Tom's sister, Pat, had died.

She remembered my wife, Janet, and still has the picture taken of the gang and Gus and Tula at our wedding in 1965.

"What ever happened to Flosh McCue?" (Flosh is correct.) That was her last question, not bad for a lady who hasn't seen us in forty-five years! She asked me if our gang was now 55 or 60 and we both laughed when I said no, try 70! Gus passed away in 1986. I asked if she'd go to lunch soon with other guys in the gang. She said she'd love to. I can't wait.

CHAPTER 37

Pancakes

Everybody should have claims to fame especially showoffs like me. Thanks to Brenda O'Keefe I have another one besides being president of the Chicago Club at John Carroll. Whereas Clyde's Restaurant in Waynesville has a motto: "Where the Home Folks Eat." Joey's Pancake House in nearby Maggie Valley should have a motto: "Where Everybody Eats." If you are going to Joey's for breakfast, the only meal it serves, be prepared to wait. The crowd gathered outside is astounding but nobody is complaining. They know when their turn comes the wait will be worth it.

Joey and Brenda O'Keefe came to Maggie Valley in 1966 from Miami Beach. Joey had been the resident manager of the Fontainebleau. They started flipping pancakes at their new restaurant at the northern end of town. It has become a landmark and a must-go-to place for the zillions of tourists who annually come to enjoy the Great Smoky Mountains National Park, which is next door.

A friend of mine, Bruce Jones (Linda's husband) and a native of these parts, happened to say that he'd never been to Joey's Pancake House. "Why would anybody wait in a long line for breakfast?" he said, "breakfast is breakfast."

I told him he had a point but he should go there one time. I explained to Bruce that the eggs were as fresh as eggs can be. The pancakes are delicious and light with lots of different toppings to choose from. The country ham is hammier, the hash brown casserole is better than your mother's, the hollandaise sauce is New York City quality and the creamed chipped beef beats any I ever had in Army mess halls, where creamed chipped beef was invented. And the fresh fruit is perfectly ripened - no need of a steak knife to cut your cantaloupe and honeydew.

I continued, sounding like I was on Joey's payroll. "The décor will remind you of your grandmother's kitchen, only its cleaner, and the wait staff are tops. They will not call you: Honey, darling, sweetie, chief, bud, boss, brother, buddy, partner or guys. (Where do these boneheads come from?) Nor will one of them say: "Good morning, young man," the rudest greeting of all if you're not a young man, and if you don't hear the hostility in that, don't become a shrink.

At Joey's it is: "Yes, sir," and "No, ma'am." They are professionals. They have manners. They smile. They are glad to see you.

When our sons and grandchildren come to visit, I always take them to Joey's. One day I took Alex and Zack and the line was even longer than usual. We put in our names, got the beeper, but soon decided we were too hungry to wait. We turned in the beeper and left.

That evening I bumped into Brenda O'Keefe at the grocery store. "Jim," she said, "I saw you and your sons outside the restaurant, but didn't see you come in." I told her we were just too hungry to wait.

She said, "Jim, my local friends don't have to wait. Call ahead and we'll have a table ready."

I was flabbergasted at this marvelous offer and have taken advantage of it many times. My guests and I walk right through the crowd and are ushered to a table with a "Good morning, Mr. Joyce." People stare and I don't care. It's a claim to fame - I can always get a table at Joey's Pancake House without standing in the famous line.

My granddaughter, Anna Kate, (Jim's child) visits from time to time. She lives in Oxford, Mississippi. The first time we walked through the crowd she asked why we didn't have to wait. I told her, with a straight face, "because your grandfather's a big shot." She nodded and smiled as she processed this information.

Another one who likes to go to Joey's with me is my mother-in-law, Jan. (The kids call her Banana.) When she visits we go to the 10:30 mass at St. Margaret's and then drive down the hill to Joey's and waltz right in. My Barbara, on the other hand, won't go with me to Joey's. Unlike me, she is modest and does not like to draw attention to herself. Just the thought of brazenly butting the line makes her cringe. Too bad for Barbara. And my sister, Mary, when she visits from Minnesota? She's right there with Banana and me.

Joey O'Keefe died in 2001, but Brenda has continued operating this super restaurant. She runs the place like a kindly drill sergeant; nothing escapes her. She is a dedicated businessperson.

One night I called to get a table for the next day. I'd forgotten to call during business hours (they close at noon) and expected to get an answering device and leave a message. Instead I heard, "Joey's," Brenda's live voice. I hesitated.

"Brenda, this is Jim Joyce. Why do you answer the phone at night?"

"Why did you call?"

"To make a reservation."

"That's why I answer the phone."

CHAPTER 38

It's all in How You Look At It

Like all married couples, Barbara and I have had disagreements beyond me crashing the line at Joey's. Some were actually quite serious like the time I got fired but didn't care. (Boy was she upset!) Most were minor, however, like what's better on meat loaf, ketchup or mushroom soup. We settled this amicably early in the marriage by making an ecumenical meat loaf - half and half. She's mushroom I'm ketchup. "You're so Midwestern," she said. The kids, wisely, ate from both ends. (What's wrong with being Midwestern?)

Now we have an on going disagreement regarding the television-shopping channel. Barbara loves it; but it has, in my opinion, just sucker deals. Her purchases are frequent and spontaneous but, in her defense, she does send most of the stuff back.

Our house is in a wooded neighborhood, which is also home to deer, bear, bobcat, coyote, fox and lesser creatures. We have two dogs, Chelli and Darby, who go nuts when one of these animals comes into the yard at night. Once, the shopping channel was hawking night vision goggles and Barbara bought them on the spot. "Now we can see what the dogs are barking at. This will be fun!" she said. They were expensive and I sulked. I have also noticed (but haven't said anything) that since she bought them, no wild animals have shown up.

Barbara is a sucker for kitchen gadgets, especially over-engineered can openers. None work as easily and efficiently as the hand-held kind you grasp, squeeze and twist. We have a drawer full of the fancy ones that even she gave up using. But I have no right to complain. Barbara makes her own money.

Some years ago she started a candy business, Steeplechase English Toffee, Inc., and does well with it. (The toffee is the best you'll ever eat.)

She's never advertised but word of mouth keeps the business growing. Pun intended.

Barbara is a purist and will not use preservatives in her candy. If she did, shelf life would be greatly extended and she would make a fortune, in my opinion. One time Jerry Joyce from the gang offered to get her toffee into dozens of Duty Free Stores in major airports. But that would have meant adding preservatives and she politely declined his offer. I could have strangled her, but said nothing because it's her business and I have nothing to do with it. I also admire her decision to not compromise freshness. (I'd have done so in a heartbeat.)

But I'm digressing. Let's get back to late night shopping where one time we did agree on a purchase. We needed a clock for our bedroom wall and she saw one on special. It was overly large, circular, and classy looking. She bought it. On the wall it looks great but there is a problem. The numbers and hands are black and the background is dark brown. We have to get out of bed and stand in front of it to see what time it is, defeating the purpose of a clock in the bedroom.

Shortly after the purchase I was on a business trip to Florida when Barbara sent the following email: "Great news! I put the night vision goggles on the bedside table. They are perfect for reading the clock!"

CHAPTER 39

Ronnie Saxon

Ronnie Saxon, Tommy Stack's Cub fan buddy, looks like a Saxon with blue eyes, blonde hair and solid physique.

We guys in the gang lived in a tavern society. Chris Quinn's was our favorite, we always started our evenings there, but Chris was ancient and around 9:30 he'd start nodding off and tell us to get out. No problem, there were lots of other taverns close by. When I was in Vietnam the guys frequented a new one, The Mirror Lounge, at 78th and Ashland. It was a cut above the other taverns in that it had live entertainment by a man named Cal Starr. Part of Cal's act was to invite someone from the audience to join him on the stage. Deals Griffin, who would become a Chicago public school teacher, was a favorite and their duets became famous on Ashland Avenue.

A few nights after I got home I went to the Mirror Lounge and bumped into Ronnie Saxon. He asked me to join him in a booth so he could "hear all about Vietnam." He was the only one who wanted to hear *anything* about Vietnam. We returning veterans were not made to feel appreciated for risking our lives. On the contrary, some people thought of us as baby killers or, worse, soft in the head for serving in that controversial war.

We sat across from each other with Ronnie asking questions then listening intently to my answers. He had his elbow propped on the table and his chin resting on the back of his hand. He was riveted by what I was saying. I was well into a story when I noticed foaming white stuff coming out of his mouth, rolling off his hand, down his forearm and pooling around his elbow. He was puking, but his head never moved and his eyes remained on me. I couldn't believe what I was seeing so kept on talking.

When I finished the story Ronnie excused himself to go to the bathroom. "I'll clean that up when I get back," he said.

"Ronnie, why didn't you go sooner?" I asked.

"I didn't want to interrupt," he said.

Only a Cub fan could be that polite (and I really appreciated it).

CHAPTER 40
Don't Lose the Paddles!

Shortly after we moved from Illinois to North Carolina, Carpenter Joyce and Janet came to visit. We decided to go white water rafting on the Nantahala River about an hour from the house. None of us had done this. Barbara elected to stay home so Jim, Janet, Alex (12), Zack (10) and I headed for the river.

An extensive briefing is given to novice rafters with two main themes: Safety: Do not get out of the raft under any circumstances! And Money: Do *not* lose your paddles or you will be charged for them.

We got on the bus with a million other people and rode upstream to a staging area. We were assigned rafts and climbed in. There were six rafts in our flotilla with a guide in only one of them, and it wasn't ours. We shoved off.

The water was rushing, there were rocks everywhere, and we had no idea how to steer. We bounced off the rocks, got turned around, water sloshed over the sides. "Holy shits!" exploded from Jim and me.

Then the worst happened. We ran up against a huge boulder, sideways, and couldn't get away from it. Water was now pouring into the raft. In a panic I told the kids to climb up on the rock. At least they'd be safe.

Jim, Janet and I now got out of the boat and into the river to push it away from the rock. With great effort we were able to dislodge it but it was now full of water and super heavy, and we couldn't hold it. It drifted into the swift current then away it went all by itself.

The boulder was, thank God, within a few feet of the shore so we got the kids off and climbed a steep bank. We started walking down a road, the river far below. Sometimes we'd catch a glimpse of our passenger-less boat, the other rafters pointing and staring at it.

But! All five of us still had our paddles!

CHAPTER 41

Republicans

One of my buddies in Waynesville was Doug VanNoppen who grew up in Morganton, North Carolina. His dad's name was Don. The next-door neighbor's name was Henry. Doug's dad and Henry started a furniture company called Henredon.

Doug was about twenty years older than me. He was a staunch Republican, of course, (they are all rich) and was an original member of the Breakfast Club at Clyde's.

Carpenter Joyce was visiting from Chicago and I took him to see the exclusive Laurel Ridge Country Club, where Doug was one of the owners. As Jimmy and I were walking by the clubhouse Doug drove up in his golf cart. I introduced him to Jimmy, and then asked the standard question, "How'd you play today?"

"Not that well," he said, "I had a 76."

I said, "I can never imagine shooting a 76." Doug, who had seen me play, said, "I can't imagine it either."

He died five years ago. Tom and I really liked him.

Doug and I had so little in common it's surprising we were friends. But we were. I bet we had two hundred breakfasts together and ten dozen lunches. What did we talk about? I have no idea, but we sure enjoyed each other's company.

I don't know what it is about breakfast, Republicans and me. The Breakfast Club has long ago ceased to exist, but now I find myself on Sunday mornings having breakfast at Shoney's with two Republicans, Thom Morgan, a business owner and Bruce Kingshill, a CPA. (They prefer to be called "Conservatives," but everybody knows it's the same thing.) When it comes to politics, economics and the government's role we agree on practically nothing, yet we like and respect each other and enjoy our time together. Life is full of mysterious forces including, perhaps especially, those that forge friendships.

CHAPTER 42

ELSA

Now, most mornings you'll find me at Clyde's Restaurant ("Where the Home Folks Eat") having breakfast. Clyde's is on Main Street in Waynesville, NC. It has been in business since before World War II.

I was not born in Waynesville, so will never be considered a home folk, but I am made to feel welcome at Clyde's. It is a clean place, the service is excellent and the food is good. An egg white omelet, grits, fresh fruit and coffee. Who could ask for anything more?

Employees at Clyde's are home folks except one. Her German accent gives her away. Her name is Elsa. When people are done eating, Elsa busses their tables pushing a cart with two plastic tubs on top up and down the aisle. Elsa is always disheveled because she works so hard. She's also the dishwasher. She wears an old fashioned hair net and is wrapped, shoulders to ankles, in an apron. She has a pretty smile, inquisitive eyes and likes to talk. Her accent's thick. You have to concentrate. (Curiously, she is not arrogant.)

When Elsa passes my table, she tells me snippets from her life, usually about her family. One day a few years ago, she was full of complaints, which was unusual. She was beset by aches and pains; back, legs, arms and so on. When she finished her griping, she started rolling the cart forward, then stopped. She turned back around and with a look of bewilderment, said, "I'm sixty-eight already!"

Now I'm sixty-eight already and as bewildered as Elsa. How could time have gone so fast? Yesterday, I'm riding my tricycle on the sidewalk of Ada Street; today I'm on Social Security. What happened?

CHAPTER 43

Last Call

No doubt you've noticed religion is never far from my mind. What with my upbringing how could it be? You can also tell I am confused about it. Nobody can prove that practicing religion by going to church, or praying like crazy, makes us better, kinder, or more loving. Nobody can prove there is a personal God who cares. Nobody can prove the divinity of Jesus. No one can prove that one religion embodies the Truth and the rest are theologically flawed, and no one knows if there's life after death. Contemplating these issues is daunting, full of "yes–buts," and they've been pondered and discussed since consciousness entered the picture.

One of the smartest guys I know is an attorney, CEO of a multi-national, a Mensa, a devourer of books of all kinds and a teller of great tales. He attended Catholic schools through college. His law school was also Catholic.

One weekend we were discussing the sexual child abuse scandal that so many Catholic clergy were part of. We expressed our disgust and shame. "Just think of all the ones who were not caught," he said, "it makes me sick. The Church has lost its way. Something rotten has set in."

Later in the weekend I was surprised to overhear him say, "...at mass last Sunday..." I called him aside and asked why he still attended mass given his current feelings. Without hesitation he said, "To cover all the bases."

This smacks of Pascal's Wager and I can empathize. I, too, still go to mass and hope that there is a next life where the injustices from this one are resolved (Palmer walking up the stream with his dead little girl; the bitter lady on Morley's porch; the young soldier who was struck by the rotor blade, etc.). Surely if there is a personal God there will be more to human existence than time on planet Earth. If not, life is meaningless, or worse – a horrible experience for millions (billions?) who were dealt a terrible hand. So you'll see my Mensa buddy and me at mass because *if* the role is called up yonder (okay to sing Protestant now) we want to be there. We are hedging our bets; living in hope; believing in a God we can't get to intellectually.

As you know, ever since I was a little kid I found mass boring, and still do, at the same time it makes me feel virtuous for attending. There is something real taking place in the church but I can't put my finger on it.

The mass is officially called, "The Sacrifice of the Mass." The ritual symbolically re-enacts Jesus' life with the emphasis on the Last Supper, The Crucifixion and the Resurrection. I can easily see myself at The Last Supper. What could be more fun than hanging out with the gang, enjoying a fine meal washed down with wine? (I'd be drinking Scotch. I hate wine.)

And I can see myself in the closed room with the frightened apostles when Jesus comes through a wall and chats us up proving He'd risen from the dead, just like He said He would. Wow! He's here! Unbelievable!

But I cannot witness The Crucifixion. How can they do such a thing to such a nice man? I climb into my gunship, bring it up to a high hover and, using the mini-guns with their pin-point accuracy, take out every Roman soldier on the hill. I then ascend to 1500' to get oriented and find Pontius Pilate's place. There it is, the biggest building in sight, and only about one klick to the west. I stay at 1500' until I am close enough to start a gun run, then I descend. At 500' I punch off the first set of rockets, which takes the roof off the main house. I continue shooting until the place is rubble and we are right on top of it. I circle around and tell the door gunner, a corporal, to clean up the courtyard, then we head back to LZ Calvary to take Jesus to safety.

Using the element of surprise, I come in low down (contour flying) and fast (hot.) When we get to the LZ, I give it a big flare to stop forward motion. I quickly put the chopper on the ground and yell to Jesus, "Get in!"

Instead of running to us, like he should, he slowly approaches shaking his head and looking at all the dead soldiers. When Jesus gets to my door, he puts his sandal on the top of the skid and raises himself up. We are now at eye level, our faces just inches apart.

"I know you meant well, Jim," he said, "But I condemn violence of any sort including revenge. You should not have killed all these people. I had already forgiven them." He put his hand on my helmet and said: "You have forgotten, my kingdom is not of this world. Now go in peace and sin no more."

He steps off the skid and backs away. When he is clear of the rotor wash I pull collective and the beautiful city of Jerusalem again appears below, but I am too upset to notice. On the intercom I ask my door gunner if he heard what Jesus said.

"Yes, sir."

"I don't get it, Corporal," I said. "I save his life and destroy his tormentors and instead of thanking me he calls me a sinner."

"Nobody understands him, sir. He's God."

The Crucifixion is the lifeblood of Christianity and we are taught that it is our sins that made it happen. As the nuns were fond of saying every sin we little kids committed drove the nails in farther. (One told us our sins caused a thorn from His crown to come out one of His eyes.) So maybe, just maybe, I am not bored at mass. My boredom may be a screen covering something far worse - extreme guilt. I'm going to think about that.

My Mensa buddy, my door gunner and I live in confusion, but I know a guy who has devoted his life to pondering God, and the heady issues that concept spawns: my brother, Bob. He believes he's got a handle on them. Bob, a philosophy professor, and staunch Catholic, has jumped over the heads of the heavy hitters of the past – Plato, Aristotle, Thomas, Kant, Descartes and the rest and believes he has grasped what they missed. A colleague said that when contemporary theologians and philosophers read his work "They won't know what to say."

His philosophy/theology "begins" (this stuff is timeless but you know what I mean) *prior* to the Big Bang. His books are available at: lifemeaning.com as well as Amazon, Barnes and Noble, etc. Type in Robert E. Joyce. If you try them be prepared to think deeply and to wonder. Bob has a powerful mind.

I thank the people in this book especially my co-author Jim. You have been the substance of my life and we now have perpetuity, first on paper, then caste in the miraculous ether of the Internet. We'll never completely disappear. That's cool!

May I propose a toast? Here's to faith, hope and charity and to what a wonderful world it *can* be.

L'Chaim. Ad pacem. Cheers.

Index